Shoeleather
and
Printers' Ink

SHOELEATHER AND PRINTERS' INK

1924–1974

Edited for The Silurians
by George Britt

Experiences and Afterthoughts
by New York Newspapermen
on the Fiftieth Anniversary
of Their Old-Timers' Society,
selected from issues of
Silurian News

Quadrangle/The New York Times Book Co.

An overall credit to Kalman Seigel
for bringing the merits of this
book to the publisher's attention.

Library of Congress Catalog Card Number: 73-90167
International Standard Book Number: 0-8129-0417-6

Book design: Jean-Claude Suares

CONTENTS

Contents

III   The Newspapers

IV   Touching on History

Contents

_____

V   Just Sit and Listen

VI   Newspapermen

Contents

INVITATION

The Society of the Silurians, Inc., collectively, has written this book, a pick-up of newspaper talk such as naturally comes out when newspaper people get together. Except for the reminders from congenial companions, many of these items might have been lost forever. We admit to a certain sentimentality in recalling them here.

As stated in the logo-title of *Silurian News,* the Society is "an organization of veteran New York City newspaper men and women who gather twice annually for an evening of good fellowship."

Why the name Silurian? The founders chose it for their own reasons, in mood or whim unspecified; the meaning today is quite either-or. One line holds that the founders, lightly viewing their senior status, referred to that antediluvian period when the crustaceans were caught in the mud—that is, when the old crabs became fossils.

The alternative theory, dating back only some nineteen hundred years, traces to the early Welsh tribe of Silures. They were stubborn individualists who never accepted Roman conquest. A commendable addition to this theory is an ancient drinking cup of larger than quart capacity, now honorably reposing in the National Museum of Wales at Cardiff.

Between geology and archaeology the significance remains optional. The choices are presented impartially in later pages herewith. However, the Society's board may have indicated its preference when it persuaded the Museum and the

Invitation

Holkham Pottery in England to copy the historic mug—although in pint-size only—and distributed these tokens to the members at the spring dinner of 1968.

The Society originated in 1924, and its gatherings were then referred to as reunions, a fit word for their generous spirit. In the spring of 1942, because of the war, it was proposed to suspend the meetings for the duration. The members fiercely voted "No": an unjustifiable hardship. Today the Silurians look to their one hundredth semiannual reunion, in 1974— fifty years of shared interest. This volume celebrates this milestone and confidently addresses the future.

The writings here brought together—mostly yarn-spinning from the inner side of the job, a bull session after the day's work, spoken by many voices—have been selected from the files of *Silurian News,* the Society's bulletin and news sheet, a semiannual publication since 1947. Although dealing with the public happenings called news, these are not news stories, but rather a semi-confidential obbligato and fresh dimension to yesterday's newspapers. Selection, of course, also means the squeeze of omission, painful especially to editors. But as all reporters understand, you can't make Page One every day and the overset is loaded with gems.

The original qualification for Silurian membership was that thirty years before, or earlier, one must have worked on a New York City paper as reporter, editor, cartoonist, or illustrator. Those 1924 charter members looked back at least to the year 1894, and this makes our semi-centennial reach today not just fifty years, but eighty.

As a baseline let us notice a small item by Silurian Watson B. Berry in *Silurian News* of November, 1949. Berry was a lawyer, although never completely forsaking journalism. In 1892, then twenty-two years old, he was a reporter on the *Tribune.* On summer vacation up north at Malone, New York,

---

he learned that President Benjamin Harrison was coming through in his private railroad car and the young man climbed aboard for the short ride to Loon Lake.

The President received him kindly, asked about his schooling, then "invited me to join him in a drink, provided I had not been brought up to be a total abstainer. I replied, 'There are few abstainers in the North country and none on the *Tribune,*' which evoked one of those extremely rare President Harrison smiles. Whereupon the President summoned his servant who brought a decanter of Scotch, two huge tumblers, and ice water. The President poured himself a stiff one and I did the same, wishing him health as we ignored the chasers. It was a great thrill, and the kick I can feel to this day."

Our early history suffers from a sparsity of detail; the first twenty-three years, 1924 to 1947, passed without benefit of *Silurian News.* Nothing could speak louder for printers' ink as against the shadows and echoes of the air waves. This also explains the absence of writings here by our early notables— Silurians such as Irvin S. Cobb, Will Irwin, Lindsay Denison, Edwin C. Hill, Charles Michelson, and the like. The loss is ours, but the Silurian bond embraces younger and older generations alike.

These pages present a valid picture of what it is like to be a newspaperman. Here you are, wearing out your shoeleather to get there and see the event while it is happening; here are your fingers inky from the moist galleys as the deadline takes over. Here is journalism itself, if you care for the word, stressing the "jour," the daily and the immediate—new as the latest edition and basic as Thomas Jefferson's rating of newspapers as preferable to laws. However studied and stylistic the magazines, here are the eyewitness basics for which there is no substitute.

Here's why the reporter thinks that some day he's going to

write the great American novel, because he himself is dealing with the elemental human excitements, the very stuff for which readers turn to fiction. Why shouldn't he string together his own unique stories the way a scholar pastes up his clips and calls it history? Here is history itself, the harsh and as yet unrecorded flashbacks of our own witnessing. Here, for example, is the almost-centenarian, Dr. Lewi—the honorary member by mutual admiration—who watched as an eager lad the autopsy on the assassin of President Garfield. We have seen the old boy at our dinners on the dais, blowing out his rings of cigar smoke like a child showing off a new toy. And across the span of time here is Vermont Royster, undaunted by change, welcoming automation and computers as calmly as the founders accepted the linotype.

These stories from *Silurian News* appeal, of course, to the newspaper tribe—to the lad matriculating in a school of journalism (the modern alternative to asking for a copyboy's job), and likewise to the veteran who conscientiously abhors the terms "media" and "communications industry." (A curse on such verbiage!) The newspaper, vulnerable as it is and subject to its perennial errors—we view it still as indispensable. We look back to our days with it as the bright romance of youth. But the appeal carries on and on, beyond newspaper men and women, to every citizen, as far-reaching as the significance of a free press. Confident in an audience rippled out beyond place or class, the Silurians present their pageant of humanity, set against its newspaper backdrop.

What's it like—what it *was* like—is only a partial reason to invite general readers. Here presented is a vital current of understanding, the view from many eyes, from viewers planted in the front row of seats.

Yes, it's anecdotal. It forever changes the subject. Read it as you would read a newspaper; if one story doesn't catch

_____

you, turn to another. The editors offer this publication in the hope that the great Silurians of our past will consider it not unworthy of themselves and that, altogether, it may reflect that Golden Age upon which rests the Society's fifty years of fellowship and pride.

—The Anthology Committee: George Britt, Kalman Seigel, William T. Brady, William A. Casselman, J. Louis Donnelly, William R. Hart, Marshall E. Newton, Oliver Pilat, Henry Senber, Ted O. Thackrey.

I.
"NOTHING HUMAN INDIFFERENT TO ME"

Hiroshima to Brooklyn
Pole to Pole
Grant to Nixon
Samplings from Time and Space

INSIDE THE INSIDE OF THE BOMB—
LAURENCE, SAVED BY A HAIR
ON EVE OF HIROSHIMA

It came out of oblivion—this story—when Dudley Martin at the Silurian governors' luncheon leaned across and asked Bill Laurence, "Do you ever see Bob Simpson, who wrote that *New Yorker* Profile about you? I've run into him recently two or three times."

Bill grinned, "That profile almost ruined me, might have cost me my life! And would never have been written if Bob hadn't been such a horse player."

A few more words and the table sensed that something was happening, and everyone began to listen as Bill went on.

"This is ridiculous," I told Bob when he told me he wanted to write a Profile about me. "They'd never run a Profile about a reporter," I said. "You'll be wasting your time." But I knew Bob had had a streak of hard luck at the race track—he was incomparably better as a copy editor than as a handicapper—and if he was trying to get back a little money from the *New Yorker,* why should I stop him?

Furthermore, I was just then living in Hell, that summer of 1944, from worry over the German's secret weapon, about which our government seemed to be asleep, which I was sure was the atomic bomb. So I told Bob what he wanted to know about myself, but mainly I told him about the apocalyptic weapon being made ready by the Nazi scientists, and the terrible fate that may be in store for the free world. "If you sell it," I told Bob, "don't drop the money on the horses."

Laurence was a Pulitzer Prize winner in 1937
for his specialty in keeping up with science,

---

*winning again in 1946 for the bomb story. He
has been showered with honors, not omitting
the first of the annual Silurian awards in 1945.
He has written books about the bomb. Yet
here is still a new angle on it as it came across
the table that day in Bill's own words, ap-
proximately like this:*

"From the German exiled scientists," said Bill, "I had begun early to get reports of the Nazis' work on an atomic
bomb, and when Goebbels would boast of a secret weapon, I
was sure I knew what he meant. I had written a long story
back in May 1940 for *The Times* about the devastating explosive power from splitting the uranium atom, as well as a
vast source of industrial power.

"I hoped it would wake up our government, but the effect
was just the opposite, it seemed. A California senator by the
name of Sheridan Downey saw in my story a threat to the coal
and petroleum industries. He had it reprinted in full in the
Congressional Record as a warning of a danger that ought to
be blocked.

"Then came Pearl Harbor. We had what was called voluntary censorship, with which all of us, of course, were glad to
comply. The Office of Censorship, among other things, sent
around a list of chemical elements—maybe a dozen obscure
elements but with uranium buried among them—asking us
not to mention anything about them. The government, we
were told, didn't want the enemy to know that we knew what
was going on, or that we were interested. Everything I wrote,
it seemed, came back marked 'Please don't publish.' I was
boxed in, feeling just frantic. Once the Nazis got the bomb

they would drop it on the heart of London and blackmail the world, all would be finished.

"Well then, suddenly in the early spring of 1945 General Groves came asking Jimmy James, *The Times* managing editor, for my services, speaking to no one else, telling him nothing, telling me nothing except it was 'for a top secret war project.' Even my wife, all she knew was the number for a post office box. I just disappeared."

[So Laurence was to be the official reporter. He was sent to Oak Ridge and all along the atomic chain, to New Mexico for the first test explosion, then to the secret base in the Pacific on the island of Tinian, finally to fly in the second of the three planes to Japan. He was the only civilian to see the bomb bay open and the bomb drop, his plane about half a mile away across the sky, to watch the dreadful fall and feel the concussion.]

"That *New Yorker* Profile," said Bill, "to which I really had not given a second thought, was now published for big attention before I got back from the Pacific. Pretty soon then, a day or two, Jimmy James sat me down to hear a story. He thought it might interest me. Immediately after I had gone incommunicado, he said, he gave orders that any inquiry about me should be referred to him. And just then from the *New Yorker* came a request for a photograph of me."

James got his friend Harold Ross on the phone. Yes, said Ross, they had a Profile of Laurence that they were ready to run. James asked for and got a set of galleys of the story and

Laurence, 1945 Profile Version

then pressed Ross to hold up publication. Ross was unwilling.

"I'll make you a bet," said James. "If you will hold it now, I promise you that it will be a much better story when the time comes to publish. If it isn't, I'll buy you the best dinner in New York. And if you admit that it is better, the dinner's on you."

"James right then was saving my life," Bill said. "At the dropping of the bomb I had been in some danger, of course. Something might have gone wrong. But here was a mortal threat, and a much worse one. If the *New Yorker* had not asked for that picture, if it had not been referred to James, if he had not been able to reach Ross and head off publication, it would have been at just that time a fatal breach of security. It would have ruined me, killed me."

Well, on the morning of the day, James telephoned Ross at home. Ross slept late and was still in bed. "Did you see to-day's *Times?*" said James. No. "Well, read it, and then call me about taking me to dinner."

That was August 7. The *New Yorker* of course got Bob Simpson immediately to fix up the story. He killed the stuff about the Nazis possibly beating us to the bomb and he wrote a new lead and put in all the detail that could now be printed. It came out August 18, twelve days after the bomb was dropped, the quickest and most timely follow-up by a wide margin that any magazine could have.

"So Ross had to take me out to the best dinner in town," James was saying. "It was champagne and caviar. The best. Never mind the wartime scarcity of meat. I had perfect filet mignon, then crêpes suzettes and ancient brandy. And Ross, the poor bastard, all he could eat was crackers and milk. He had ulcers."

"And the Profile would never have been written," said Bill, "if Bob hadn't been losing his shirt at the Jamaica track."

—WILLIAM H. LAURENCE, April 1968

BROOKLYN, TOO, MIGHT HAVE
HAD ITS HISTORIC BANG,
ALMOST AND IF . . .

The memory that stands out most strongly in my long tenure as an Editor of the *New York Journal-American* revolves around the construction of the tunnel which today brings water from the Catskill Mountains into Brooklyn.

I have no records at hand to give me the precise date, but it must have been in the middle 1930s, when I sent my staff reporter and cameraman out to photograph the progress being made by the sandhogs.

At that time, the East River section of the tunnel had been completed and the crews were now pushing the diggings toward Prospect Park via downtown Brooklyn. The section was deep underground, for it had to pass under several levels of subways and the maze of criss-crossing sewer mains.

There had never been a newspaper picture taken of the subterranean aqueduct, so Tom Prendergast, the combination photographer and reporter, was happy to get the assignment. His zeal was soon blunted by the foreman of the works who declared that photographers were absolutely forbidden on the premises.

He returned to the office, defeated but determined to try again despite the odds that were against him. So he took his camera to the spot again one midnight, figuring that the foreman who had halted him would not be on the job, and the night foreman might be more elastic in his interpretation of the regulations.

But this fellow proved to be worse, from Tom's point of view. He said taking pictures of the vast operation, deep under the streets of Brooklyn, was absolutely dangerous, and if he were even caught talking to a newsman with a camera, he would be summarily fired.

Up to that time, no one had told Tom what the danger was and not believing there was any he never asked. But being young and ambitious, he resolved to try the boss of the middle shift, to get exclusive pictures that would fill the reader with wonder.

So he went to the spot about nine o'clock one night, and when he was stopped he asked to see the chief foreman. This bossman was a little more folksy than the other two, and he was in a conversational mood. He told Tom all about the work, accomplished with what was considered phenomenal speed. It was then that Tom sprang his question, "What is so dangerous about taking a picture around here?"

"The reason is that this big chamber is filled with dynamite, nitroglycerine, and other volatile chemicals for blasting, and the air is explosive from the fumes that permeate every cubic inch in here." As a convincer he added, "Even your lungs are now filled with it and if anything happened, you'd be blown inside out. Now, to take pictures, you'd have to use a flash light, and you know what that would do."

Tom told him that open flashes from powder were passing out and that he had with him the newfangled flash bulbs that could not do any harm. The man said he'd stick to the regulations anyhow, and that was that.

So I told Tom I'd go with him next time, to see if I still possessed my old powers of persuasion. We decided that the middle shift showed the most promise, and there we found the affable boss, again on the job.

Well, I spoke to the guy for half an hour, and when I saw he was weakening, I asked him to take us out of the chamber to a safe spot where smoking was permitted. He agreed, and

---

Tom brought forth his bulbs. Now, these first flash bulbs were about the size of a forty candlepower electric bulb, very much larger than the kind in use today. Each bulb had within it a small sheet of what looked like aluminum, beaten to the thickness of tissue paper. It was this which gave the bulb its super-light, and it glowed red hot for about ten seconds after the flash was made.

Tom set off about a dozen of these, and the foreman was amazed at their safety. Not one bulb split open during the demonstration.

"All right," the foreman said, "get your camera properly set up and focused, and I'll let you take one shot and then you go."

We re-entered the cavern where Tom set up the camera so he could shoot the picture with one hand as he set off the flash. After a minute he yelled, "O.K., here goes."

With that he flashed the bulb. It cracked into a million pieces, the metal foil glowing in the open.

The foreman nearly collapsed and we were all transfixed.

The mishap could have blown all of downtown Brooklyn off the map. Somehow or other it proved to be harmless. But neither the *New York Journal-American* nor any other paper ever got the picture we were after.

—JOHN W. NEWTON, March 1971

(Footnote:—Modern methods apparently avoid similar dangers.)

1909, NORTH POLE
THE HOTTEST STORY

The North Pole in the early 1900s stood as inaccessible as the moon, yet it was still the great magnet for adventure. Then within a single week, down from the Arctic ice came word at last from two expeditions—the rival claims of Dr. Frederick A. Cook and Commander Robert E. Peary—setting the public ablaze with hero worship and partisanship. Two of the reporters on this prize news assignment, Edwards of the *Herald* and Meriwether of *The Times,* forty years later set down their recollections for *Silurian News.*

Yes, Cutthroat Competition

Early in September 1909, bulletin after bulletin clattered out of the Morkrums: *

"I have discovered the North Pole!" "I discovered the North Pole April 6, 1909!" "I discovered the North Pole in 1908!" First Cook; then Peary; then Cook; then dead silence from Peary. Cook had waited a year and crossed the Atlantic to send a bulletin. Peary had wirelessed as soon as he could get through the ice to Labrador.

Someone was lying. Reporters had to find Peary, and a grand scramble followed. Roy W. Howard (Scripps-Howard Roy) and I were first from New York to reach Sydney, Nova Scotia. A dozen others were there from Canada, two or three from Boston. They ganged up on us: "The UP and New York *Herald* have hooked up!" They spurned us, spied on us day and night; wouldn't let us out of sight. Every man was trying to charter a ship on his own; but captains wouldn't go up through the Strait of Belle Isle, "graveyard of ships,"—too many icebergs.

One rainy Saturday evening, Roy and I sneaked across the Bay on the last ferry to North Sydney where the Canadian Cableship *Tyrian* had put in with orders to take newsmen out to find Peary. Next day, free from our "enemies," and with bottled reinforcements, we went to Captain Dickson; begged him, between to-yous, to up-anchor and go out at once. He acted as if on the point of doing so when our "enemies" barged into the smoke-filled ward-room and spiked our foul conspiracy. All of us returned to Sydney. Monday, eighteen of us went back to the *Tyrian* to find the captain had received official word:

> Await the arrival of the six o'clock train Monday from Montreal with more correspondents.

"Captain, that'll bring fifty more; maybe some sob-sisters!"

"Sob-sisters? Women? My Gawd, I can't bunk all you men. What'll I do with the women?" The suggestions offered indicated that knighthood was out of "flour" completely.

"Captain," we counseled, "this cablegram says await the arrival of the train. Nothing more. Doesn't tell you to take extra people aboard the *Tyrian;* doesn't even mention the *Tyrian*. As soon as that train is in officially, you can go out—can't you—and not disobey orders? Inferences don't go in any man's orders. You know that!"

"Why—That's right. I hadn't thought of that."

And, when that train was reported in officially, just at six o'clock the *Tyrian*'s screws turned—and we went right out—with only eighteen thinly-clad correspondents. I remember with us were Barton Curry of *The World*; Robert Welles Ritchie, *The Sun;* Carl Brandeberry, the AP; Arthur Constantine, *Boston Herald;* Fred Thompson, *Boston Post*. The *Tyrian* met up with Peary at Battle Harbor, Labrador; it was the only ship to reach there, despite many after-claims of reporters that they went up on a trampship.

We found Peary agreeable. We loaded up with thousands and thousands of words and returned to Sydney to find we had left behind forty or fifty gentle souls who were ready to cut the guts out of eighteen grinning space-grabbers.

Only one man brought out of Battle Harbor a souvenir of moment—Barton Curry. He bought at the little shanty-store a handsome seal-skin bolero—and a straw hat!

—DELT EDWARDS, May 1949

(* Morkrum: telegraphic printing system, named for manufacturer, Morkrum Company of Chicago.)

Best-Laid Plans Blow Up

The Peary story is to me a bitter memory. *The New York Times* had financed Peary's expedition to the Pole and as a member of the staff I had written the preliminary matter. Then the flash from Battle Harbor, "Have got O. P." I had all of ten minutes to catch a train.

In Sydney, N. S., the newspapermen rapidly assembled. Time wore on. Then one day a tramp steamship, groping for a cargo, appeared in harbor. I was one of the first to inspire the idea of chartering that tramp and proceeding forthwith to Battle Harbor and was so sure my paper would approve that I didn't ask authority, merely wiring I had committed *The Times* to its share of the charter and was going with the expedition.

Then, as lines were being cast off, came a hurrying messenger with a telegram for me. It was from the then part-owner of *The Times,* under whom I had served on the N.Y. *Herald,* who had brought me to *The Times* and who was handling the

Peary story. It was a peremptory order to withdraw *The Times* from the charter and for me to remain in Sydney, adding that my unauthorized act would have nullified all arrangements made with Peary and by which *The Times* was to have the exclusive account of his expedition. The message added that I was to arrange for an open wire to be held in readiness for instantaneous transmission of the Peary account when he arrived in Sydney. I had to make a pierhead leap for shore.

On the following Sunday some two score correspondents came swarming into Sydney fairly bursting with a two-hour interview they had had with Peary at Battle Harbor. Doubtless the explorer would have carried out his arrangement with *The Times* had not old Doc Cook bobbed up with his claim of discovery. This so enraged Peary that he emptied himself of every detail of his expedition.

And not a *Times* man in that group! Here was newspaper disaster. In an effort to retrieve it I thought of some representative of an afternoon newspaper whose matter would be made stale by the fact that the day was Sunday. I found one, opened negotiations; yes, he would let *The Times* have the story at double space rates. I wired the offer to *The Times,* marking it for the attention of the executive handling the Peary matter. He was absent and the wire went to managing editor Van Anda.

Now, Van, a master of sarcasm and wholly unaware as to why I was loafing around Sydney, instead of being with that expedition, employed some of his best sarcasm authorizing this staff writer of *The Times* to buy the story of an expedition *The Times* had financed. Van is now dead and so far as I know he never knew the inside story. This is the first time I have told it.

—WALTER SCOTT MERIWETHER, May 1949

RADIO TO BALLOONS, 1923,
AND FROM ANTARCTICA, 1930

Silurian Wagoner was tapped by General Electric to direct its pioneer radio news bureau out of Station WGY Schenectady, one of the first ten such stations on the air. "It was my job," he recalled, "to keep WGY prominently before the public and make it one of the best-known stations on the air." Which he did, as the two memoirs following indicate, and made history as well.

Winning the Race

Schenectady is but a small city, compared to New York, Pittsburgh, Detroit, Boston, Buffalo, Cleveland, and Chicago, all of which were among the first ten. We had no hopes of competing with such metropolitan cities for talent but we did have one asset they lacked and that was short-wave facilities. It seemed our only hope and I decided to make use of them. Short waves could travel thousands of miles, which popular broadcast stations could not do.

One of the first stunts I arranged was broadcasting the national balloon race on July 5, 1923, and furnishing special weather reports to one of the teams. The race started in Milwaukee that year.

General Electric had just developed its first tube receiver and its engineers were too busy to assign me a technical assistant for my trip to Milwaukee. So I packed one of the new tube receivers and left alone. I had previously arranged with the U.S. Army to try out radio reception in its entry in the race, which was to be piloted by Major Ora Westover, later to become Brigadier General commanding the Army air forces.

In those days it was necessary not only to have a long

aerial but a good ground, generally provided by a piece of metal pipe driven into the ground outside your home. Not until I arrived in Milwaukee, did it occur to me that a balloon provided no means for a ground. This was but two days before the race, a Saturday and a Sunday, when General Electric was closed. No one around Milwaukee could offer any help. As a last resort I took my problem to Marquette University nearby. The professor of electrical engineering explained I needed a counterpoise. I had never heard the word before and had no idea what it meant.

"Where or how can I get one?" I asked, still hurried in the shortness of time.

The professor explained it would not be too difficult to build one. All I need do would be to line the inside of the balloon basket, which carried the pilot, with PURE copper fly screening. Elated, I rushed back to Milwaukee but my troubles were not over. I visited a half dozen or more stores before I could find pure copper screening. They had bronze and other kinds. Copper was too expensive and didn't sell.

Then to find a tinsmith to solder the ends of the screening, for the professor had told me it must be a complete circuit. Despite the fact it was a Saturday afternoon I did locate one and by midafternoon the counterpoise was ready.

I was all fixed also with aluminum aerial, 300 foot of copper wire on a reel which could be wound and unwound from the balloon basket. It was the trailing antenna type used by army airplanes in those days.

Now for the test and to "instruct" Major Westover in the use of the equipment. My room was on the sixth and top floor of the Planters Hotel. I mounted the screening on top of chairs, to somewhat duplicate conditions in the basket above ground, and threw the aerial out of the window. To my great relief it worked. Through cooperation with the army department in

Washington I had arranged for special weather reports to be sent me, giving wind conditions at various altitude levels, which were radioed every hour to the balloon.

Major Westover won the race and in his official report he paid high tribute to the help radio and the weather reports had been in deciding on the best altitude to keep his balloon going in one direction and not get caught in a reverse wind that might take him back where he started from. Major Westover landed up near Quebec in Canada and the radio receiver lies buried in Lake St. John as it had to be cast overboard with other instruments to lighten the cargo and keep the balloon from landing in the water. The event received nationwide publicity. It was the first time that radio had ever been used in a balloon race.

—CLYDE D. WAGONER, January 1963

—Admiral Byrd actually flew over the South Pole on November 29, 1929. This first personal contact with him was made some three months afterward. (Already, in May 1926, he had been first to fly over the North Pole.)

Byrd's Living Voice

"Hello Dick! How are you? This is Clyde Wagoner speaking from up in Schenectady."

"Hello, Wag! How grand to hear your voice again! Everything perfectly fine with me," was the cheerful and quick reply of Admiral Richard Evelyn Byrd over a short wave, long wave, telephone line setup that had been arranged by General Electric for this epochal broadcast, connecting Schenectady with Dunedin, New Zealand, a distance of some 9,000 miles. The time was 7:30 A.M. on March 11, 1930, in Schenectady, N.Y.

It was the first that anyone in this country had heard his voice since he left in 1929 on his first expedition to Antarctica. *The New York Times,* which had Russell Owen as a correspondent on this hazardous expedition, had received radiograms from Admiral Byrd by way of its own short-wave station but its facilities were not capable of bringing in voice communication.

Present and participating in this history-making two-way broadcast were the late Adolph S. Ochs, publisher of *The New York Times,* and his son-in-law Arthur Sulzberger. Both chatted with Byrd and Owen on this broadcast which was carried by an NBC network of 40 stations, from coast to coast.

That was perhaps the greatest thrill to occur in my 50 years of newspaper work. Until we heard his voice, no one really knew whether he had survived the rigors of the South Pole despite the receipt of radiograms by *The New York Times* bearing his signature.

My voice from Schenectady reached Admiral Byrd direct in Dunedin. But New Zealand did not have adequate facilities to transmit his voice direct. Instead, his voice traveled 600 miles in the opposite direction from Schenectady before it started its journey across the Pacific. Byrd spoke before a mike in station 4YA, which sent his voice over land wire and 16 miles of submarine cable to Wellington. There Station 2YA, operating on long wave, relayed his voice to Sydney, Australia, where short-wave station 2ME transmitted it to Schenectady.

The broadcast as mentioned previously took place on March 11, 1930. It was 7:30 A.M., early spring in Schenectady. In Sydney it was 10:30 P.M., same day, but early autumn. In New Zealand it was 12:30 A.M. the following day.

—CLYDE D. WAGONER, November 1961

: 18 :

DAYS OF INNOCENCE:
GROMYKO AND ZIPPER

Twenty years ago when I proposed to a network that the new United Nations rated coverage on a permanent basis, my then boss took a dim view. "Who cares?" he said. "It won't produce news. It's just a do-gooder organization that won't last as long as the League of Nations."

Today the United Nations is still very much alive and kicking, in spite of all predictions to the contrary. As for producing news, UN Headquarters keeps occupied the more than 200 members of the UN Correspondents Association.

The UN Assembly had its first organization meeting twenty years ago this winter at Church House in London. In March 1946, the Security Council had its first meeting in this country. It had the use of Hunter College's Bronx campus, until then a training station for WAVES.

The gymnasium had been transformed into an impressive Security Council Chamber. You would never have suspected that the eleven council members were sitting on a platform over the swimming pool. This past spring in Oslo, Trygve Lie who was then Secretary General told me he sometimes got so exasperated at the Council that he often wished he could press a button and tumble them all into the pool.

I am one of the few working correspondents still covering the UN who was present at the opening meeting of the Council. Charlie Grumich headed up the AP team. I believe Harrison Salisbury, now of *The Times,* was the UP chief, but *The Times* itself at that time had no permanent bureau head. Jim Reston and Bill Laurence were there at the beginning, and Tom Hamilton, back from the Navy, came in early summer after a brief Washington tour and stayed for nineteen years.

John Rogers headed the *Herald Trib* at Hunter, and his number one man, Pete Kihss, now of *The Times,* I used to see poring over the day's documents as we rode down to Manhattan on the subway.

The East-West clash began with the first meetings of the Security Council. Iran complained that Russian troops had not evacuated their firm World War II positions in North Iran. The Iranian ambassador, a short, serious man with black hair brushed up in front, whom we nicknamed Mickey Mouse, brought the complaint to the Council and Soviet delegate Gromyko, in some apparent confusion, walked out of the Council meeting.

The late Frank Begley, who died on mission in Cyprus this year, was an ex-police chief from Connecticut and directed UN security. Frank met Gromyko in the men's room and escorted him as he headed toward the building exit. At the door, just before they were to see the waiting photographers, Frank suddenly foresaw an international embarrassment.

"Ambassador Gromyko," said Begley, "your zipper is down."

Hastily Gromyko adjusted his dress, then, both men grinning broadly, they stepped through the door to meet the photographers. The cameramen wondered what was so funny about this international crisis, and only years later did Begley tell the story.

By the time the Assembly of fifty-one countries convened in September, the Sperry plant at Lake Success was ready. Half the building was turned over to the UN, and a brick wall was built between it and the busy factory still working on Navy contracts. Two of the Sperry workmen were in my radio booth in a committee room on one of the first days at Lake Success.

"Strange," said one. "On our side of the wall we're making

new weapons for the Navy, and on this side, they're making peace."

When the full Assembly met, it did so in the New York City building at Flushing Meadows left over from the 1939 World's Fair. It had been used as a skating rink, and for the past two years it has been the City's Fair building again. Around the edges were the press cubicles.

There I saw a wonderful tribute to a great lady. When Mrs. Eleanor Roosevelt walked into the hall to take her place with the American delegation, every delegate in the room arose in her honor in a completely spontaneous demonstration of respect for her and for her husband. It was most moving because it came from the heart of the world.

The delegates ran up road mileage in those years. Their offices, including that of the United States at Two Park Avenue, were in New York City. They had to drive twenty-odd miles daily to Lake Success. Then after a committee meeting, they might all pile in their cars and go back ten miles along Grand Central Parkway to the Assembly building at Flushing Meadows. Then they might have to return to Lake Success for an evening committee meeting, and eventually back to their offices and apartments in New York.

It all seemed somewhat exciting, but it did not make for efficient conduct of business.

One pleasant feature of the Lake Success arrangement was that the delegates' lounge, with a semi-circular bar in the center, was situated between the press area and the meeting rooms. The most direct route from our offices to the Security Council or the various committees lay only one foot from the bar. We could not help meeting and mixing with delegates and secretariat members at that focal point.

It was there that Ambassador Yakov Malik of the Soviet Union and Ambassador Philip Jessup of the United States continued their informal conversation, begun in the men's room, which eventually resulted in the lifting of the Berlin blockade. When the new buildings on the East River were completed at the end of 1951, and reporters and diplomats had to walk to one end of the complex for refreshment instead of catching a quick one on the fly between conference rooms, liquor consumption dropped. Some of the fun was missing as well.

People in later years have tended to criticize the organization because it was not a panacea for all the ills that afflict the world. The United Nations is no better and no worse, no stronger and no weaker, than the relations between the great powers. But I think that even in those early days at Hunter College, if we had known that twenty years later, the United Nations would have remained vigorous, growing, a true means to bring all countries great and small together to consider their common problems, most of the reporters and diplomats would have been well pleased with the future.

—JOHN MAC VANE, October 1965

EICHMANN'S TRIAL DRAGS ON . . .
THE PRESS MINUS TRAINED SEALS

After all the learned literature that has emerged about the Eichmann trial in Jerusalem in 1961—almost a lifetime ago —I have concluded that I can best serve my fellow Silurians by sticking to the news coverage of this trial of global interest and historic import. I don't think any editor believed before the trial started that it would last for more than three weeks. It began early in March and after three months we correspondents were wondering if it would ever end. It did— in mid-December.

As far as I was concerned, as the *Herald Tribune* correspondent, there were two principal figures in the trial. One was Adolf Eichmann of the twitching, ravaged facial mien, sitting in his glass cage. I don't think that he once in all that long trial ever let his eyes meet the eyes of any of the press people or any of the spectators. He was, as everybody knows, convicted of sending several millions of innocent Jews to the Hitler extermination facilities in several countries.

The other principal figure who quite naturally concerned me sat near the front of the press room downstairs, an enormously large room with accommodations for 600 correspondents from all over the world. This other man consigned at least as many millions of words to a facility on West 43rd Street called *The New York Times*. There, cynical cable desk men routinely exterminated thousands of these words with zig-zags of their pencils. I would hear afterwards from this man his laments about those atrocities, and for those I would enjoy a hearty laugh. For this man, Homer Bigart, my competitor, had broken at the outset of the trial what was to me a sacred code, usually honored by *Times* men.

That code was, no *Times* man should write his story without first consulting with the *Herald Tribune* man on what he was using for his lead. To be sure, this is not taught in journalism school but it does serve as a safety device to save wear and tear on the nerves; in short, a therapeutic measure. I had known Bigart from the time he was a skinny boy reporter fresh from Hawley, Pa. sometime during the late twenties or early thirties. By the time of the Eichmann trial he had acquired—thanks to his enormous expense accounts—a portly distinction that many a United States senator could envy. In the courtroom sessions in Jerusalem we usually sat together, exchanging whispered comments on various personalities in the trial—on how well or how badly Eichmann looked that day, about peculiarities of the legal zealots of both the prosecution and defense staffs, and even about the judges.

The courtroom itself was new and beautifully equipped, with slanting elevation of seats as in a theater, and earphones at each seat giving a choice of testimony in any one of four languages—Hebrew, English, French, or German. We needed to make only casual notes because the efficient Israeli Press Department was supplying full transcripts in the same four languages, and doing it so fast that usually we could be marking the transcript sheets within less than an hour after the words were spoken. In the first few days seats were assigned to the correspondents.

But after three weeks a hundred or more trained seals had departed and thereafter we could sit wherever we chose. With that freedom of choice there was in the beginning some vying among the press to get in the front row left, where you would be sitting within a few feet of the prisoner in the cage. But after a while all the correspondents got sick and tired of looking at that shell of a man and preferred to sit far away from him.

The sessions were long and arduous, running from 9 A.M. to 6 P.M., with a scant hour's break for lunch. But we could go downstairs to the press room at any time and watch and hear the courtroom proceedings from about a dozen closed-circuit TV sets attached high along the walls. In the morning when that code-smasher, Bigart, and I would settle down in adjoining seats, he would flip over the blank note paper and display to me underneath, firmly attached to his clipboard, a document of his own devising. At first glance it looked like an astrological table, a mixture of calendar and mathematical data. Complicated as it looked, all it was really was his daily, updated, calculated estimates as to when the trial would end and he could go home. I wish I had put money on those projections because he was never right, not even up to the final week.

My trouble with Bigart came at the end of the day's session and the rush downstairs to the typewriters. On some days the testimony offered ten or a dozen possibilities for good, smashing leads. On other days it would be so totally repetitious of what we had written before that there seemed to be no natural lead to the story.

The TV and radio characters who had to go on the air each night were infinitely curious about what both *The Times* and the *Herald Tribune* would be headlining about the trial in the next morning's papers. I would see them down front trying to pump Bigart and then they would come ankling up to see what I was writing.

For example, Martin Agronsky of NBC would slither over to my table with a cheery, "Hey, Bob, what did you think of today's session?" "Why, I thought about the same as Homer Bigart thinks about it." "What does he think?" "Well, Martin, I saw you down there picking his brains, you tell me." "He said practically nothing." "We can't do business on that basis,

Martin." "Well, he liked that next-to-the-last witness." "Yes, but what angle?" To make a long story short, I might or might not get a hint as to what Bigart was doing, but that crafty competitor had caught on fast and had initiated his own counter-espionage.

I was always the next-to-the last man to leave the press room for a late dinner at Fink's Bar, the newsmen's hangout not far from the courthouse. The last to leave always was Bigart. As I would stroll past him I'd say, "Keep it short, Homer, remember they're cutting it in New York." He'd say, "Bob, for God's sake save me a seat at Fink's." Dave Rothschild, the genial proprietor, always had a table for Bigart and me.

Soon Bigart would appear and sit down and order a beer and look at me with great innocence and ask, "What did you write tonight?" I would say, "Come on, Homer, hand them over." Then he would reach in his pocket and pull out his blanksheets and hand his story to me. And I would pull out mine and hand them over to him. You never saw two more concentrated guys anywhere than we were for the time it took us to absorb each other's first take of copy. Sometimes I would groan in despair. Sometimes it would be Bigart who displayed symptoms of faint, and sometimes we'd both grin and throw each other's copy back, because we had written the same lead.

Oh, it was a great trial, Hannah Arendt and her high-flown abstractions notwithstanding. Believe me, she wasn't around that courtroom very long. It was a fair trial, the fairest I had ever seen, and I am an old trial reporter. Watching Eichmann for nearly a thousand hours I came to believe he didn't care about dying in the end. All he cared about, I think, was to maintain his phony posture of a brave German officer who acted under orders, and to go to his death without whimpering so as to hold the respect of his sons in Germany and South America. He was never a real German officer.

Just before the trial, I had visited five of the extermination camps which remain as museums of the atrocities, including the worst of all, Auschwitz in Poland. And I had gone to Linz in Austria, where Eichmann was born and grew up. I had talked to many people there, notably his brother, a lawyer and a seemingly honest man. Eichmann came from a respectable family. But Eichmann was a maverick.

The police showed me photographs of him at the time he was preparing to leave Linz to join Hitler's Brown Shirt street fighters who were torturing the Jews in Berlin before the conflagration of war. Eichmann looked young and clean, with a mean, devilish, good-looking face. He did die without a whimper, and his ashes were strewn from an airplane over the blue Mediterranean. If that seemed too good an end for him, it was because the Israelis did not want any part of his remains to pollute the sacred soil of Israel.

—ROBERT S. BIRD, October 1968

OLD N.Y. PRESS CLUB
—GIANTS IN THOSE DAYS

It was in 1869 that a few adventurous spirits in the daily newspapers of old New York City founded what they called "The Journalistic Society." Dana of the *Sun* wanted to meet Greeley of the *Tribune* and Jennings of *The Times* wanted to study Thurlow Weed of the *Commercial Advertiser*. Bennett of the *Herald* desired to study all of them at short range, in an era when editors used verbal scimitars on each other and made their personal quarrels matters of public notice. But these gentlemen never showed any actual desire to get together. The civilization of that day did not call for an outward smile and an inward enmity. It was all the same inside and outside; the gentlemen on the editorial top never met.

So adventurous reporters, led by James Pooton of *The New York Times,* William N. Penney of the old *New York Daily News,* William H. Stiner of *The Tribune,* George F. Williams of *The Times* and Charles A. Bladen of the *Herald* formed The Journalistic Society in 1869, incorporated in 1872 as The New York Press Club. They hoped to bring the editors together, also a few authors, and let them mix with the reporters. That was the foundation of a social and charitable organization that for a long period was the first to entertain all foreign celebrities and to have as its guests at its annual dinners, every president of the United States, from Grant to Coolidge.

The beginning of the club was in two rooms on Tryon Row, a site now covered by the Municipal Building. These rooms were over a saloon and restaurant, which fed the members of the Society food and embellishments by means of a dumbwaiter. There Greeley went, after some urging, to meet

Jennings, the powerful intellectual editor of *The Times,* who had started the war on the Tweed ring; Dana of the *Sun;* Demas Barnes, the Brooklyn publisher of *The Argus;* Thurlow Weed, the elder Bennett, Theodore Tilton of the *Golden Age,* Henry Ward Beecher, and Williamson of the *Sunday Dispatch,* and Caldwell of the *Sunday Mercury*—all looked each other over and also became acquainted with some of their own reporters. Williamson and Caldwell were big toads in the puddle in those days, for the dailies did not issue Sunday newspapers. That was the real beginning of the Press Club.

Then along came A. Oakey Hall, Mayor of New York, but a silent owner of the *Daily News* together with former Mayor Wood. With them came Robert Bonner of *The Ledger;* Henry M. Stanley, the African explorer; Thomas Nast, the cartoonist, Henry Villard of the *Evening Post;* George W. Childs of the *Philadelphia Ledger,* Bret Harte, Mark Twain, John W. Mackey, founder of the Postal Telegraph and young Thomas Kinsella, later to become famous as the editor of the *Brooklyn Eagle.* With such dignitaries interested in its progress, the club had to move from its quarters over the saloon and take a pretentious place at 115-17 Nassau Street.

Thus it prepared for its first annual dinner in Moquin's, on Ann Street. Bayard Taylor, Richard Henry Stoddard, poets; Grant White, exemplar of all that was good in English writing, and William Winter, famous dramatic critic were the speakers. But William M. Tweed was ungracious enough to escape from Ludlow Street Jail that night and while ex-Mayor Oakey Hall was replying to a jest from the Rev. DeWitt Talmadge, the dinner was broken up by calls for the reporters and the editors.

* * *

The next annual dinner was historic and successful. It was attended by President Grant, General Sherman, and General Phil Sheridan, and was held in the St. Nicholas Hotel. Without notes of any kind, President Grant delivered a classic speech that marked him as a notable public speaker and wit. Newspapermen were the victims of his wit that evening, as he said:

I suppose you will expect me to say something about the press of New York, the press of the United States, and the press of the world. I confess that at some periods of my life, when I have read what you had to say about me, I have lost all faith and all hope. . . . But since a young editor has spoken for the press and has fixed the lifetime of a generation of newspapermen at about twelve years, I have a growing hope within me, that, in the future, the press may be able to do some of the great good which we will all admit it is possible for it to do.

I have been somewhat of a reader of newspapers for forty years. There is one peculiarity I have observed and that is that in all of the walks of life outside the press, people have entirely mistaken their profession, their occupation. I never knew a mayor of a city, a councilman of a city, any public officer, any government official; I never knew a member of Congress, a senator or a president of the United States who could not be enlightened in his duties by the youngest member of the press.

I never knew a general to command a brigade, division, corps, or army who could begin to do it as well as men far away in their sanctums, and I have wondered. I was very glad to learn that the newspaper fraternity was ready to take, with perfect confidence, any office that might be tendered to it, from president to mayor, and I have been astonished that citizens have not given it to them, because they might have known that all of these offices could have been well and properly filled.

I hope that when the new generation comes up, about twelve years hence, I shall again dine with the Press Club of New York and that I will see that those of this generation, who are so well fitted to fill all of the civil offices, will have all been accommodated, until at last there shall be nothing left for them to criticize.

Something unusual developed from this dinner. Grant, Sherman, and Sheridan insisted upon a return affair, at which they would be the undisputed hosts, and they selected Delmonico's uptown place for a buffet supper. . . . It was a stand-up feast, in which the three distinguished men insisted upon passing food and drink, and in being real privates in the ranks. An after-result was that Col. Amos J. Cummings, a Civil War fighter, but then a distinguished member of the *Morning Sun* walked off with Gen. Grant's overcoat. Cummings was six inches taller than Grant and the overcoat he left draped down to the shoes of the distinguished Civil War General. The exchanges were made next afternoon at Delmonico's, at Chambers and Broadway, with adequate apologies. The truth was that the hospitality of the Union generals, in uptown Delmonico's was so overwhelming that Colonel Cummings had become quite indifferent to the fit of his overcoat.

President Grant, with humor that so long had been unsuspected, held a court martial and fined Cummings a luncheon for twenty-five at Sutherland's chop house next afternoon. George F. Williams, who had been a confidential messenger between Grant and Lincoln during the Civil War, with the rank of major, presided at the court-martial luncheon.

* * *

The club enjoyed ever-increasing popularity with the press and public officials as the years passed. Joe Howard, opera critic for the *Herald* and American reviewer for the *London Times,* held that the club's finest feature was what he called its "Comradicity." Joe was its president for four terms and ought to have known.

It was in the Press Club that William C. Cowan, organizer of the City Hall Reporter's Association, then political writer for the *Star,* boxed four rounds with Theodore Roosevelt, while the latter was Police Commissioner. Later, as President, T.R. was the club guest at dinners on five occasions. It was in the club, too, that Murat Halsted stirred up a hilarious situation by getting Henry Watterson worked up on the meaning of the Democratic Party. There also Bret Harte, with his inevitable pipe, suggested to Mark Twain that he, Twain, would make more money at bricklaying than in composing alleged humor. Joseph I. C. Clarke of the *Herald,* author of "Kelly, Burke and Shea" good naturedly needled Herman Ridder of the *Staats-Zeitung* on the inferiority of the German race, to which Amos Cummings would joyfully agree, while Barclay Gallagher, Eastern Manager of the Associated Press, would generously except those Germans who had emigrated to Ireland centuries before.

Caleb Dunn, famous versifier of the seventies and eighties, would stir Thomas Kinsella of the *Brooklyn Eagle* into a satirical mood by denouncing the humor of Mark Twain as a factory product, while William Cullen Bryant of the *Brooklyn Times* acted as peacemaker. That was what Joe Howard meant by the club's "comradicity."

The genuine spirit of the club in those early days was shown when Andrew Bonar, a member, deeded to it a plot for one thousand graves, in the highest and most beautiful spot in Cypress Hills Cemetery. Next came the establishment of a small widows' fund. The first beneficiary was Mrs. Frederick Hamilton, whose husband, in his zeal as a reporter, boarded a yellow fever ship for the old *Daily News,* in the early eighties, and gave his life as a result. The club also had six hospital beds, as a result of generous contributions, one of $10,000 having been made by Joseph Pulitzer. As the years passed, the club also built up a splendid library for the reference needs of newspapermen, but lack of space later necessitated transfer of its bound newspaper files to the Hall of Records, City of New York.

In its history, the club had entertained men of distinction from all parts of the world. Stanley, Peary, and Shackleton, the explorers, were among them. The great actors of Europe, from Sir Henry Irving on, were welcome guests. There was never a tightening of the lines. On the same night that Parnell and Davitt were guests, the club, learning that the recent Lord Mayor of London was in New York, invited him also. A similar situation arose when former President Roosevelt returned from Africa. At that time, John Redmond and his brother Will, the Irish leaders, with their colleague, Devlin of Belfast, were in the city. They promptly accepted the club's invitation, whereupon, it developed, that the last previous Lord Mayor of London was also in the city. He accepted. It was a night of great hilarity. At one point, London's previous Lord Mayor, rose to remark that he thought some of the jibes in the songs about Colonel Roosevelt were wholly out of place. A moment later Colonel Roosevelt requested a song that lampooned him worse than any of the others and promptly joined in the chorus. That subdued the ex-Mayor of London. That was the spirit of the New York Press Club in its heyday.

—JOHN A. HENNESSY, May 1953

: 33 :

Silurian Hennessy was 13 years old when he began work on a newspaper, as office boy at *The Times,* of which his father afterward became city editor. From 1900 to 1912 he himself was managing editor of the *Press;* his revelations of municipal corruption were a major factor in electing John Purroy Mitchel to be Mayor in 1913. In 1916 he published his book on state politics, "What's the Matter With New York, a Story of the Waste of Millions." He died in 1951, 91 years old. The foregoing article is from his sketch written for a program of the old Press Club. The club lapsed in the 1930s, and the New York City Reporters Association became its heir and successor.

NIXON, THAT FATAL DAY,
CRYSTAL BALL FOGS UP

It was a sunny, brisk day in November, Richard M. Nixon was flying in from Dallas, and the press was reluctant to leave the press room in the International Arrival Building at then Idlewild Airport. The arrival was clear across the terminals area, too long to walk and too short to drive. But make it we did, UPI's Hank Logeman and AP's me.

I always enjoyed meeting Nixon, then out of office and trying hard. His manner was unfailingly friendly, a trifle anxious and uncertain, but always professional.

It was bright and pleasant in the American Airlines terminal, and we had no difficulty finding Nixon. President John F. Kennedy was in Dallas and Nixon seemed quietly pleased that the airport press in New York had time for him.

"Was there much of a crowd in Dallas when you took off?" we asked in a context which escapes me now.

The slow, cautious smile, the appraising Quaker eyes, the ready, perhaps forced smile but still a smile.

"Oh, no. The crowd was occupied elsewhere."

"What about Vice-President Johnson in the coming election?"

"Kennedy will have to drop him," said Nixon, the professional politician answering a headline-oriented question. "He'll have to do it to keep the liberal vote."

The smile again, the handshake, and he was off to Manhattan by taxi, an also-ran, out-of-it. We dictated our stories and made it back to the comfortable, air-conditioned press room, whose sealed windows faced on the busy ramp, our private, exciting backyard—a constant scene of far-ranging airliners taxiing to disgorge.

Then the flash, and the telephones ringing. President Kennedy shot! Soon the man Nixon said would be dumped had been sworn in as President.

I remember the unbelievable moments that followed. Persons in the terminal, who had followed the tragedy over radios, glared with suspicion when I sought their reactions. A few demanded to see my credentials, something which hadn't happened to me in years and almost never at the airport.

We did not know it then, but Camelot was over. This was the dawning of the age of Secret Service.

My late wife, Doris, and I were currently presenting the Idlewild Players in Rostand's "The Romantics" in Hangar 17 at the airport. The Players were our hobby, our indulgence.

When we numbly gathered at the hangar a little later, the building guard gave us a withering look.

"You're not doing the play tonight?" he challenged.

"Of course not," we said. "We just want to talk."

What's more, no audience came. America was hurt. It had been stabbed in the heart. Dumbly, numbly, it mourned.

Republican or Democrat, I don't think we miss Camelot, really. It wasn't that real, but a bright concept, a fixation which affection and idealism made seem real.

But the present cynicism and all the rest, they aren't healthy either. We can still remember, though, and not a few of us, that wonderful lift when we really loved the man we called the President.

—TOM DEL VECCHIO, October 1972

II.

ALL IN THE ROUTINE

Infinite Variety,
And Laughs With the Sweat,
And Non-Routine Comradery,
—Oh Well, Bull's Eyes, Too

IF NORTHCLIFFE ACTUALLY HAD
SHOT HIMSELF, WHAT SAYS YOU?

I had one very narrow escape from death in the first world war when a lone German aviator swooped down upon me as I was foolishly climbing up to an observation post in broad daylight. He emptied his machine gun twice in my face—I could see his red mustache, he was so close —but somehow he failed to hit me. Then I had some pretty thrilling experiences with the Black Hand after doing a Sunday story about them, forty or more years ago. But I guess I never had to think faster than when I was alone with Northcliffe in his study and he started to shoot himself. As no one had any inkling he was crazy, I should have been hanged for murder as sure as snakes, if I hadn't distracted his attention. So I guess that was the time I got the greatest thrill. The doctors cured my cancer all right, but damned near killed the guinea pig! For months now I have been fighting the same kind of anaemia that so many people died of in Hiroshima. But I am putting up a pretty good fight, and although I may not be able to get round to your next dinner it will not be for lack of trying. Here is the story you asked for, there is nothing the matter with my brain. (The author died the following March—1949.)

Had I been placed on trial for the murder of Lord Northcliffe in 1920, I should have taken the stand in my own defense and testified as follows:
After lunch, on Thursday, May 13, Sir Campbell Stuart

called me up and asked me to ring the chief at his house in Carlton Gardens. I did so and Northcliffe asked me to dine with him that evening. He told me to come a little before five o'clock as he had some work he wanted me to do.

I reached the house at 4:50 p.m. and was at once shown upstairs to where he was working all alone in his study, a large room with two windows. A long table stood behind a sofa in the middle of the room, piled with papers. From the couch on which he was reclining the chief waved at me the noon editions of *The Evening News,* one of his own papers, and *The Evening Standard* that belonged to Lord Beaverbrook.

"Tell me which of these two rags is the worst!"

I sat down, took a sheet of paper, listed from memory the principal news stories of the day. Then in parallel columns I gave marks to the papers according to how they had handled and headlined the news. If the judgment of both editors as to the value of a story was against my own, I corrected my list to meet their view. This done, I went through the papers to see what exclusive stories they had and what current news items supplied by the agencies they had spiked.

Then I turned to editorials, compared them as to topical interest, punch, and style of writing, looked over the cartoons and illustrations. In an hour I was ready. Lord Northcliffe's paper was way below its rival. As I had known the chief for twenty-five years, I gave it to him straight. He was furious, took my notes, verified my findings, and called up the editor of *The Evening News.* There was some delay in putting the call through and Northcliffe, who usually had good command of a bad temper, began to show signs of impatience. By the time the connection was made, he had worked himself into a rage, shouting his criticisms into the telephone, telling the editor he was disgusted and wanted to see him the next day.

He replaced the receiver, turned to me and inquired: "Where did you learn to do that?"

I told him such comparisons were daily routine on *The New York World;* that wherever the late Mr. Pulitzer was, on his yacht *Liberty,* at Cape Martin or at Bar Harbor, he always had the papers compared for him. Lord Northcliffe was greatly interested: "Go on, tell me all about Pulitzer," he said. I explained that when on *The New York World,* I had been Mr. Pulitzer's guest for a few days at Bar Harbor and had learned much about life on the yacht from his secretaries, Captain Norman Thwaites, George Pollock, and Alleyne Ireland, whose *Reminiscences of a Secretary* give a vivid picture of what working for Mr. Pulitzer was like, and I was able to hold the chief's attention for more than an hour.

As always, when his interest was aroused, Lord Northcliffe was excited, and in a silly effort to impress the chief with my own descriptive powers I ended by dramatizing the absolute helplessness of the blind genius who was entirely dependent on others for everything that made life worth living to him.

A strange look, a haunted look of fear that I had never seen before, came into Lord Northcliffe's eyes, and he rose trembling all over. "If I had been Pulitzer," he said "I would have shot myself!" Then he went over to a cupboard between the two windows and taking out a glass jar filled with alcohol, showed me the cancerous growth that had been removed from his thyroid.

"Look at that!" he shouted. "Damn the doctors! And now they won't let me out of this house. Here I am all day shut up between these four walls! What difference is there between that and being blind? I am often tempted to end it all, to be rid of fools, to get some peace! My God, I will!"

His voice had risen harsh and unnatural. He laid the jar

down on a small table near his couch, pulled out the drawer, and seized a service revolver, before I could do anything.

Whether or not an English jury would have believed me, whether or not the eloquence of counsel could have saved me from the gallows, I do not know. But I saw the danger in which I stood. I was alone in the room with Northcliffe, the natural assumption would be that we had had a row and that I had killed him. There he stood with a gun in his hand, at any moment he might raise it to his head. I thought hard and quick.

"Chief" I said, as calmly as I could, "did you see that cartoon of yourself as Napoleon?"

"No, where?" he asked. I pretended to go through the mass of papers on the table, and Northcliffe put down the gun and came to look with me. In a flash I was between him and the weapon. I was safe. A moment later the valet announced that dinner was ready. We walked downstairs to the dining room, and as we took our seats the Chief said: "Henry, you must not let me get excited."

—HENRY NOBLE HALL, November 1948

"LITTLE EGYPT" OF HOOTCHY-KOOCHY FAME, ONE LONE REPORTER'S STORY

Following my coverage of the trial of Harry Thaw in 1907, the *Evening World*'s city editor, Charles Chapin, kept me hopping furiously all over the city in search of human interest. I even had to work every second Sunday at Police Headquarters.

Reporters assigned there were supposed to run down all "police slips" of arrests and other happenings for the Monday papers, and the *Evening World* would not be behind the mornings.

Chapin used to reach the city room at 6:30 to get the jump on the evening papers, particularly Hearst's *Evening Journal*. Chapin wanted all copy in for his first edition so it could be out on the streets by 9 o'clock.

One dull, freezing Sunday, about a year after the Thaw trial, the reporters at Headquarters were glancing casually, if at all, at the incoming slips. They were more interested in poker. I didn't indulge, having been brought up by great card-playing parents. Almost hating the sight of playing cards, I spent my headquarters time reading the Sunday papers.

I was itching to get out on the street when along came a slip from the Tenderloin stationhouse in West 30th Street. A woman had been found choked, dead for ten days or so, in an uninviting tenement house in 37th Street just west of Seventh Avenue.

"That's nothing, Dodge," the other reporters said, "forget it!"

But I had my reasons. "If there is anything to it," I replied, "I'll let you know!"

Working together on many murder stories, I had come to know Chief Coroner Harburger very well. "JULius," as we called him, was hell-bent for publicity. He wanted to see his name in every other line of any stories in which he figured officially. At that time, incidentally, the law gave the coroner precedence over the police.

JULius and I became so friendly that he called me his "personal secretary," and had bestowed on me a badge similar to his own, together with some engraved cards bearing the coroner's official crest.

Outside of Police Headquarters, I phoned JULius about my story at his home nearby, and he invited me over to have Sunday dinner with the family. When I declined, he wanted to go uptown with me. This I didn't want, so I assured him that I'd call him from the scene.

When I arrived at the address, I found a policeman standing guard outside. I showed my Coroner's "credentials" instead of my press card. He waved me inside and called up to another policeman who was stationed outside the apartment door to say the coroner's assistant had arrived.

The body had been dead for days and days, no doubt of that. My first bit of business was to open wide the two living-room windows. After I hung my head outside in the freezing air, I walked back to the bedroom alcove where the body lay. The woman had been choked and the marks were on her. But I was also caught immediately by the pastel portrait, standing on an easel, of a female dancer, and it was the same woman. I recognized who she was. She was the famous "Little Egypt," the sensation of the Chicago World's Fair. My parents had taken me to the fair and my curiosity had picked up everything to know about her.

Behind the easel picture was a desk; the top strewn with torn-up letters, and I stuffed the pieces in my pocket.

Once outside, I phoned JULius and suggested he visit the scene of the crime. I also told him about the letters and that I would call him again once I had read them. Then I picked myself a desk at the old Herald Square Hotel in 34th Street and went to work. Soon, I had put together enough pages to clue me in unraveling a story.

The letters chiefly consisted of a correspondence between lawyers in Manhattan and in Buffalo. The Buffalo lawyers, acting for a wealthy client in that city, had been trying to locate and make a financial settlement on Little Egypt. Years before, it appeared the client, then a student at Yale, had met the dancer and their acquaintance blossomed into romance; they had become engaged—ring and all. Then Little Egypt learned that his parents had firmly opposed his marrying her. She returned her ring and said she never wished to see him again. She never did.

For years he bombarded her with letters, addressing them by her real name and sending them care of her last-known address. She never answered the letters nor the messages sent by the Manhattan attorney who knew, somehow, of her various locations.

For a while she earned a modest income from posing for artists. But, as her friends died off and her physical qualifications for modeling began to fade, Little Egypt turned to prostitution.

She set herself up in the cheap tenement and there now she lay, strangled by a client who evidently wanted more than "a good time." The flat had been ransacked for jewels or money; even a hole had been cut in her mattress in the search for something valuable. The killer had shown no apparent interest in the beautiful portrait and ignored the torn-up correspondence.

With the story shaping up in my mind, I headed for the building downtown where the local attorney had his office. Remember, it was Sunday and the building locked up tight. A watchman answered my ring of the front door. I talked fast and furious to impress him that it was a matter of life or death for me to get the lawyer's home address. No use. As the watchman started to close the door, a dollar bill appeared and disappeared into his hand. Then he asked what he could do. I told him to take me up to the law offices and stand over me while I looked for the home address and phone number of the man I sought. I had remembered that there is usually a desk directory kept handy alongside office switchboards.

There was indeed such a book and I quickly noted down the data I needed.

From the first pay telephone I could find outside I put in a call to New Rochelle and reached my man. When I told him about Little Egypt and his torn letters he agreed to hurry into town and meet me, close by Grand Central Terminal.

From this meeting I hurried back to the *World,* and when I told the assistant city editor what I had, he told me to start banging it out. Then the city editor of the *Morning World* rushed in and immediately got busy on the Buffalo law firm.

The story on the Buffalo end was pulled together by the *World's* local correspondent and a reporter dispatched by first train to that city. For nearly a week, *The World* and *The Evening World* carried front-page Little Egypt specials from both Buffalo and New York.

—WENDELL PHILLIPS DODGE, March 1972

Note: This is a truly inside story, as old clippings show. Other papers of the day—cleanly scooped on this sensational murder—took a sourgrapes attitude, choosing to publish a prettied-up account provided by Little Egypt's embarrassed family. Her true name, by the way, was Katherine Devine.

LADY LUCK WAS A LADY
AS EDWARDS HIT IT AGAIN

Old Broadway was just simmering down for the night when the two big bronze men at the big bronze clock over the front door of the *New York Herald* began whamming out the hour. Late strollers lined the curb to listen. It was the night of May 28, 1914, late and just turning into May 29, when the deep-toned peals died into a bulletin in all the newspaper offices:

"Canadian *Empress of Ireland* sunk."

Bulletins were slow. Ten or fifteen minutes later another bulletin:

"*Empress* on her side just off Rimouski. Rammed by freighter *Storstadt.*"

George Daley was news editor; Bob Dill night city editor. They jumped together in a conference and then fast, they ordered reporters: "Call Grand Central and find out where Rimouski is"—"You find out how to get there."—"You get the steamship people out of bed; get pictures; all the info." Etc. etc. etc.

Bulletins came very slowly; not more than three or four by two o'clock in the morning—and very skimpy at that.

I was taken off the night city desk and ordered to cover the story. "This looks very bad," George said to me. "Bob says it's OK for you to go. Now, go home and get some sleep; if it holds up I'll call you; not otherwise. Don't forget your camera."

George woke me at 4 o'clock: "Train out of Grand Central at 5; get it. I'll meet you at the train with plenty of money. This is a whale of a story. You'll have to get your tickets at Quebec for Rimouski. Maybe you can catch the newspaper train that will be going out when you get to Montreal."

I caught the newspaper train in Montreal. Aboard already

were 225 or 230 news and camera men—and they all had tickets clear to Rimouski. We arrived at Quebec at eight o'clock in the morning. I jumped off the car steps to chase to the depot for my ticket to Rimouski.

At that moment the conductor of the Rimouski train, just in, told my conductor: "They're bringing all the survivors in here on the next train; and all the bodies, by river on a battleship—"

And that news train went right out that moment, with all the news group—reporters and camera men—and on the way to Rimouski which was 250 miles out the peninsula east and no way to get back to Quebec until the next day.

And I was left ALONE, the only news or camera man there. It just happened. I hadn't arranged it.

I went to the Chateau Frontenac, freshened up, got coffee. I did not have to wait long. Here they came, just hundreds of them. Among the first to arrive were the Rev. James Wallett, Essex, England and J. H. Cash, Nottingham, England. They were the last to go off the rolling side of the *Empress*. Then came Mr. and Mrs. Thomas Greenway, of Toronto. They jumped off the *Empress* arm-in-arm; were separated; each thought the other lost; were reunited at the Chateau Frontenac. Stories like that on every hand. The crowd of reporters at Rimouski had to work by one telegraph wire, amid a swarm of confused officials who were forced to break up boxes to make crude coffins for the victims.

Now, down to the pier where they were bringing all the bodies, flags at half-mast; crowds around, just like it would look for weeks. And to the railroad with my films: "Five dollars if you will get these to the *New York Herald*," I offered a conductor.

"Been reading the *Herald* for forty years. Do it for nothing. I connect almost immediately with a New York conductor friend. He'll get them there." He did. They turned out beautiful, sharp shots. "The first pictures from the wreck" all across the *Herald*'s front page.

By Saturday evening, I had a complete story on the wire, thousands of words. About half-past eight I was walking out of the Western Union when four New York reporters in a bunch met me. I did not know any of them.

"Well, here we are," they said, "what can you do for us?"

"I keep carbons of everything I write. You can divide them up. You have very little time. Go to it."

They were Johnny Jones, *New York Sun;* Earl Hadley, *Evening Sun;* Harold Vivian, *American;* William Curtin, *Tribune.*

After that, we all went to the Chateau Frontenac for a letdown. About 4 the others went to bed. I took a shower, freshed, then went down to the dock. It was deserted. I sat on a box for a time, then a lone man came from the *Storstadt* which had put into dock.

"Do you happen to know about the wreck?"

"Well," he returned agreeably, "I was the officer of the deck on the *Empress*. I saw it all!"

And no one had met up with him. He was the only one who did have the story. And again, it was all mine!

His story, briefly was: "There was a low-lying fog all over the Gulf. We heard the *Storstadt* coming. She was blowing her whistle occasionally. We figured she was proceeding at her usual speed—even in the fog—and at night. We signaled for her to slow down, but she didn't slow down. We repeated our signals. She ignored them. In a few minutes I saw her mast lights coming over the fog bank. She was coming so fast I knew she would hit us. Nothing could have prevented a collision. She hit us hard on starboard and we started to roll over almost at once.

"Passengers were jolted out of their bunks. Those below had no chance. The stairways from below always Y out at the top. When a ship rolls one stairway turns up until it is almost overhead. The other turns down into the water. There was no way to get down to any of them or for anyone to get up. Naturally there was a bedlam of the doomed. Many persons jumped overboard and were drowned. And there were so many little children, drowned in their sleep."

Sunday afternoon May 31 two ships brought all the bodies up the St. Lawrence. A small white ship, hardly bigger than a tugboat, carried the children, and back of it a huge battleship, coming slowly, it seemed caressingly. In the dim sunlight, looking down from the Heights of Quebec, the two ships looked for all the world like a big mother hen slowly trailing and guarding her chicks.

At the decorated pier, the bodies were placed on long table-high platforms inside. The bodies of the adults were mostly in open top boxes, or crude coffins, the best that could be found in the emergency. The bodies of the children, more than 300 of them, were assembled in one section. They were in small packing cases or paper cartons; some of the children were so tiny they were in shoe boxes with their feet sticking out the open ends.

As the husky sailors came across the gangplank, each with one or two small boxes on one arm and one or two on the other, tears streamed down their faces. Nor did they attempt to check them. The people watching were in tears, too. It would have been a hard soul that could have kept a dry eye while watching the heart-breaking parade.

Someone has said that death by drowning is easy, that your thoughts are of pleasant things. But that was not true in this case. Faces and twisted bodies of the adults showed pain.

With the little children it was different. There were no expressions of fright or pain on any of them—any of them. Evidently they had been drowned in their sleep—and quickly. And—on the face of each one was the smile of a little cherub.

—DELT EDWARDS, October 1970

(In loss of life the *Empress,* with 1024 dead, is exceeded only by the *Titanic* among peacetime ocean disasters.)

GIRL AFOOT IN THE TENDERLOIN—
OLD-TIME POLICE REPORTER RECALLS

That section of New York City from the north side of 14th St. to the south side of 42nd St., bounded on the east by Fourth Ave. and on the west by Eighth Ave., was the famous Tenderloin. Most of the leading hotels in the early 1900s were in that district and nearly all the theaters. There were also many bawdy houses and gambling houses. In the days of the Raines Law hotels, every drinking place had ten rooms for rent and every corner seemed to house a saloon.

The Tenderloin police station was on the north side of 30th St. midway between Sixth and Seventh Aves. One of the most troublesome problems was the great number of unescorted women who patrolled the streets at night, mainly the avenues. Plainclothes policemen were always on the prowl, and week-end nights they would arrest 50 to 75 women on the charge of loitering. These were never in a cell very long; most of them had arranged for bail before their arrest.

All the morning newspapers assigned men to the Tenderloin, even the Bennett *Herald,* the only paper with its home base in the district. Newsmen went on the job at dusk and did not quit until 2 or 2:30 a.m. The chief news source was the Tenderloin police station. Directly across from the station on the ground floor of a tenement the reporters rented a two-room office and installed private telephone wires to their offices!

To reporters who gave any thought to the question, turning these women out on the streets again after a professional bondsman furnished bail at cost of $5 each and then fining another $5 or $10 the next morning in a police court looked like a futile way of handling the problem. It only made the women work harder. So when it became rumored around that someone with police blessing was opening a night club for the social outcasts, it seemed a sensible sort of undertaking.

This first night club of the Tenderloin, the Haymarket, started under the management of a young man with a scar on his face who was reported to be a former policeman's son. Anyway, he had sufficient money to take over an unoccupied building, formerly a museum, on the southeast corner of Sixth Ave. and 30th St. There was a good-sized dance floor and on three sides a balcony wide enough to hold tables and chairs.

The Haymarket prospered from the start. The boss would not stand for any rough stuff, and if a woman was even accused of robbing a man in the place, he never let her in again. He also barred the male friends who at first tried to lounge around to see how their women were doing.

Nevertheless, there seemed to be just as many women as ever sauntering the streets and getting booked at the station.

From our reporter's office there in 30th St. we used to watch one particular girl, quiet and neat, regular in her habits, going along every evening at dusk and returning at 1:30 in the morning. She wore dark clothes and always a sailor hat, white or brown or black, and she always carried a book under her arm.

We assumed that she had some sort of service job, working nights, probably in a hotel. That impression held for a year until someone spotted her sitting at a table in the Haymarket. From then on when she passed the office some reporter or other would always say hello.

You could set a clock by her quitting time. But one chilly fall night here she came, hurrying homeward around midnight.

"You are early," said a reporter to her. "What's the trouble?"

"I guess trouble is my name," said the woman. "In the powder room of the Haymarket last night I knocked a bottle

Shoeleather and Printers' Ink

----

of poison out of the hand of a young girl who was about to drink it. She had just learned she had an incurable disease. She was broke and homeless. I took her home with me. This morning I sent for a doctor. The woman who owns the house knows my business. She stopped the doctor and found out what was the matter with the young girl. Now she has ordered me to get her out of the house today or get out myself. That is why I am hurrying home."

"Maybe I can help," said the reporter. "I'll see if I can't get an ambulance to take her off your hands early tomorrow."

In those days there was a sort of general manager who seemed to run Bellevue regardless of who was medical head. He was a one-legged genial cuss who thrived on helping anyone in trouble. Before noon that next day he sent the ambulance and took the sick girl to the hospital on Welfare Island.

Early that night the woman, still carrying her book, halted the reporter and thanked him for helping to get the sick girl to the hospital.

"I want to say good-bye," she said. "I've had enough."

"Why did you bother with that young girl?" asked the reporter. "Did you know her?"

"No, I did not know her. But I have a daughter about her age who is finishing her education in a convent. I did what I could for her because I hope God will have someone help my own daughter if she is ever in trouble. I am going home to my daughter now."

"Where is your home?"

"Don't ask me, or my name, please. Try and remember me kindly as I will remember you."

"Answer me one question before you go. Why did you always carry a book under your arm? I see it is Victor Hugo's *Notre Dame*."

: 54 :

_____

"The book was my protector. I have never been arrested. The type of policemen who arrest women on the street are book-shy and I discovered that early in my career."

—DAN SLATTERY, October 1964

The author, an honored charter member of the Silurians died at the age of 91, in June, four months before his story was published. The manuscript was yellowed and a note said, "written fifty years ago and never printed. It turned up when I was going through a lot of junk."

DISTRICT SHACK CELEBRATES
WITH KEG OF BOOTLEG BEER

Today's reporters are sober young married men who commute to the suburbs and have no time for the hell-raising of the old district men. Here is change indeed since the days before electronics and radio cars, especially before Repeal.

The district men covered their territory from the district shack, chiefly police news. Each of the papers then kept a man in the Bronx, Harlem, East and West Side, Bellevue, and headquarters, besides the Brooklyn crews which had a flavor and identity of their own. They might not write their own stories but they could pull out the facts like a vacuum cleaner and feed them to a rewrite man with nothing missing.

None among them was a greater man than Dan Madden of the *New York American* down at Bellevue, the hero and almost the ruination of a party at the East Side shack. Dan was one of the neighbors' children who had graduated from copy boy to district reporter. The party was to welcome back Jim Lewis of the *World,* who had been out ill for several months.

The shack was on the ground floor of a brownstone, a couple of doors from the East 51st St. station. The windows had bars, the entrance was a grilled iron door underneath the stoop, a setup practically identical with 90 out of every 100 East Side speakeasies.

For our party we arranged to get a half barrel of beer from a Third Avenue speak and asked Madden to get the Morgue wagon to transport it. The Morgue wagon we had in mind was an inconspicuous black panel truck with no marking on it. They also had a beaten-up old ambulance at Bellevue, used to haul stiffs from the hospital to the Morgue around the corner. It tickled Madden's Irish sense of humor to get a uniformed driver and the old ambulance for our beer.

You know what happens when you stop an ambulance on a New York street. Well it did. We rolled the barrel out of a side door of the speakeasy, tossed it into the ambulance and yelled at the driver to get going before the crowd got any bigger. Madden sprang onto the jump seat across the rear. As the ambulance swung around the corner at a good clip, the keg rolled all the way back and smacked Madden in the rear end, knocking him out into Third Avenue. His yell slowed the driver, but a look at the crowd convinced us that it was no time to stop.

We pulled up outside the shack and a bigger crowd gathered. Quickly we rolled the keg in, closed the door, and pulled down the curtains.

In a moment there was a banging on the window and a voice, "Open up, this is the police." We knew it couldn't be any of our friends from next door. After all the Captain had been invited to the party. It was one of the Special Service Squad who was sure he had caught the precinct's protected speakeasy. The Special Service Squad operated independently, and part of their job was to catch the precinct men who were blinded to a barroom by the sight of Hamilton's engraved portrait.

We called the station house and asked for somebody to take off our necks the guy who was hammering on our window. Eventually our pals persuaded the Special cop to leave.

However, there was a firehouse half a block away and those firemen had not needed the commotion to tell them "free beer." They piled in almost immediately and we could see our supply vanishing. Then Jack Kenney of the *News* and

Johnnie McIlkenny of *City News* slipped out and pulled a fire box. When the signal tapped out on the alarm in the shack, the firemen yelled "That's our call," and dashed to the fire-house. They never got back in and the party proceeded.

Having no place to put the beer barrel to keep it cold we had propped it up on a couple of cakes of ice on a desk. It lasted well, until our offices gave us good-night at 4 a.m.

The next evening when we came in, there was a huge puddle covering the floor and a note from the landlord, "Move at once."

—MARSHALL E. NEWTON, April 1965

STAG FILM BACK WHEN—
STOPS A MIDNIGHT CROWD

Back in the thirties the East Side shack was in a store on 51st St. near Third Avenue, a dirty little place with bare wood floor-space for the four wretched police reporters who inhabited it.

To endure our shame in private we had strung a cheap cotton curtain about halfway up the window, and we'd sit around nights watching disembodied heads bobbing up above the curtain to get a glimpse of us. The neighborhood word said we were bookmakers—how else explain four men who opened their shop at 7 p.m., stayed to 4 a.m. and sat around for nine hours doing nothing but playing pinochle while waiting for the phone to ring?

The shack has long since disappeared, and the corner is now occupied by—of all things—the national headquarters of the Girl Scouts of America. (I sometimes shudder to think what would happen if some of the "girl scouts" who dropped in to see how the newspaper boys were doing were to visit the present occupants of the site.)

At the corner of Lexington Avenue, now occupied by the Summit Hotel, was Loew's Lexington, a movie house that originally had been an opera house; and midway between Lexington and Third Avenues, across the street, the old station house.

I covered the beat for *The Times;* the other guys worked for the *Herald Tribune,* the *Mirror* and the City News Assn. We had a lot in common, including economic status—$35 a week, give or take a buck or two. But there were the Stork Club, El Morocco, and the Versailles Restaurant where we were frequently "house guests" (freeloaders) and could rub elbows with the affluent.

In those days crime laboratories had not yet come into full bloom, and detectives maintained a string of stool pigeons to whom they gave amnesty for petty crimes together with dope and sneaky pete (cheap wine). We reporters referred to the dicks as sleuths and attributed to them fantastic powers of deduction whenever they made a significant arrest.

In return, the sleuths would show their gratitude in numerous ways. One time they raided a stag party and gave us enough film for a two-hour show. They used to call such films French movies; now they rate them X and show them in "art" theaters. In any event, we quickly borrowed a projector and prepared for a showing. I drove up to Ruppert's Brewery, then at 9th St. and Third Avenue, and got the beer.

We borrowed glasses from the bar across the street in return for inviting the bartender. Then we stopped into the station house and tipped the word to the detectives, the lieutenant at the desk, and the duty sergeants that we were having a movie at midnight when they came off duty. There was an assistant district attorney in the station house and we asked him too.

Now picture the scene. The damn store was crowded when all four reporters were in it. And there must have been 30 people in there that night. We put the beer barrel on the table and we had to put chairs out on the sidewalk to make room for all the standees. The table alone held 8 people. I was working the beer spigot, and we passed the glasses over each other's heads.

First, we doused the lights and tried showing the picture on the dirty brown wall. No good. So we turned the projector around and threw the beam on the window curtain. We got a clear image.

For the next two hours we drank beer, smoked, and watched fornication performed in endless variations. The air got stale and so heavy with cigarette smoke that tears streamed down our faces. But, I am proud to say there wasn't a sissy among us—every man stayed to the end.

When the last inch of film had been ground through the machine someone threw on the lights and opened the door. It was unbelievable; the smoke billowed out as from a fire; we come bursting out with it onto the sidewalk—and into sheer amazement.

It seems that Loew's Lexington had let out its last show about midnight, the same time we started ours. Homeward bound moviegoers passing the shack could clearly see our show through the cotton window curtain. And that stopped them—some 200 people, men and women, standing there across the street as in silent appreciation. They had been standing there for two full hours.

No one appeared shocked by what they saw; no one had gone into the nearby police station to complain against the obscene performance; and no one was surprised to see police officers, whom they surely recognized despite street clothes, come trooping out of the shack. After a while, realizing the show was over and not just in intermission, they went home.

—RALPH KATZ, March 1970

MIKE, THAT GRAND OLD NAME,
& THE GREAT MEN WHO WORE IT

The importance of being Mike, for a district man, could doubtless be exaggerated, and there were other good ones named Harry or Bill or maybe Percy, but the Mikes seemed to have it. Anyway, Mike is a good starting point for a round-up on the old-time district man, now largely obsolesced by electronic journalism and the roving radio press car. In his day he kept the paper tuned in to the raw stuff of life, a man of ingenuity and deep loyalty, a principal hero of shoptalk.

Mike Haggerty of the City News Assn., *Herald* and *Times,* began at the age of 17, retired from *The Times* 20 years ago after 51 years of it, and will be 88 next June. His son on *The Times* thinks still that newspapers are here to stay. The City News started Mike at $12 a week, with $3.50 allowance for expenses. Among stories he covered were the burning of the steamer *General Slocum* at Hell Gate, 1030 dead, and Harry Thaw's shooting of Stanford White at Madison Square Garden.

Another marine story, Mike covered on horseback—policeman's horse. Mike then was working out of the Morrisania Police Station, 160th St. and Third Ave., the Bronx. A call from the office told him a Fall River boat on a weekend excursion—(Mike called it a "bed boat")—was grounded just off Barretto's Point, somewhere near Hunts Point. The police captain had already driven off to the scene in a surrey, and how was Mike going to get there?

Well, Mike had a friend on the desk at the station, and the friend told the sergeant to have one of the men lend Mike his horse. Mike had ridden bareback a little, but never in a saddle, and he distrusted the contraption. So the desk just ordered the sergeant to go along to steady him. "The sergeant had a hell of a time," recalls Mike, "keeping me from falling off." However, he covered the story and came back in the captain's surrey.

Another of the famous Mikes was Mike Finnegan, long indispensable at Headquarters, concluding with the *World-Telegram*.

Mike was covering a conference with Commissioner Valentine about a series of hassles over police refusal to honor press cards. His report to the office went like this:

"The Police Commissioner said that when he signs the police card, that means that every officer should honor it even if there was a great confla—, if there was a big conflag—, even if there was a hell of a fire."

Mike was a reporter and not a writing man, so he was a bit panicked when some joker on the desk of the old *Telegram* phoned him at the police headquarters shack and said the paper had a new rule: each district man would have to turn in a feature story once a week. Other men at the shack offered to help him out, and one of them wrote an interview with an old-time cop.

When the story arrived at the old carbarn in Dey Street, the prankster on the desk guessed what had happened and promptly called Mike. "This is such a good story, Mike," he said, "that we are taking you off police and putting you on features." Without benefit of counsel, Mike confessed.

A third top-ranker of the name was Mike Clary of *PM*, among other papers. He could assume a presence of vast dignity. Taking out and adjusting his goldrimmed pince-nez attached to its black silk ribbon, he would question an eyewitness on the scene as if he were at least a deputy commissioner, scooping up facts by the shovel full. (For another pride of the name, Mike Claffey of the Journal-American, see page 287.)

The master in that line was Oscar Herdman, lobster police

headquarters man for the *World-Telegram,* who many times saved the first edition by a bold technique of his own. Homer Thorne, lobster city editor, would call Oscar and say, "We haven't a headline in the shop. Dig up something!" Oscar would go over the morning papers and pick out a New Orleans kidnapping, a Hollywood shooting, or a Denver mayhem, and phone police headquarters in the selected town. "This is Herdman, calling from New York police headquarters," he would say. "Anything we can do for you in crime?" And some bored lieutenant, flattered by the call would talk freely, often disclosing an arrest or a new clue that the local papers and wire services did not know because the morning newspapermen had gone home to sleep and the evenings had not shown up. And Homer would have an eight-column headline.

—March 1967

MINUTE HANDWRITING CHECK
CATCHES LINDBERGH KIDNAPPER

The task of the night editor of the *Evening Journal* (later the *N.Y. Journal-American*) in the midthirties was comparable to that of a magician pulling rabbits out of a hat. Lockup time was 2:30 a.m.; presses start 50 minutes later, while the a.m. papers still were replating. Yet his edition always had to appear exciting with fresh news. It involved a constant burrowing for exclusive stories.

I held down that job in those days. In the hope of picking up some tip that would lead me to the cherished scoop, I used to check in with the city desk in the afternoon, after the Wall St. final. My city desk contact was the late Al Williams, whose record for longest service on the paper, has yet to be equalled.

When I phoned on the afternoon of Sept. 20, 1934, Al's voice was hysterical. "All hell is loose," he shouted. "They've caught the Lindbergh baby kidnapper. A guy called Richard Hauptmann. Passed out ransom bills. A bushelful was dug up in his garage."

"Any other evidence?" I asked. "That's all so far," Al replied. "Everybody's on the story."

Ransom bills found on a man did not necessarily prove he had climbed a ladder into the Lindbergh home, stolen the child out of the crib, and killed it. Evidence was needed to tie him more tightly to the crime.

I had a hunch.

"How about getting samples of the suspect's handwriting to compare it with the ransom notes?" I asked. "Maybe at the Motor Vehicle Bureau?" "Good idea," Al replied.

When I arrived at the office that evening, Al was riding the most extensive coverage in years. He handed me the schedule, adding: "We've got his driver's and auto license applications."

I ordered blowups of the license applications and the ransom notes. Then we phoned Scott E. Leslie, the handwriting expert whose testimony had helped convict the notorious underworld kingpin Waxie Gordon, to learn if he would be home later that night.

Jittery lest Leslie unwittingly spill our secret to the police or another paper, we refrained from tipping him off that we had handwriting specimens of the Lindbergh suspect. For the same reason, we delayed our call on him as late as our deadline permitted.

The minutes dragged endlessly. Finally, Sid Livingston, the paper's legendary police reporter, took the documents and drove to Leslie's home in Brooklyn where he found him asleep. At midnight Sid phoned: "The same man wrote them all. Leslie recognized the similarities in one look."

We wanted more than one look. The story had to be convincing—and libel-proof. "Sid," I said, "please have him examine the scripts thoroughly, analyze each letter separately, pinpoint the identical markings." I hung up and ordered Joe Harrington, our star rewrite man—later a notable contributor to the *Saturday Evening Post*—to clear his desk for the big story.

Soon, Sid was on the phone again. "Leslie has checked the writing by every known test. There's not even the shadow of a doubt." "Give the story to Joe," I said, "and hang around there. Keep Leslie amused. We want to read the story to him when it's finished."

The City Edition of the *Evening Journal* began to roll at 3:20 a.m. on Sept. 23, 1934. An 8-column red "extra" topped the masthead, and beneath it splashed bold 8 column 240 point banners:

"WRITING LINKS SUSPECT TO LINDY
BABY-KILLING"

The main story ran 2 column measure with a 60 point readout saying: "Prisoner Penned Kidnap Note, Says Expert" and in column one, another story in 48 point type: "*Journal Pins Ransom Note to Suspect.*" Under the headlines, between the stories was a 5 column cut of Hauptmann's application for a driver's license, and below it two 2½ column cuts, the ransom note that had been left at Lindbergh's home and the note that led to the $50,000 ransom payment. Balancing the layout was a 2½ column head shot of Hauptmann.

Except for the bundles rushed to the out-of-town trains, no paper was allowed out of the press room until the 8 a.m. delivery began. We waited for the other afternoon papers to arrive. They had routine follow-up stories about the prospective arraignment of Hauptmann.

The scoop turned out to be of major significance. Hauptmann had alibied that a friend had left him some packages before going to Germany, had died, and he had opened the packages, found the money, and began to spend it. He had no idea they were the ransom bills. He pleaded innocence.

Our scoop presented the first bit of evidence to shatter his plea. It placed him both at the murder scene and in the ransom deal. It tied him to the "crime of the century" as if he had made a written confession.

—LOU SHAINMARK, November 1961

MAFIA-WATCHING NOT TOO UNSAFE—
IF PLAYED STRICTLY BY THE RULES

"What do you hear from the mob?" has become almost a standard teasing greeting I get from acquaintances, relatives, cops, and Federal agents since I became *The Times*'s Mafia-watcher nearly six years ago.

Running a not-very-close second in number of times asked is: "Don't those Mafia guys ever try to hit back at you because of all those things you write about them?"

Truth is, I hear nothing of any consequence directly from the mob. To be sure, in the tedious hours of waiting outside grand jury rooms or in courthouse corridors during trial recess, the social amenities are observed and there is small talk among reporters and the more urbane bosses of organized crime. During one such recess Carlos Marcello, Mafia boss of Louisiana, beaming with pride because Jerry Greene of *Newsday* spoke highly of Marcello's restaurant, told us: "If you're ever down my way, call me up and I'll meet you at The Plantation."

The best stories about organized crime, including the inner politics of the organization, result from just piecing together bits of information or conjecture obtained from different official sources (not always in agreement), checking records of unsolved murders or of trials deemed too insignificant for the newspapers to have covered, and then putting the jigsaw puzzle together.

Some of these, like *The Times*'s first take-out five years ago on the infiltration of organized crime into legitimate businesses, required more than a month of research including visits to Washington and other cities. Others, like the first in-depth exploration of the Joe Bananas "family," involved a tour of the Canadian municipal constabulary, provincial police, and the Northwest Royal Mounties. (The office wouldn't send me to Italy, but I'm dreaming up a project that I hope will get me to Rome, Naples, and Sicily—Arthur Gelb please note.)

Mafia-reporting involves a problem of ethics. When we describe a racketeer, who may have a police record as long as his arm, as a "Mafia boss" or a "capo" or "consiglieri," are we guilty of McCarthyism? No one has ever been proved in court to be a member of the Mafia because it is not a crime to be a Mafioso. Men of the Mafia have gone to prison for extortion, murder, and other crimes, and for conspiracy (the most effective legal weapon so far). But always it has been for a specific crime, not for membership.

The major difference between McCarthy's public denunciations and the current labeling of Mafiosi is that the former were based, for the most part, on nebulous and unevaluated "information," while the identification of Mafiosi is backed by electronic evidence.

Federal, as well as local, investigative and enforcement agents have freely given to reporters whom they trusted some of the information gleaned from eavesdropping and from informers. Their rationale, which I have accepted in the main (with only a lurking misgiving), has been: "We know, beyond any conjecture and out of their own mouths, that these guys are members of a secret brotherhood that is undermining our whole social and economic system, corrupting public officials and levying tribute in one way or another on every consumer, workingman, businessman, and taxpayer. Until we are able to send them to prison, we need the help of the press. That keeps them off balance and puts a crimp in some of their enterprises."

In a somewhat Quixotic approach, my editors decided recently that I should, when referring to a Mafioso as such, ask him if he was a member of the Mafia and report his answer (if printable). To my surprise, it worked, but under only special circumstances.

Carmine (The Doctor) Lombardozzi, Mafia "money mover" in the Carlo Gambino family, a specialist in investing racket profits in legitimate businesses, was testifying in behalf of a real-estate associate who sought reinstatement of his license which had been revoked for improper practices. It so happened that Lombardozzi, about whom I had written many stories but whom I had not met, had been making inquiries about me from one of my colleagues at a perjury trial in Brooklyn.

"He was asking what kind of fellow you were," my colleague told me, "and then he inquired about your health."

During a recess in the hearing, I approached Lombardozzi and said: "I'm Charlie Grutzner from *The Times*. I felt I should say hello because you've been asking about my health."

The Mafioso's face, under a crown of waved gray hair, creased into a broad smile.

"Charlie," he said. "I'm glad to know you. I've been reading your stuff."

Here was my opportunity to ask the question. "If what they say about me were true," he laughed and answered, "I'd own half of New York. I wish I did."

It made a good quote in the story. After the hearing resumed, he turned several times in his seat on the spectator bench in front of me to make remarks about some of the witnesses. As he left, he said: "Give my regards to Jack. We must have a drink sometime."

I don't know what response a similar question would get from someone like Michele (Mike) Miranda, the grim, tight-lipped septuagenarian consigliere in the "family" of the late Vito Genovese. During weeks of almost daily encounters outside a Queens grand jury room, Miranda only glared at reporters.

By contrast, Santo Trafficante, who became one of the Mafia bosses in Florida after Castro chased him out of Cuba, was as genial as the greeter in a government casino. Trafficante's father had been a boss in Cuba before him. He had grown up in luxury, was well educated and accustomed to the social graces.

Learning that Nick Pileggi, who was covering the hearing for the Associated Press was of Italian parentage, he expressed surprise that the fair-haired newsman had his ancestral roots in Calabria, from which Trafficante had sprung. There was an instant rapport and discussion about the Old Country, which Pileggi had visited.

Once before, I had occasion to put the question about membership in the secret brotherhood. In 1965, after the U.S. Supreme Court had slammed the door on the imprisoned Genovese's hopes for reversal of his narcotics conviction, there were meetings in the underworld on his successor as head of the "family."

One name the police picked up was that of Frank Saverio Celano, a 69-year-old retired restaurateur. Celano had never been arrested for anything more serious than card- and dice-playing. Now he was regarded as a possible "sleeper"—who could manage affairs without the notoriety attached to Miranda, Jerry Catena and Thomas (Tommy Ryan) Eboli—who eventually became the "caretakers" of the "family's" enterprises.

I found Celano in his modest, second-floor apartment nestled between industrial lofts three blocks from Police Headquarters. The slim little man had been named by Valachi, the Mafia turncoat, as a "soldier" under Genovese and was listed by the

F.B.I. as a loan shark. He was wearing red-and-black striped pajamas as he came to the door. "Well?" he said.

I told him there was talk around town that he might be in line "to run Mr. Genovese's enterprises while he's away."

"That's crazy," he said. "There's nothing like that. There's so much crazy talk going around. I have nothing to do with that."

He shut off further questions by saying: "I have nothing to say—you wasted your time." But his tone wasn't hostile. I believe he was secretly pleased that his name had come up, even as a longshot.

The Times carried the story on Page One as it might have reported on a prospect for vice-presidency of A.T.&T.

Oh, yes, that second question I'm sometimes asked, about possible reprisals from the mob? I have never had even a hint of anything more ominous than Lombardozzi's inquiry about my health—and I don't believe he carries any ill-will now.

I once asked Ralph Salerno, the police department's Mafia expert (since retired), whether he, whose testimony had sent men to prison, had any fear of reprisals.

"No, they wouldn't hurt a law-man or a newspaperman as long as you don't play along with them and then try to double-cross them," he replied. "They realize we're doing our job, like they're doing theirs. Besides, they know it would hurt their image to hit a cop or a reporter."

Another time, when I was chatting with John F. Malone, district chief of the F.B.I., I told him what Salerno had said. Malone smiled and said: "He's right in a general way, but if you ever see someone monkeying with your car, call me before you step on the starter."

I'm inclined to accept Salerno's analysis. But if I see someone tinkering with my car, I'll call Malone.

—CHARLES GRUTZNER, April 1969

CATS HAVE NINE LIVES APIECE
AS EVERYBODY OUGHT TO KNOW

As I have always said, the events of that morning were Elmer Roessner's fault, because when he sat at the *World-Telegram*'s city desk he taught me always to report my story in the form of a headline. Another maxim of his was that if an assignment didn't pan out, a good reporter would find—if possible—a substitute story.

"Whatever you have, sum it up as a headline," Rosie would insist. "That way, whoever is on the desk can size up your story immediately and get on with other things."

A flash came in from City News (remember them?) that a fire truck and school bus had collided, on Third Avenue and 17th Street, as I recall. Joe Brady, on the desk, sent me to cover the story pronto.

"Take a cab," Joe said, an order almost unheard of then.

I took a cab, arrived at the scene, and found only that a fire truck and a regular city passenger bus had done a little scraping, but the bus had gone its way and the fire truck was parked outside a saloon. The firemen were in the basement sealing off an ammonia leak and disposing of two cats that had died of the fumes. My assignment had not panned out, but there was another story. I called the desk and, of course, got Joe Brady.

Mindful that I was a Roessner disciple, I said, "18 Lives Lost, Two Cats Dead."

It was Rosie's fault that I had gotten a substitute story. It was Joe's fault, too, that he didn't catch my headline in its entirety. My only sin was pride of authorship. I had become too caught up with my own catchy headline to realize that the headline in reverse, "Two Cats Dead, 18 Lives Lost," would have saved a lot of people a lot of trouble.

The next thing I heard from Joe was: "Give it to Allen Smith in short takes."

Allen got on the phone and said: "Give it to me fast."

Allen was an exceptionally fine rewriteman and good in every respect. So I said: "Eighteen lives lost today when two cats . . ."

"What?" asked Allen. "Repeat that."

I did. He mumbled something that sounded profane and then shouted "Hold on."

Pretty fast then, Allen was back on the phone, saying in the usual prefunctory way: "The desk wants you to come right in."

I didn't realize that it was a "forthwith" summons. As I neared the office, still unwittingly innocent, I met reporters coming up Barclay St. on their way to assignments. The first one gave me a brief account of what had gone on.

Joe Brady had yelled to Bert MacDonald (who had succeeded Rosie) and to the famous Bo McAnney (the managing editor who *never* got angry) what he thought I had turned in.

Copy boys were lined up to relay my story from Allen to the desk and from the desk to the copy desk. All photographers were called to the city desk on the double. Reporters were rounded up to go hither and yon as the story required. All were to take cabs, never mind expense.

The presses were just about to be stopped. Then Allen straightened out all concerned on what I really had turned in.

Well, I thought it was funny. So did my fellow reporters. They all laughed, but their quizzical looks should have warned me that there was a storm in the offing.

I went on to the city room and walked up to Bert with a big grin on my face. About the only thing I remember of that morning then was that Bert took one look at me and said: "Wipe that grin off your face."

Things really are foggy after that. I don't know if Bert said anything else, if anyone said anything at all, but I do remember that I was surrounded by editors, big and little. I remember distinctly that I never had seen Bo wear the look he was wearing. Looking back, I have a hunch that this is the one time the great McAnney could not find words. Everyone just seemed to stare at me as if I were the bastard at a family reunion.

I don't recall having another assignment that day. It wasn't until late afternoon when I was up around the city desk, invited or uninvited I cannot say, that Bo spoke to me.

"Murray," he sighed, "if everyone or anyone had gotten off on that story, if it had cost us in any way, you would have had to pay every penny of that cost."

Then I realized what Rosie had done to me.

—MURRAY DAVIS, March 1966

"ALICE DEAR, I WANT TO PRESENT THIS YOUNG MAN FROM THE CITY"

An obituary published shortly before Christmas brought to mind a story I worked on in the early 1930s. Subject of the obit was a retired minister, 89 years old, once hereabouts the original guru of nudism.

A morning paper, so long ago, reported a nudist camp up the river, actually open and operating. My assignment, from Elmer Roessner, I think, was for independent research among the nudes—probing into, so to speak, their rationale.

At Poughkeepsie I got a taxi, heading over toward New Paltz. I'd made my date by telephone, and there waiting for me on the porch of a roadside farm house sat the Reverend Doctor himself, amply clothed in shorts and shirt. He pointed to a rocking chair and expounded his philosophy, all about his conversion to nudism and his hopes for the movement. Finally he said:—

"The best learning, naturally, is first hand. Why not join our group this afternoon down by the lake—if you feel it would be psychologically possible?"

This was the point, what I had come for, so I followed the Doctor to a fairly large farm chicken house, now freshly whitewashed—the undressing room. Then in flawless camp uniform we walked down the slope back of the house. The crabgrass had been recently cut, and the jabbing stubble held my thought sternly to barefoot level. At the lake we came upon two or three dozen men and women of assorted ages nuding at leisure in the sunshine, in and out of the water. En masse they appeared to me less psychological than if we had come upon them singly or in pairs. They were certainly not the types that Titian painted.

The Doctor led on to a small pier thrust out into the lake,

and here, indeed, stood a girl looking exactly the way a nudist camp girl ought to look.

"My daughter Alice," said the Doctor, and then to her, "Alice, dear, I want to introduce a young man from the city who is joining us for the afternoon."

I took her hand and assumed, as far as possible, a calm and casual attitude. I'd never experienced a paternal introduction quite like this, but it got my instant OK. Alice was about 18, the right size and shape in every detail, and her smile was pure sugar. My assignment however, was professional, not aesthetic. Regretfully, I let go her hand, gargled a few nothings, turned with dignity, and dived into the lake. It was a spring-fed lake and refreshingly cold. I can still feel that cold water.

Going about my work, I talked to a good many of the nudes. I joined a canoeing couple and viewed from the lake the practicing nudists around the shore. Reporting in the nude presents one positive inconvenience, the absence of pockets for notepad or pencil. One must depend upon photographic memory for each detail and nuance. Perhaps after thirty-five years it is only nostalgic yearning.

My story, let me add, was no journalistic prize. No worse, however, than others I have written. I waited several days to see it in print. Then Rosie told me the desk had decided just to skip nudism. At that period, after all, not psychologically possible.

—GEORGE BRITT, April 1969

PRIZE RINGSIDE SEAT FROM
PRESIDENT PAYS OFF IN WINK

There were no Castros or Castroites in Havana back in the spring of 1915 when Jack Johnson gave up his heavyweight title to Jess Willard after twenty-six grueling rounds. I don't mean to say that there were no political plottings or assassinations. Cuba always had plenty of those.

At that time Cuba had one of the nicest men as president that the country ever enjoyed. He was Menocal, educated at Cornell University, and an honest and dedicated man. He didn't store away any government funds in Switzerland or elsewhere as others had done.

I was able to meet him under rather enjoyable circumstances. I was there as a representative of the United Press to cover the fight. But I got there very late.

Already the Associated Press, the International News Service (an organization I later was with for forty-three years) and the *New York World* were all on the scene when I got there. They had reserved ringside wires and there were only three circuits. The government controlled all communications. I argued and bellowed and roared but I got nowhere. I tried to set up a wireless circuit to New York. That failed.

Extremely unhappy, I knew that Roy Howard, president of the United Press, who had sent me there, would not accept any excuses. Someone had given me a guest card to the American club. I could think of nothing better to do than to go over to the American club and drown my sorrows.

Standing at the bar nursing that beer and feeling pretty low I suddenly became aware of a big raw-boned chap standing near me and eyeing me with a puzzled look.

"What's the matter, son?" he said. "You look as though you had lost your last friend."

I didn't need any encouragement to tell him my sad tale.

"Oh, that's ridiculous," he said. "Menocal is a good friend of mine. We'll see him and get this fixed up."

With that he stuck out his hand and shook mine vigorously. "I'm Cap Rice," he said. "Everyone knows me. I'll be glad to help. Who are you?"

I told him. I didn't know then he was the justly famous Cushman A. Rice, whose fabulous story led Richard Harding Davis to write "Captain Macklin." Rice was Macklin in the flesh.

A West Pointer, he had led revolutions in Honduras and had bought hundreds of acres of Cuba sugar and tobacco land. This, despite the fact that his father was one of the richest men in Minnesota. The father owned a string of banks.

Rice had started for the front door. I meekly followed along wondering to myself whether I was a fool and being taken for a ride or whether this fellow was really legitimate.

I soon found out. As we stepped out of the club the doorman blew a whistle and up rolled a big Italian limousine, driven by a liveried chauffeur. Rice gave him directions in Spanish but I could make out enough to know that it was the presidential palace. Reaching there Rice hopped out of the car and strode vigorously up the steps and into the building. I followed but it was difficult to keep up with the long-legged Cap. He strode by secretaries, some of whom raised their hands as though to say "wait a minute." Rice paid no attention. He walked directly into President Menocal's office and started right in talking fast.

"This is an outrage," he proclaimed. "Here is a man representing thousands of newspapers all over the world. (How Roy Howard would have liked that.) They tell him they have no wire to the ringside for him. What are you going to do about it?"

There was a gleam of amusement in Menocal's eyes. "Well Captain I think we should let the man speak for himself. By the way who is he?"

Rice came as near to blushing as I ever later saw him. He whispered to me "what did you say your name was?" Menocal heard him and laughed heartily.

"Introduce yourself," he told me, "and tell me your story."

I did and in a minute he was on the telephone talking to the government engineers. He ordered a ten-pair cable run out to the race track where the fight was being held. After two or three conversations he turned to me and said:

"Rest easy, Mr. Faris. You shall have your wire. I have given orders that you have the first selection of where you want to sit. The wires will be installed by six o'clock tomorrow morning."

I was still pinching myself to make sure it all wasn't a dream as Cap and I made our way out and back to the American club, where we celebrated.

But I was still in so much doubt that I arose very early the next morning—the day of the fight—and took a taxi out to the race track. The ring had been built right under the finish wire on the track.

The man in charge reacted instantly when I introduced myself. It was "si, si, Senor" all the way. He had received the President's message. He conveyed to me the idea that I should select my seat. As the fight was scheduled for noon I figured that the most comfortable seat would be with my back to the sun. So I took a seat on the west side of the ring. I think the late Herbert Bayard Swope who was covering the fight for *The New York World,* drew the seat on the east side and he stared into the sun all afternoon. Frank Menke got there and grabbed the seat on the south side, which wasn't too bad. The AP had the one on the north.

All in the Routine

Of course it is history that Willard won with a knockout in the twenty-sixth round. It wasn't a real knockout nor was it a "frame" as some writers, even including the late Damon Runyon, one of the greatest, said. Johnson took a terrific lacing. The fight was scheduled to go forty-five rounds. I am satisfied that Johnson simply figured that there was no reason why he should go on taking a beating for another twenty rounds.

When Willard dropped him in the twenty-sixth round he fell right in front of me. I could have raised up from my seat and touched him. I swear that with his face turned to me he gave a big wink. He was not out.

—BARRY FARIS, April 1962

And here is a footnote about Rice from *Silurian News* of October 1962:—

Rice had a penchant for newspaper men. He sought their company and they, in turn, thought mighty highly of him.

One of his friends braced him one day with this question:

"Tell me, Cap, why is it that the great majority of your close friends are newspaper men?"

Rice lost no time in replying.

"I'll tell you, son," he said, "it's because the percentage of lice among newspaper men is far lower than in any other type of the human race I have ever met."

: 81 :

HOW TO MEET A CAST OF STARS
IT'S EASY—WRITE ON SPORTS

I was never a theater-goer in my twenty-five years as a sportswriter for a simple reason. During the theatrical season, which corresponded fairly closely with basketball, ice hockey, indoor track, and boxing seasons in New York City, I usually spent about five nights a week sitting in a press seat at Madison Square Garden looking at a contest in one of the above-named sports. That gave me little chance to watch the stage stars behind the footlights on adjacent Broadway.

Even so, I had a wide acquaintance with stars of stage, screen, and radio, as the saying went before the days of TV. I didn't have to watch them act. They came out to help me watch sports events.

In the days when they played ball games by daylight George M. Cohan was in his regular seat at the Polo Grounds or the Yankee Stadium every afternoon except Wednesdays and Saturdays when he had matinees. At the Polo Grounds he sat in the last row of the lower grandstand between home plate and first base. At the Yankee Stadium he sat in a mezzanine box, front row, also between home plate and first base. He always had his crony Sam Forrest with him, and many an afternoon I spent with the two of them, looking at the ball game and listening to George tell of the great players of the past whom he had known.

I met DeWolf Hopper and Wilton Lackaye and Louis Mann at the ball games, too. In fact, I didn't have to leave the press box to meet Louis Mann. As sportswriters know, his insistence on displacing Hughey Fullerton in the press box away back at the play-off game between the Giants and Cubs in

1908 led to the formation of the Baseball Writers Association of America to protect the working press against strolling players. They let Louis back into the press box at intervals later, but only on uncrowded days and as a great privilege.

Among the other red-hot rooters I regularly encountered at baseball games were Tallulah Bankhead, Joe E. Brown (who was a good ball player himself), Raymond Massey, and Bill Frawley. The Giants were Tallulah's team but she was a regular cheer-up visitor to the Gehrig home in Riverdale when Lou was slipping into the shadows.

You never knew where you would meet this cast of characters. It would depend on the city in which their shows were playing. And what sports they preferred. You might meet Bill Frawley at Wrigley Field or Shibe Park or Yankee Stadium. Walter Huston walked with a couple of us while we were following Bob Jones, Walter Hagen, Johnny Farrell—the ultimate winner—in the national open golf championship at Olympia Fields near Chicago in 1928.

I met Bing Crosby just where you would expect—on a golf course. It was at the Winged Foot in Larchmont but for the life of me I can't remember which tournament it was because they have had a lot of big ones there.

At an Army-Columbia football game at Michie Stadium, West Point, the man next to me in the press box was Pat O'Brien, the movie star. "I'm scouting Army for Notre Dame," he whispered. He didn't like what he saw. Army ran all over Columbia.

Tom Meighan, another movie star of older days, followed Gene Sarazen almost like a caddie around the golf course in half a dozen open or P.G.A. championships. Until he retired to Beverly Hills, the veteran actor and playwright Frank Craven used to share a suite of hotel rooms with a group of us covering the amateur and open golf championships in different parts of the country. On several occasions we roomed together. He was a delightful companion. It only goes to show that the way to meet a notable cast of characters is to get a job as a sportswriter and stick at it.

—JOHN KIERAN, March 1967

BATTLE OF THE LONG COUNT— SNAFUS ALSO IN EXCESS COUNT

When I was a young lad and greener than my ancestry, I enlisted in the sports department of *The New York Times,* then a quasi-military group that was run with battlefield precision by Col. Bernard St. Dennis Thomson, the sports editor. The Colonel left nothing to chance. He planned everything to the minutest detail. And when he snapped out orders, the troops said, "Yes, sir," and obeyed.

In early September, 1927, a major campaign lay ahead, the return bout between Gene Tunney and Jack Dempsey in Chicago for the heavyweight championship of the world. Scouting parties already were on the scene.

John Kieran was there to write the new Sports of the Times column which I was to inherit in 1942. Jim Harrison handled a general lead each day. Dick Vidmer covered Tunney's training camp at a Chicago suburb and Jimmy Dawson was with Dempsey. Two weeks before the fight the Colonel summoned me to his command post.

"Young man," he snapped, "you are to leave for Chicago in the morning. Interest in this fight keeps mounting and I want you to help out the others in any way you can."

"Yes, sir," I said.

"Your assignment on the fight itself," he said, handing me a mimeographed sheet that placed every line, complete, "will be to dictate the blow-by-blow. In the year you've been with us, you've gained a lot of experience with blow-by-blow descriptions from Madison Square Garden and the fight clubs. Forget that this will be the biggest and most important fight you'll ever see. Dictate slowly and evenly to the telegraph operator. Don't panic."

"Have no fears, sir," I said. "I won't panic." Oh, yeah?

So off I went to Chicago for the loneliest and most miserable two weeks I ever spent in my life. Kieran, the bird watcher, was up at dawn every day to study bird life along the lake front. The three others arose late after studying Chicago night life.

At that time I barely knew any of them and was even less acquainted with the other sports writers. So I wandered about, unhappy and alone. But that's how I learned about the gigantic snafu.

One evening Vidmer filed his story on Tunney's training and encountered Gene afterwards. He asked about the next day's schedule.

"I won't train at all tomorrow," said Tunney. "I'm taking the day off."

"Good," said Vidmer. "I'll take the day off, too. I'll write another story tonight, give it to the telegraph operator and tell him to file it at 5 o'clock tomorrow. Meanwhile, I'll be in Chicago, having fun with the boys."

In Chicago the next day Vidmer encountered Dawson.

"What the hell are you doing here?" said Dawson.

"Tunney didn't work out today," said the airy Vidmer. "I wrote a story in advance and left it with the telegraph operator to file this afternoon."

"You fathead!" screamed Dawson. "I'm covering Tunney today. You're covering Dempsey. We've switched camps. Didn't you get Thomson's telegram with the new orders? You must have skipped out before it arrived. You're in trouble already for sending an extra Tunney story. You better stir your stumps or you're in a worse mess by not filing on Dempsey."

Vidmer foraged around and pieced together a report on Dempsey's activities. In the lobby on his way to the telegraph office he ran into a Chicago writer who buttonholed him and drew him off into a corner.

"I hope you got the biggest story of all, Vid," said the Chicago friend. "We just heard about it today. Dempsey had secret training in the moonlight last night."

He supplied details. Vidmer raced back upstairs, the unfiled Dempsey story in his pocket, and wrote another story about the secret training. He ran to the telegraph office and sent off this new Dempsey piece, on top of his Tunney story of yesterday's writing, already gone. Smug and happy, he came back to the hotel. The first person he saw was Dawson.

"How did you do with Dempsey?" said Dawson.

"Great," said Vidmer. "You won't believe this, Jim. But Dempsey had a secret workout in the moonlight last night and that's what I wrote about. I've already sent it."

"Ye, gods," moaned Dawson, or words to that effect. "I scooped everyone on that last night. We've already printed my account of it."

The stunned Vidmer groped for a chair. He had sent one full story on Tunney, another on Dempsey's secret workout, and in his pocket was the still unsent Dempsey story. He staggered to Western Union and turned in this one, the third for the day "By Richard Vidmer."

Thomson shot back a long telegram that made Vid's hair curl: Vid would be fired if he didn't offer satisfactory explanation instantly. Vidmer's only defense was the truth. It took him a thousand words to tell it but it saved him from the Colonel's firing squad.

This has to be a sports record for snafus. That I also had one fortunately went unnoticed. I had spent a month at Speculator with Tunney in July, and he was so kind and helpful to the green kid during this preliminary training that I grew to idolize him. What solidified my position with Tunney was that he could not abide the only other sportswriter in camp, Westbrook Pegler, columnist for the *Chicago Tribune*.

My blow-by-blow dictation at the fight was beautifully dispassionate, accurate, and complete—until Dempsey toppled Tunney in what was to make this the Battle of the Long Count. When Tunney went down, I shot up to my feet, the dictation forgotten. A picture long hung in Madison Square Garden of that episode. I was the only ringsider standing, with mouth wide open and a horrified expression on my face.

The blow-by-blow description, mine, made the front page of *The Times*. Every round is a model of simplicity, clarity, and evenness—except the famous seventh. I sure shortchanged the customers on that one. The longest round had the shortest description. I wouldn't panic, eh? I certainly did.

But at least it didn't get me in trouble with my commander, Col. Thomson. He never was aware of it. The only member of the troops to gripe him was Vidmer, the man who produced three different stories on the same day.

—ARTHUR DALEY, October 1965

As Helpful Friends
Congest the Cables

Arthur Daley's story in last fall's issue about the contretemps over the Tunney-Dempsey fight copy reminds me that many of our members must have similar tales of copy mix-ups which they could put down for the *Silurian News*. I recall the story along that line told with glee by old-timers on *The Times* staff about Lee Spears. He was traveling with some diplomatic mission aboard ship to South America where the cable rate for press copy was astronomical, and he fell afoul of the hospitality. Four friends, each too much a gentleman to make any reference to what they were doing to anyone else, filed a story in Spears' name to the office. Freddie Birchall the night managing editor, saw the stories coming in, realized the tolls and knew what had happened. He fired off a message to Spears, "We believed you the first time."

Then there was the time during the 1924 Democratic convention when Jim Hagerty took care of Charley Michaels's assignment, when Charley wandered astray. After he turned in the copy Joe Tebeau, in charge of the convention coverage, roared out, "Who wrote this story? It wasn't Michaels."

Jim confessed that he had written it, explaining that he thought Michaels was delayed. "I knew it wasn't Charley's copy," said Tebeau, "I have been looking forward to copy-reading his story all night." Michaels always turned in copy wondrous to behold. It made good sense when it was deciphered, but it was filled with interlineations, skipped letters in words, open spaces, words and sentences exxed out, at first glance looking like the meanderings of a child who couldn't write. No other copy looked like his.

—MARSHALL E. NEWTON

"GET HIM TO THE CHURCH ON TIME" —A DIRGE OF GUILT-SMITTEN PALS

The overworked and underpaid news staff of the *Daily Mail* of Montreal gave a gay party in 1915 in the city's most fashionable restaurant for one of its associates. This gallant young gentleman was an Englishman, one of our bright and eager reporters. He was about to marry a beautiful English lady, who had been residing in Vancouver, British Columbia. A week or so before the party she had sailed for Montreal for the wedding. The Panama Canal had opened the year before, and her ship was to be the first to transit the Canal from the Canadian West to the East Coast. So the trip was news for the Montreal newspapers.

Another reporter arranged the party. What promises he made and how he did it remain a secret, but as no one on the staff could afford a good dinner with wines and cigars, it had to be on the cuff. We were young then and more concerned with a night of fun than with journalistic ethics. The restaurant lived up to its reputation. We had a good dinner, plenty of liquor, and excellent cigars. It was on Saturday night, and Sunday newspapers were not published in Canada.

When the dinner was over, a substantial number of the party decided to take a look at night-life in Montreal, and of course the prospective bridegroom went along. The city in those days was wide open. Estimates of the number of brothels ran as high as 5,000, and they came in all varieties. Some even provided drinks and music.

Enough of the staff was able to report on Sunday to produce the Monday morning editions. Some had headaches and others hangovers after the night of fun, but all agreed that the party had been a grand success. There were even suggestions that it be made an annual affair. This was the height of optimism, for the *Daily Mail* soon passed into journalistic oblivion. Consternation came earlier, however, when it was learned that the bridegroom-to-be had contracted a violent form of venereal disease, and that same day the *Daily Mail* carried the news that the bride's ship had just started to transit the Canal.

Ardent discussions in the city room considered how long it would take for a cure, and if any cure could be complete and permanent. The consensus was that no cure was possible before the ship would arrive. There was speculation as to how the marriage could be delayed and how the happy bride could be entertained on her arrival. A collection was taken up to pay the physician who had started treatment on the bridegroom. A feeling of doom pervaded the entire staff. All felt guilty.

Then—providentially—a landslide in the Culebra Cut blocked the bride's ship in the Canal. Hope and joy returned to the city room. Stories about that disaster were published daily and posted on the bulletin board.

It developed then that it would take weeks of dredging, a blessing beyond the fondest dream.

So began the most fantastic of races, the race between the physician in Montreal Hospital to clean up the prospective bridegroom and the engineers of the United States Government to clear the Panama Canal. There were high hopes from day to day, and times of deep depression. Just when it looked as if the *Daily Mail's* boy would be licked, there was still another slide at Culebra. There were rumors of prayers being said for still more slides, and reports of bets placed on the result. There was even talk of a pool on the day the ship would get free again.

For the bride's ship finally to reach the Atlantic took almost a month, and for it to enter the St. Lawrence and dock at Montreal, a couple of weeks more. So we won the race. The bride arrived. The marriage took place on time, and every member of the *Daily Mail* staff was relieved of his worry. There were celebrations, of course, and some drank to excess in their joy, but that was all.

It should be told also that the married couple lived happily together and later moved to Toronto, where the bridegroom became in later years one of the most distinguished editors in Canada. Amen!

—NEIL MACNEIL, October 1964

MR. OCHS DROPS IN FOR CHAT
JUST AS PRESSURE GETS HOT

My first night in charge of the production of *The New York Times* was in the first week of June, 1930. I was 39 years old and the youngest man up to that time to put *The Times* to press. I was deeply impressed with the responsibility of directing the staff and fully conscious of the prestige of *The Times* and its reputation for completeness, accuracy, and fairness.

It was an average news night and I got a good start on my work and kept well ahead of the flow of news. At 10 p.m. I had things pretty well cleaned up and was due to go to the composing room in a quarter of an hour for the closing of the first edition. And then Adolph S. Ochs, the owner and publisher, walked up to my desk.

Mr. Ochs was in the habit of dropping in to visit the news department after attending a dinner or some function. He loved to chat with the news editors about the news and their work, but always sought not to disturb them. What is more, he never to my knowledge interfered with the news coverage. He prided himself on the fact that his editors were free to use their best judgment in presenting "all the news that's fit to print," "without fear or favor."

"Don't let me interfere with your work, Mr. MacNeil," he said, as he took a seat beside my desk. "Go right ahead with what you have to do."

He then inquired about the news of the day, and after being informed, he went on:

"I have a little test that I give, that I should like to try on you."

I was not too sure what this meant, whether he was serious or otherwise. Neither was I too sure of myself. My previous acquaintance with him had been limited.

"A friend of mine had a horse, a valuable race horse," he

declared. "He was mighty proud of that horse, which had been bred in his own stables and trained under his supervision. He entered that horse in one of the important stake races of the year. He carefully supervised the horse's training for the race and watched his workouts on the track. Finally the day of the race came. My friend arrived early at the stable to see the horse and to be present when he got his morning work-out.

"When he got there the night watchman said there was a bad omen and that he should not race the horse that day.

" 'The omen,' said the watchman, 'is that I dreamed last night that the horse was leading the race and stumbled and broke his ankle and had to be destroyed.'

" 'That's nonsense,' said my friend, and ordered the horse to be run. He ran and he won, easily. Then my friend went back to the stable and fired the watchman.

"Why did he fire him?"

I made several hesitant replies. My mind wasn't there but was concerned over the approaching edition. To each reply he responded: "Wrong."

Then to add to my embarrassment he added, "I tried this out on Marian, my young granddaughter, and she solved it at the first try."

"Did you put it to her as you put it to me?" I asked.

"Exactly," he replied, "but I should add that I tried it also on her father, and he flunked."

After some more floundering by me, he inquired, "Do you give up?" I did.

"Well," he explained, "he fired the night watchman because he had been asleep on the job. Wouldn't you?"

With that he had a good laugh and left happily for home, and this relieved editor proceeded to the composing room and put the first edition of *The Times* to press.

—NEIL MACNEIL, October 1966

BOSS CHAPIN'S ARREST FOR MURDER: GUESS WHICH REPORTER COVERED IT?

Nearly thirty-five years have passed since Charles Chapin dominated the *Evening World* city room with his cold gray eyes and high-pitched voice, but he still remains the most vivid character and talked-about personality of old Park Row.

The latest story about him comes from Emmet Crozier, who worked on the *Evening World* in the spring and summer of 1918, just before the tragic events that ended Chapin's career.

Crozier, who served as second vice-president of the Society of Silurians in the administration just ended, writes:

"The old man was not as harsh or sarcastic to me as other old *World* men recall him. He did keep me sitting idly in the city room for a week after he hired me, giving me an occasional trivial paragraph to rewrite, or ignoring me entirely; but that was just the silent treatment he gave all new reporters. When I had been broken in, he called me up to the desk one afternoon and assigned me to a regular beat—the old Federal Building, United States District Courts, and the Department of Justice.

"Thereafter for several months I was very busy. I saw the old man only a few minutes when I checked in each morning, and talked to him once or twice a day on the telephone. He scolded me occasionally for being late with copy, but for the most part our relations were tranquil, if not amiable.

"During the summer I got an offer from George T. Hughes, city editor of the *Globe*—a day rewrite job—at $10 a week more than I was getting on the *World*. So I walked up to Chapin's desk one afternoon with a carefully rehearsed speech. The *World* was a great newspaper and I was proud to be a member of its staff. I hoped to continue working under the great gilded Pulitzer dome; but, meanwhile, the *Globe* which was a good paper, too, had offered me $10 a week more. I reviewed my pleasant relations with the *World,* my hard work in the Federal courts, and expressed the hope that the *World* would meet the *Globe* offer and keep me on Park Row.

"The old man listened to me in silence. When I had finished, he said:

" 'How much did you say they'll pay you?' "

" 'Fifty dollars a week. But I'd rather stay on the *World.*' "

" 'Um-mm. Well, that's a good salary for a young man. If I were you, I'd take it.' "

"He said I could finish the week out and then, with a perfunctory nod, dismissed me.

"That was Thursday afternoon. I cleaned out my desk at the *World* Saturday and drew my final week's salary at the cashier's office. When I walked into the *Globe* office the following Tuesday to begin my new job, Mr. Hughes called to me:

" 'Crozier! Don't hang up your hat. Come over here, I have an assignment for you.' "

" 'Your old city editor, Charles Chapin, killed his wife at the Cumberland Hotel a couple of night ago,' " Hughes continued, as I stood before him. " 'He had been missing for forty-eight hours, wandering around the city and has just given himself up at the West Fifty-first Street Police Station. Go up and cover his arraignment at West Side Court.' "

"So my first assignment for the *Globe* was to watch my former boss, the most famous city editor in New York, stand at the rail in the shabby courtroom and mumble his 'not guilty' plea to the charge of murder, and then go back to the *Globe* office and write about it.

"I told Gene Fowler about that last encounter with Chapin in police court, at a Silurian dinner a couple of years ago. Gene listened thoughtfully to the story, and when I had finished, he shook his head, deeply impressed and groping for words.

"'My God!' he said, 'I never had any of that kind of luck with my city editors!'"

—EMMET CROZIER, May 1954

TWO MEN NOT ENOUGH
FOR FOOLING CHAPIN

Charlie Keegan told me this story:—When Chapin was city editor of the *Evening World,* he became suspicious of the way one of the reporters was covering his assignment. So he gave this reporter an assignment to interview someone in mid-town.

When the reporter had left the office, Chapin called Charlie Keegan to the desk, told him what assignment had been given the other reporter and said, "Charlie, I want you to follow him, without his knowing, and come back and tell me just how he covered the assignment."

Charlie left the city room and headed for a bar that was frequented by the *World* crowd. He knew he'd find his fellow reporter there, and did. Charlie climbed on a stool and told what Chapin had said.

After a drink or two both went to Room 9 or what preceded Room 9 at City Hall. They gabbed for a while, then both took a subway uptown. The first reporter got his interview and he and Charlie took a train downtown and to the office. Charlie followed the first reporter in by a few minutes, went up to Chapin and reported that the first reporter had done a good job but had to wait a few minutes to interview the subject.

"Charlie," Chapin said, "you take six weeks off without pay. I had someone following you."

—MURRAY DAVIS, October 1967

SPINNING FOR HIS STORY WITH GANDHI; THAT'S WHAT IT TOOK

I am a mild, self-effacing man who never could cast himself in the melodramatic role Hollywood often assigns a newspaperman. Yet, like others of the craft, I have used artifices and maneuvers to get a story, as while in New Delhi in 1946 for the *New York Post*. I joined Mohandas K. Gandhi's spinning class in order to obtain an interview with him.

Gandhi regarded hand-spinning as the panacea that would lift India's peasants out of the rut of poverty. He not only preached that gospel but put it into operation by promoting the use of a simple, cheap, portable wheel on which to spin cotton thread.

Following his example, politicians and intellectuals discarded their machine-made clothing and wore homespun shirts and loin cloths whose thread they had spun on Gandhi's wheel. This coarse and somewhat itchy material not only became the height of fashion but a symbol of India's struggle to free itself of British rule.

Gandhi, then 77 years old, seldom talked to one reporter. If you had a question you could get him to answer it if you joined the entourage which accompanied him on his daily walk each morning at 5:30. It was my hunch he would see me alone, once he learned that I was seriously interested in learning to spin.

I had the good fortune to be the only American in a spinning class of 33 in a tent across the street from Gandhi's quarters in the Colony of the Untouchables. The course consisted of seven three-hour sessions taught by three young men one of whom was Kanu Gandhi, grand-nephew of the Mahatma and the only one who spoke English and gave me instruction. We sat on the ground, each with his own spinning wheel, an ingenious device enclosed in a portable wooden box. One half of it contained the spindle driven by two wooden wheels. The other held the iron rod for ginning, sharpened bamboo stick for carding, and a bamboo rod for rolling the sliver of untwisted thread.

It wasn't hard to learn even for one as manually clumsy as I, and within three days I was spinning 25 yards of thread per session. Once each day Gandhi, dressed in a homespun loin cloth, his hands resting on the shoulders of two maidens between whom he walked, visited the class. He remained long enough to beam his infectious, toothless smile through steel-rimmed spectacles and then walked out as we beamed back.

At the last session, suddenly I became aware that my fellow students were spinning like mad. But not knowing why, I just waited until I heard the excited voice of Kanu Gandhi calling across the room to me: "Hurry! Get busy! This is a final test, a test against time."

Well, I threw the wheel into high so to speak, but never caught up with those ahead of me. Consequently I flunked.

Kanu blamed himself for my failure because he had not told me in English when the others learned in Hindustani that there was to be a test. He offered to give me another but I declined. Thereby I became eligible to join the thousands of Indians who, being unable to complete a college course either for lack of money or ability, put on their stationery, calling card, or sign on the front door, their names followed by "Failed A.B." or "Failed M.D." or failed what have you. Thus I am privileged to use the degree "F.S." (failed spinner).

Fortunately it did not prevent Gandhi from seeing me two weeks later.

I have seldom felt self-conscious in the presence of a celebrity but I was ill at ease when Kanu Gandhi, who also acted as one of the Mahatma's secretaries, ushered me into the thatched hut which served as Gandhi's office and bedroom. He lay on a cot about six inches from the floor, his body covered by a sheet of homespun. At his side, a few inches higher, was a desk, the only furniture in the room. Gandhi reclined throughout the interview because it was at this time every day that, for therapeutic reasons, he kept a mud pack around his stomach. He motioned me to sit down and I did—on the floor.

I don't know whether it was his smile or his complete serenity, or the fact that both of us were spinners. Anyway my nervousness quickly vanished and I felt I was sitting with an old friend.

I told him I was ashamed that I flunked the course and Kanu interrupted by assuring Gandhi that while I was not a speedy spinner, the quality of my thread was first class. That brought another of his heart-warming beams and we then talked for an hour about India and its intricate problems and how he planned to live to 125 to help solve them.

A little over a year later that man of wisdom, humility, and dignity was assassinated.

—ANDREW A. FREEMAN, March 1967

III.

THE NEWSPAPERS

Why Get Sentimental?
But. . . .
Somehow the Old Rags
Instilled a Certain Affection

NEWSPAPERS OF YESTERYEAR?
VANISHED, BUT NOT FORGOTTEN

One sunshiny day in 1923, Harry (whose byline was H. I.) Phillips, Ray McCaw, then city editor of the *Globe,* and myself were sitting around the dinner table in my home after a game of what, in a Pickwickian sense, we called golf. In a moment of extravagance I had opened a bottle of champagne and we were about to take the first sip when the telephone rang.

William Shillaber, one of the owners of the *Globe* was at the other end of the wire. He apologized for interrupting me at dinner and then gave me the startling news that the *Globe* had been sold to Munsey, who would sink it. He instructed me to put the oldest paper in America to bed for the last time on Saturday. When I returned to the table with that news, the flavor of the champagne had sadly deteriorated.

Munsey extinguished the *Globe,* which was making money, to rid *The Sun* of its competition; which was, itself, one day to sink into the arms of Roy Howard and the *Telegram.* The *Mail* folded in due time to make way for the *Graphic,* which also folded. The *Herald* disappeared into the sober and solemn columns of the *Tribune.* The *American* quit and finally *The Morning* and *Evening World.*

Something like a general gasp of horror ran around Park Row when *The World* stopped its presses. I was in Egypt, just boarding a barge for a ship home, when I heard my name being called frantically and looked up to see Jay Darling running toward me. When he got within earshot, he shouted breathlessly: "My God! Have you heard the news? *The World* has been sold." That event had an extraordinary effect upon the mood of the newspaper world.

When I reached Paris, the British-American Club asked me to talk to them at luncheon and explain what it all meant. The disappearance of *The World* was something comparable to the sinking of Gibraltar into the sea. These citadels of news were very large employers of newsmen, and the question arose—What would become of all the poor wretches thus hurled into unemployment? The answer is not without interest. But I attempt an answer only for my old staff on the *Globe*.

I always remember with a warm feeling Van Anda, then managing editor of *The Times*. He called me and asked that I give him the names of the best men I had and to send them up. And, he added, he would take quite a few even though he might not need them all. One of these men—Ray McCaw, our city editor—went there and retired only recently as night managing editor of *The Times*.

Harry Phillips got a phone call from John Tennant of *The World,* who signed him up at twice what he was getting on the *Globe*. But instantly Munsey claimed his services. Phillips had a contract with the Associated Newspapers, which the *Globe* operated and which Munsey acquired. Munsey filed suit against *The World*. Phillips was distraught. Finally *The World* told him to stop worrying—he was on the payroll and if he had sense he would get on a boat and take a nice trip to Europe, which he did.

But Phillips, who had a gift for worrying, insisted on exercising it. Munsey won the suit against *The World* and Phillips went to *The Sun* with a heavy heart, where with ever-rising honorarium, he has been spreading good cheer and lighting the horrors of the editorial page with his long years of wise and wonderful nonsense.

Another frightful casualty was the late Bob Ripley. He was getting about $200 a week as a sports cartoonist and providing an occasional contribution called "Believe It Or Not." He, too, was tied up with Associated Newspapers. Munsey knew this but he refused to use Ripley's cartoons. Two months later, Rip called me and asked if I would intercede with *The Sun* to get at least "Believe It Or Not" in once a week to give him a New York stand. I called Keats Speed who told me he would like to use Rip's work, but Munsey said he wouldn't have such stuff in his paper. Less than a year later the Hearst people signed Bob up at some fabulous sum almost beyond belief.

However, the chapter supplied an interesting comment on man's capacity for pessimism and his equally great capacity for the rebound. Most of the top men of the *Globe*, despite the overcrowded market, went on to fame and riches. Wes Stout became editor of the *Saturday Evening Post*. Bill Chenery, the *Globe's* chief editorial writer, became editor of *Collier's*. Bill Flynn, of the *Telegraph*, became editor of another weekly which has since folded. Bruce Bliven became editor of the *New Republic*. Another editorial writer, Maxwell Anderson, at the time was writing a play, using the public library as his study. It turned out to be *What Price Glory*.

—JOHN T. FLYNN, May 1954

GENERAL ORDERS FROM J. P.,
THE WORLD TO BE LIKE THIS

In 1911, while cruising southward from New York on his yacht Joseph Pulitzer was taken ill, and, in the harbor of Charleston on October 20, he lapsed into unconsciousness and died.

A little over a year before his death, in a letter to our Honorary President Charles M. Lincoln, at that time managing editor of *The New York World,* Mr. Pulitzer summarized his ideals for *The World* in these words:

"Concentrate your brain upon these objectives:

"1. What is original, distinctive, dramatic, romantic, thrilling, unique, curious, quaint, humorous, odd, apt to be talked about, without shocking good taste or lowering the general tone, good tone, and above all without impairing the confidence of the people in the truth of the stories or the character of the paper for reliability and scrupulous cleanness.

"2. What is the one distinctive feature, fight, crusade, public service or big exclusive? No paper can be great, in my opinion, if it depends simply upon the hand-to-mouth idea, news coming in anyhow. One big distinctive feature every day at least. One striking feature each issue should contain, prepared before, not left to chance.

"3. Generally speaking, always remember the difference between a paper made for the million, for the masses, and a paper made for the classes. In using the word masses I do not exclude anybody. I should make a paper that the judges of the Supreme Court of the United States would read with enjoyment, everybody, but I would not make a paper that only the judges of the Supreme Court and their class would read. I would make this paper without lowering the tone in the slightest degree.

"4. Accuracy, accuracy, accuracy. Also terseness, intelligent, not stupid condensation. No picture or illustration unless it is 1st class both in idea and execution."

May 1948

"NO ROOM FOR DULLNESS,"
HEARST DEMANDS THE BEST

How many of the present generation of newspaper men—and women—know that William Randolph Hearst, Senior led the parade by literally years in making newspapers lively, tightly edited, and of compelling general interest?

Having worked under his banner for forty-seven years the writer certainly can testify to the brilliant leadership of this giant among newspaper publishers who has been so inaccurately portrayed many times by writers who believed they could fathom his genius.

I am writing this because I have just finished going through literally reams of instructions that Mr. Hearst sent out to his editors and publishers over the years. For the benefit of those who are coming along today and have made news writing their careers I want to quote from some of the instructions that passed across my desk during the more than forty years I sat at the helm of the International News Service news desk.

One metropolitan newspaper recently has been making a great deal of fuss about dull newspapers with a slogan along the line of "Newspapers Don't Have To Be Dull."

Well, please note what Mr. Hearst wrote to his editors many, many years ago:

"There is no room for dullness in today's newspaper. There is no room for excess verbiage. There is no room for elaborate writing."

And he followed that with these statements:

"There is a difference between writing windily and writing breezily; and that difference has got to be recognized.

"There may not be room for so many dull papers, but there certainly is room for a bright and brief paper. . . ." In 1939 Mr. Hearst laid down to his publishers and editors a document which he called "First Principles".

It read in part:

"Your paper must have the dominant circulation.

"Circulation is the seal of public approval.

"The only way to get and KEEP the dominant circulation is by the merits of your paper.

"The first essential, therefore, is a good paper—the best paper.

"Never economize on your product. Economize on your PROCESS, but not on your PRODUCT.

"Efficiency is the best economy. To cut the product is to confess inefficiency."

And from personal experience I can testify to how important Mr. Hearst regarded the following word he sent to his editors:

"Have a good exclusive news feature as often as possible. PAY LIBERALLY for big exclusive stuff and encourage tipsters. Get reporters with acquaintance.

"When a big story must get in all the papers, try to have notably the best account in your paper."

And time and again he told his writers and editors: "Don't allow long introductions to stories or involved sentences.

"Don't repeat unnecessarily. Don't serve up the story in the headlines and then in the introduction and then in the box. Plunge immediately to the interesting part of the story."

And this one is something every news writer in the world could profit by in a tremendous way if he followed it religiously:

"DON'T ALLOW EXAGGERATION. IT IS A CHEAP AND INEFFECTIVE SUBSTITUTE FOR REAL INTEREST. REWARD REPORTERS WHO CAN MAKE TRUTH INTERESTING AND WEED OUT THOSE WHO CANNOT."

—BARRY FARIS, October 1962

MYRTLE AVE. TO THAW TRIAL,
VIA THE ROLLER SKATING RINK

My career in the Myrtle Avenue Police Court was hectic. I had to be there at 9 A.M. on the opening of Court, and as I lived in Manhattan, and went by subway to Brooklyn Bridge and then by Myrtle Avenue "L" to Washington Avenue, I had to get up about 6:30 A.M. When I did not, the other boys would cover me, Hammond of the *Eagle,* Nash of the *Times* and Bastable of the *Standard Union.*

Back in 1905 there were four active newspapers published in Brooklyn—*Eagle, Citizen, Times,* and *Standard Union.* Few of them ever published a "beat" or "scoop" because there existed among all of us an unwritten rule to share the news with each other in case any man missed a story.

Each paper had different rules as to words which reporters might not use. For us on the *Citizen,* the ban included: "All to the mustard," "He's got a lot of Moxie," "23 Skidoo," "Knockout drops." "Aber Nit." " 'Raus Mit Ihm," "Rubberneck," "Annie Oakley," "Tommy," "Get a Horse," "Isn't That Peachy," "Floaters," "Lead Pipe Cinch," "He's a Lobster," "Sky Pilot," "Tell it to Sweeney," "Land of Nod" (describing Philadelphia), "Protect Her Honor" and the use of "St." and "Ave." for "Street" and "Avenue".

The ban on the word "honor" was caused by a story, written by a leg man on the *Citizen* about a rape case in which he said, "She fought for her honor three times last week and lost every time."

I covered the Police Court for about a year. Two of the Magistrates were Alexander Geismar and John F. Hylan, who later became Mayor. About noon I would leave the court and race back to the city room to type out my grist of news to be

set before the paper went to press at 2 P.M. All were then
free until evening; everyone got a night assignment.

After covering the night assignment, you had to write the
story in longhand, and then ride down to the *Citizen* Building
at Fulton and Adams Street and put the copy in the big mail
box at the entrance.

The afternoons were our own, and most of us devoted them
to recreation. We had friends in the theaters. Marie Fitzgerald
was press agent for the Spooner Theater, Eddie Bader represented Keenan's and most of the others including Percy
Williams' Orpheum would pass us in if we showed our reporter's police card. We were also frequent patrons of the
Claremont Roller Skating Rink where all reporters were invited in free.

The leg men spent many hours there. George Chambers of
the *Citizen,* a great ladies' man, used to specialize in teaching
the girls to skate. "I like to teach the girls right from wrong,"
he would say, "but I teach them wrong first." Kent Stiles of
the *Eagle* was also an aficianado of the rink, as was Teddy
Stitt of the *Standard Union.*

One source of profit to leg men was free transportation on
the Brooklyn Rapid Transit lines. Eddie Hungerford was the
press agent for the B.R.T., and whenever there was a bad
trolley or elevated accident, we would swarm over to his office
on Montague Street. Eddie would be ready with a written release absolving the Company and would ask us to print it
in full. We would conclude by inquiring if he had any tickets
on hand and he would give each reporter a book of tickets
good for 100 free rides on the B.R.T. Of course, each ride
was charged to our papers at a nickel apiece, so eventually
we wound up $5 ahead.

Everyone on the paper was directed to write a story each
week for the Sunday supplement, preferably on a matter of

local interest. I was in the Brookyln Public Library once when I came across the account of the American soldiers who were captured by the British at the Battle of Brooklyn Heights and were confined on a prison ship in the East River. The ship was so crowded and the food so bad that most of the prisoners died. I wrote the story and suggested that a monument be erected to the memory of what I termed "The Prison Ship Martyrs." Astonishingly, some of the civic organizations took up the cry and the Prison Ship Martyrs Monument was erected in Fort Greene Park facing the waterfront where it still stands.

After covering the Myrtle Avenue Court for about eight months, I was assigned to Brooklyn Police Headquarters with a modest raise in salary. Some of the Headquarters reporters were well known. I remember Burr of *The Sun,* an elegant dresser who paid $100 for his custom-made suits, an unheard of extravagance in those days. Eddie Reilly, the lawyer who afterward defended Hauptmann in the Lindbergh kidnapping case, came into the press room frequently. If any reporter referred a criminal case to Eddie in which a fee was paid, the reporter got an order for a suit of clothes, good at "Schlang, My Tailor" on Myrtle Avenue.

One day we got news a freighter in Erie Basin was afire. One or two could cover the story and give it to the others so that Police Headquarters could be covered if anything big broke thereafter. John Early of the *Eagle* and I volunteered.

Learning that the crosstown trolley line was out on acount of the fire, John said "Let's run for it" and we started down Smith Street and ran all the way to Erie Basin. We were so winded we could hardly walk.

The following week John Harman, the city editor, assigned me to the Harry Thaw trial. I was given a seat in the front of the Courtroom, just behind the counsel tables, next to Charley

---

Somerville, the cartoonist for the Hearst newspapers. I telephoned in the story each night to our rewrite man, John Mahoney, a brilliant Irishman, who had it double leaded on our front page.

Harry Thaw sat with his lawyers at the counsel table, paying no attention to the testimony. He spent most of his time looking backwards into the courtroom, smiling at and flirting with the female spectators seated there. In the meantime Charley Somerville, when not drawing pictures of the trial scenes, made pencil sketches of all his fellow journalists.

—EDWARD CAREY COHEN, October 1969

TRIBUNE'S TALL TOWER FALLS
AS PAPER, UPTOWN, FOLDS

On April 25, 1966 when the *New York Herald Tribune's* skeleton staff rattled down to new quarters and an uncertain fate on Barclay St., there seemed to be one promising augury on an otherwise ominous horizon. Looking up Park Place, the handful of those who were working out the strike against the merger could see a remarkable building across the thin, spring green of City Hall Park. It was of red brick and gray stone, with accents of dark mansard roof and patinaed copper, and high up, under a great clock the name: *New York Tribune.*

This was the "tall tower" that Whitelaw Reid had built to confound the skeptics, when Horace Greeley died in 1872, after his disastrous campaign for the presidency, taking nearly half the *Tribune's* circulation with him to his grave in Brooklyn.

To a very large number of *Tribune* subscribers, the founder was the paper. To another substantial group it was, however independent its course, the personification of that Republican party which Greeley had been so instrumental in founding. They followed the great editor and his paper through very sharp turns of doctrine, building up to a circulation of some half a million during the Civil War. But they could not follow him into opposition to President Grant for all the scandals of his adminstration, and when Greeley died little more than a month after his decisive defeat at the polls many despaired of the journal he had founded thirty-one years before.

Joseph Bucklin Bishop was a young editorial writer under Greeley's successor, Whitelaw Reid. Bishop tried to explain his connection to an elderly friend in one of those rural areas where the *Tribune* had been the law and Greeley its sole expounder. "With the *Try-bune!*" exclaimed the friend. "Does it print yet? I thought Greeley was dead!"

It was in the teeth of this sentiment, and after a bruising battle for control, that Whitelaw Reid, with a young associate John Hay, started to rebuild the *Tribune*. He began by going ahead with plans that had been laid before Greeley's death, to give New York's most influential paper a worthy home.

The new structure was designed by an architect well known in his day—Richard M. Hunt. It drew inspiration from abroad marrying a Florentine campanile to mansard roofs. Labor troubles (prophetically) delayed construction. The staff of the *Tribune* moved to temporary quarters on Spruce St. in May 1873, and did not officially acquire their new home until the paper's 34th birthday, April 10, 1875. But they had much to be proud of.

The Tall Tower was, it was boasted, "more strongly built than the temple of Paestum or the aqueduct of Segovia." What is more, its height of 260 feet was exceeded, in New York City by only one other spire—that of Trinity Church.

The finishings were, in terms of newspaper architecture in that day, superb. The composing room was high up—on the ninth floor. Just below it was Whitelaw Reid's sanctum, complete with a wood-burning fireplace and a black onyx clock in the Egyptian style that was to be a feature many years later, of the managing editor's office on 41st St. In the city room, said an envious writer from Philadelphia, there was "real water," and, in general, "there isn't an editor-in-chief in the city as well cared for as the humblest reporter on the *Tribune*."

In the basement of the Tall Tower (prohibitionist Horace Greeley must have disturbed the sod of Greenwood Cemetery!) was a beer saloon, which achieved something of a reputation as "a jolly good place to lunch." And there was a new Hoe web press that could run off 16,000 to 18,000 *Tribunes* in an hour. Despite the facilities in the basement for lubricating and speeding up production, however, the *Tribune* in its new home was more sedate than in Greeley's rambunctious days.

This was largely due to Whitelaw Reid. He was a driving newspaperman, with a record of sensational beats behind him. He had been instrumental in securing (through association with a London newspaper) the best American coverage of the Franco-Prussian War. He had also encouraged the city staff to such feats as running a panel house (of the kind where prostitution was mingled with robbery) to expose police inefficiency. But as the guiding force of the *Tribune* he began to lay ever greater emphasis on culture and politics. He bought poems from Walt Whitman ("A Death Sonnet for Custer" . . . $10) and articles from Mark Twain; he had Henry James as a Paris correspondent and a superb critical staff. The *Tribune* drew praise from the literate and became a Bible for High Republicans (the flirtation with the Democrats ended in 1876). But the colorful characters of the Greeley era, the sort who were hired and fired by James Gordon Bennett Jr. with such erratic speed, or who were coaxed into brilliance by Charles A. Dana, were seldom seen in the Tall Tower as the *Tribune* shook down into sober prosperity.

A city editor of the last two decades of the 19th century, too, was something of an oddity in the respectable *Tribune* establishment. Arthur Bowers could bellow like a Bull of Bashan (or a Lessing Engelking) and he could be as overbearing as a character out of *Front Page*.

The Tall Tower was not subjected to the sudden shakeup that afflicted Bennett's *Herald* or Pulitzer's *World*. Men regarded a post there as a permanency (this tradition only really disappeared with the paper itself) and that may have been one reason why the annals of the Tall Tower are rather slim. Things did begin to change when the turn of the century

---

brought deficits, and, in due course brought a young Ogden Mills Reid to stir the dust of the Tall Tower. Men of promise began to drift in—John Marquand, Deems Taylor, Heywood Broun, Robert Benchley, Franklin P. Adams. The lunchroom —which moved up toward the top of the building while the city room moved closer to the street—took on something of an Algonquin Round Table flavor. Wits from *The Morning World* (whose golden dome flourished over the *Tribune*) would join their fellows on the *Tribune*.

There was a new city editor now, the antithesis of burly Bowers—George Burdick, a quiet, shy man who concocted a sovereign antidote for reportorial buck fever. William E. Curtin uncovered a big smuggling story (he was, for years, the ship news reporter)—one that brought both his city editor and himself under a contempt citation for refusing to reveal their sources. Curtin, as the story goes, fussed about with new leads and corrections until Burdick tapped him on the shoulder with the salutary injunction: "Mr. Curtin, just one word after another!"

There were many others who graced the Tall Tower in its twilight—Denis Tilden Lynch, William Orr until his triumphant departure for Hollywood, and Emma Bugbee, who came to the *Tribune* fresh from school and left it 55 years later, when the move to Barclay St. presaged the end. These were the years of the Rosenthal murder, the sinking of the *Titanic,* and the beginning of World War I—which changed so many things.

Whitelaw Reid died in 1912; Ogden, with the energetic assistance of his wife, Helen Rogers Reid, took over. With the war and the newspaper consolidations by F. A. Munsey, the paper's circulation began to rise. In 1921, the *Tribune* joined the *Herald* and *The Times* uptown, beginning construction of a new plant on West 41st St. This was occupied in

1923, just before the purchase of the *Herald* opened a new chapter. The Tall Tower remained on Newspaper Row as a reminder of the past.

It still stood, apparently as firm as the temple of Paestum, when the *Herald Tribune* moved downtown again in 1966. But on closer inspection it was clear that it was only a shell. The windows stared emptily, and large signs read: "Demolition by Jay Wreckers." During the long, hot summer, a web of scaffolding spread over the doomed structure, like spiders spinning a shroud for some desiccated squirrel in an attic.

It was plain, as the paper's fate darkened steadily, that there was a kind of macabre race on to see which would disappear first—the *Herald Tribune* or its former home. The paper won the race. Only the tower itself had vanished, with its old, proud title, when John Hay Whitney announced, on Aug. 15, 1966, that the *New York Herald Tribune* would never publish again.

—HARRY W. BAEHR, October 1966

The *Herald Tribune* did go on by way of merger—the *World Journal-Tribune* (or *"Widget"*) down Barclay St. from the old tower, until the total demise on May 5, 1967.

PARIS HERALD OF THOSE DAYS—
MECCA FOR YOUNG REPORTERS

It was twenty years ago that I breached the doors of the *Paris Herald*. In those days it was the indisputable domain of Eric Hawkins, a diminutive one-time British boxer who in his years as a newspaperman stirred us all with a friendliness, aplomb, and integrity, that could come only from the heart. Wrapped into Eric and his orbit at the old shop, 21 Rue de Berri, was a mystique and sentiment that will always affect those who served in the greatest years.

It's fair to say that there was only one of him and, for those who knew him, no one like him. He died in late 1969, and had been semi-retired for several years. But he still went to the office every day.

You know how it is when you land in a new place. You have a lot of gall. You don't know you're supposed to wait your turn. It was like that when I first arrived in Paris in 1949, just off a Black Diamond Line freighter. I had a suitcase, a rucksack, a typewriter, and wore the only fedora I owned in my life. I was on my way to Grenoble to the university. But being in Paris, I marched straight to the *Herald* and reported for duty.

No one threw me out. It was just like Larry Dame had told me. I had been a sports writer on the *Boston Herald Traveler,* and Larry had whetted my desire to go to Mecca.

Larry had been on the *Paris Herald* in its most famous days—the era when *Herald* reporters could dig Lone Eagle Lindy out of a back room in the Paris Embassy when no one else could find him, or if news was lacking, could turn a large ripple on the desolate island of Yap into a tidal wave of magnificent proportions and thus come up with a lead story that everyone else seemed to have missed. (The *Chicago Trib,* which then published a daily in Paris, picked up the Yap story the next day, by which time the *Herald* editors had moved on.)

At any rate, Eric Hawkins seemed not to think it unusual that I should come steaming in unannounced. We talked about the paper and my plans to write and ski in the Alps. Eric introduced me to Bob Sage, who said he would like travel pieces, which I furnished forthwith.

Thereafter I was for a year at the University of Grenoble, then back in Paris again, getting married to a French girl, and trying to figure out whether to head for the States or stay on. I did the *Cour de Civilization* at the Sorbonne with many other ex-GI's. Finally, Eric sealed my happy fate: Bob Yoakum was leaving, I was taken aboard. That was late summer, 1951.

Eric was a small man. He had fought as a featherweight under the name Kid Hawks. He wore dark double-breasted suits. Despite his tiny-tim figure, he had presence—one of those people who really didn't look around, just came in and sat down. People looked at him.

Eric had a front office and came in at ten or so for his general chores. He would go out for lunch and again for dinner, coming back about 9 P.M., into the City Room.

Eric's sit-down was a desk that was kitty-corner and next to a door. Just a few feet from it was the big table where bound volumes of the *Herald* could be taken down and spread out. The cyclists, the mobile copyboys of the paper, also held forth there between missions. They were a genial crew, in knickers that bagged deep below the knee.

The cyclists had a special rapport with Eric. There was Big Paul, gaunt and huge, with cap and dark glasses. He would often broach a mini-dispute with Eric. "Mais, Monsieur Hawkeens," he would begin. Eric was short-shrift on plaints, not even annoyed. "Allez, allez," he would say, hardly looking up.

There was Robert, my good friend. He had boxed in the 1936 Berlin Olympics. A great guy. He and Eric got along well. They had been in the ring. Jean, whom Eric had designated to be lord of the supplies, was the third cyclist. Jean gave us one pencil a week, and there was the funny day when he stooped to retrieve something and there was a cascade of virgin pencils from his upper pocket.

Eric's first chore every evening was to look over the make-up sheets with Jim Knight. And he would chat with the rest of us, according to the occasion, the people on the copy desk, or with me or Vincent Bujega, the resident reporters. He had that way of saying, "why don't you . . ." that makes one want to do it his way. The late Pye Chamberlain Sr. was there also, a real gentleman. His son, Pye Jr., is a radio reporter.

I think Eric treasured his nightly stints. The office was at once talky and purposeful. No one really fooled around, but there were jokes and asides in the air.

Eric saw this: the night that Bujega was working away— Vincent being a Maltese and a highly literate soul—when the door burst open. A man advanced. Booge was in his line of fire.

"I'm a Canadian," the man boomed, "and I'm incensed at the editorial on Canada. You have insulted my country. You're a bunch of Americans sounding off. . . ."

You could see it coming with your eyes closed. Booge put down his pipe and drew himself up. "My deah sir," he said crisply, "don't complain to me. For I am a British subject . . . like yourself."

The last four or five words carried some force. I'll never forget the visitor's startled step back. The rest of it was blah.

It was a rather bouncy place, too. In the back room we had recording equipment operated by students. Correspondents around Europe phoned their copy to the *Herald* for transmission to the New York office. For a while one of the recording room crew was a delicious redhead. One of her many suitors was an ardent South American who one night pursued her into the City Room, only to have her wheel around and deck him with a Coke bottle.

I don't think Eric had any special handle on people. He was a newsman, interested, moving around, sizing up, zeroing in, lavish or sometimes curt.

Others around the desk in the 1950s were Roy McMullen, Tom Dorsey, Jules Grad, Tommy Thompson, Jan Hansbrouck. Every colleague had been there since World War II, and Bob Sage had been in France for 32 years. There was an expatriate mood that I wasn't sure I wanted to live with forever. Walter Kerr, then European chief correspondent for the *New York Trib,* and I got to talking one night at the California Bar, across the street. He was saying, if you work for an American paper, you ought to work the home base once in a while, and somewhere in there I made a decision. After five years abroad and three plus with the *Paris Herald,* I would go home again.

I was able to return to Paris, and I saw Eric many times more, the last being in the 1968 summer. I found him still keeping on top of what was going on in politics and press, a mainstay of the Anglo-American Press Association. But Eric was unhappy at my leaving, those years before. He felt so close to the *Paris Herald,* he couldn't understand. Once you were on the *Herald,* you belonged to it and it to you.

That sentiment is still with me. I'm sure the others will say the same. I can remember the old desks that, shoved together, made up the copy desk, the rather gritty interior, the faded photographs of past glory on the walls. But even while I was there a new order came in. A functional copy desk was set up

---

and the pictures were taken down and the walls painted. It was in those years past that I saw Eric's saga begin to enter into the halls of time. But let us never forget. . . .

—MARSHALL PECK, March 1972

AS BRONX AS BRONX ITSELF—
AS O'FLAHERTY AS O'FLAHERTY

The *Bronx Home News* headline for the Bolshevist uprising in November, 1917 was BRONX MAN LEADS RUSSIAN REVOLUTION. Leon Trotsky had been a resident of the Bronx.

"An account about a Bronx child bitten by a dog will sell more papers than a murder in Chicago." In this faith lived and prospered the most rugged individualist of its day in Metropolitan journalism.

Names filled the *Home News*. Bronx personal columns, "Bokays & Brikbatz" and "Whyspers" were jammed with names. Weddings and anniversaries, births and birthdays, baptisms and bar mitzvahs, cellar clubs, women's clubs, political clubs, social and fraternal organizations, sermons and communion breakfasts—these were the *Home News*. They lifted an initial $1,000 investment up past a $1,000,000 valuation.

The man who set and applied this formula—J. O'F. by name—appeared daily in an ink-stained knit jacket with yawning holes in the elbows and so faded that no respectable *Hobo News* staffer would itch for it. He haunted the editorial room nightly, dousing lights over unoccupied desks, imagined by new employees to be the janitor. He was, in fact the owner and publisher, the man who started the paper in January, 1907 and who carried it to success, regardless of the depression, until his death April 20, 1939, the one and only James O'Flaherty, Jr.

He would have been 65 in a few days. The paper was bought by the *New York Post* in May 1945, and the name itself survived only four years more.

Tall and thin, his long face supported by a determined

chin, the publisher stared over a closely pruned moustache, his wide earnest eyes confirming his expression of averageness. His falsetto voice was short-range, but he guffawed readily, "Hoh, Hoh, Hoh." His constant query was "How the deuce—?" The image he firmly maintained was that of a commoner, keyed to life's simplicities, immune to the kick of plus plutocracy.

O'Flaherty was born in Manhattan's Lower East Side, but after he finished the public schools and had two years at City College he mapped a Bronx detour to a Park Ave. penthouse.

After college he worked a few years for James, Sr., who had an ad service that included 300 dailies and weeklies. The father kept a downtown Manhattan office and a small printing shop in the Bronx where he set ads and made matrices for clients. The son saw opportunity in the Bronx and Harlem advertisers. So he took a job with the old *New York News* and learned the routines of reporting and newspaper advertising.

One of O'Flaherty's early assistants recalls when he was a young bachelor. He slept in the loft of his father's print shop when he worked on publication dates almost around the clock, and looked the part. However, "soon after his marriage he donned new conservative clothes that fitted him, including a necktie neatly hanging from a wing collar of washable celluloid."

Stamped from middle-class dies, he exhibited, especially in his later years, a phobia at exposing his opulence. There could be no doubt of his uneasiness as a millionaire, trying to conceal his wealth, seemingly covering his tracks. He also practiced a discriminating and untiring generosity, strictly sub rosa.

If an employee standing by happened to ask for a light, he would go into an elaborate fumble. Minutes would pass as he dug into the pockets of that hole-ridden knit jacket, finally to produce an old-fashioned kitchen match.

One of his oddities, which may have helped him escape from perplexities uncommon among other men of means, concerned his motor car. It was an imposing Lancia, complete with chauffeur. Starting with salutes from the Park Ave. palace guard, his early morning drive to the Bronx almost invariably ended at Melrose Ave. and East 149th St., a couple of blocks from the *Home News* office. There he descended, to walk the rest of the way. He liked to hike, he said. But the shiny limousine was never parked within sight.

The obvious profits of the *Home News* along with his own rising standard of living doubtless suggested to him that employees might complain that they were underpaid.

The publisher adhered to the Golden Rule, beyond a doubt, but his early editorial pay scale was anything but 14 karat. Yet as a pro-labor man, he did not resist the Newspaper Guild and was the first New York daily publisher to sign a Guild contract.

There were at least 100 reporters and editors in the early 1920s when I was there. Many of these reporters had been carriers who left delivery routes to become reporters in the same areas. As carrier-reporter the youth was paid 25¢ an inch as a stringer.

More than half the staff were fledgings, hired at $20 weekly, and raised $2 or $3 occasionally; when someone getting more, quit, another was hired for less.

The copy desk for years worked a double-trick weekend, both Saturday afternoon and Sunday papers. Each man received $1 dinner money, no extra pay.

O'Flaherty's Women's Pages and Sports Pages swelled the egos and the happiness of Bronx readers. The publisher had played baseball and football at City College and courted tennis throughout his life, once serving as vice president of the New York Tennis Club.

Telephones rang far into the night to give sandlot scores. O'Flaherty himself often answered the telephone, only to call the nearest reporter to take the information. If he saw that the reporter called was reading proof or doing something else he could do, he would take over while the reporter got the information.

The Bronx Chamber of Commerce came alive only when sparked by J. O'F. He was the first to drive for an uptown bridge to New Jersey, the George Washington Bridge. He asked for the Tri-Borough bridge long before other papers.

O'Flaherty expressed his religious faith through charity. Tenant evictions for nonpayment of rent produced the common sight in the early twenties of homeless families with their furniture set out on the sidewalks. The publisher was attentive to these cases in *Home News* territory. He would send an assistant to investigate, and on his report would provide shelter, food, and funds. He never failed to help employees caught in financial difficulties.

—JOHN B. DONNELLY, April 1965

JOHN DONNELLY DIES;
THE STORY GETS AWAY

John B. Donnelly of Tribes Hill, N.Y., a contributor whose profile of James O'Flaherty of the *Bronx Home News* brightened these pages last spring, died suddenly on August 24 at his home. He was a native of Amsterdam, N. Y., and his first newspaper job was with the *Amsterdam Morning Sentinel*. Besides the *Bronx Home News* he worked in New York on *The Wall Street Journal* and the *Telegram,* concluding with 26 years as public relations director for IBM.

A few weeks before he died, he outlined a story for the *Silurian News,* one of the liveliest reminiscences we shall never read. We have only this paragraph from his letter:

"I am most anxious to write about the long day I suffered with the spirits in an unsuccessful effort to interview Mark Twain. Emil Gavreau gave me the assignment. He was then managing editor of the Hartford *Courant,* where he showed his yen for the offbeat before he became M. E. of the *New York Graphic* which he hippodromed from a nearby bar . . . Now recently I've had a breezy letter from a celebrated spiritualist medium to whom I had recalled that when I couldn't get in touch with Mark's spirit, the city editor said, 'I knew he went to Hell.' The Reverend contradicts this, saying he has communicated with the humorist and that he is a spirit of great influence in the other world. I'm writing the medium again. Perhaps he can get Mark to say something."

—October 1965

: 130 :

HIS OWN IDEA OF HEAVEN—
A FORMER CUB LOOKS BACK

If I could only recapture the excitement of that wonderful first year, when I achieved the dream of working on a big time paper in New York! Every day was better than the one before. I have asked the Almighty to let me choose my own idea of Heaven (unless He has other plans for me) and that idea will be to be back in New York in 1919, a cub reporter on the *Herald.*

On January 6, that year, I came to New York to Seek My Fortune and checked in at a Times Square hotel then known as Wallick's, long since razed. That night, as I lay abed wondering whether I could land a newspaper job and if so, keep it, the big chewing gum sign on the building across the street kept blinking into my room, as if to say, "Go back to Saratoga, Buster, and quit trying to crash big time." Indeed, as I lay there listening to Times Square roaring up against my window, New York did not sound like a world that intended to be my oyster. Quite the reverse.

Jack Donlon, a Saratoga boy who had Made Good, was night city editor of the *Herald*—the old *Herald.* Next day I went to see Jack about a job. He gave me a letter to Hood McFarland of the *Tribune.* I saw Hood and he was polite but said he didn't have anything just then but if I'd leave my name, etc. I reported back to Donlon and he gave me another letter, to Jack Gavin of *The World.* Gavin said he didn't have anything just then either but if I'd leave my name, etc. I went back to Donlon. He said "Oh, hell!" and cut the Gordian knot by persuading Bill Willis, city editor of the *Herald,* to give me a job. Thirty-five smackers a week, every week! That night I blinked right back at that gum sign.

When I reported for work Dick Silver, the day city editor, asked me if I had any particular specialty. I had about a dozen specialties, for during my seven years on the *Saratogian* I had done everything from ladies clubs, politics, and police courts to (in August) turf expert. But I told Dick I hoped to become a drama critic. Dick laughed heartily at this and gave me my first assignment, to do a story about the crowds of relieved Germans who were rushing to re-deposit their savings in the Central Savings Bank on Fourteenth Street. This story made the paper, almost uncut, though that may have been a kind gesture by Donlon, to give me confidence. After that I got no more than a stick or so until they gave me a column on the return of the *Leviathan* with the 27th Division troops, in March. I went down the Bay on that assignment and met two reporters who became, in time, old friends—Bill Beazell of *The World* and Bruce Rae of *The Times*. I came to New York with the idea that every reporter was a Richard Harding Davis constantly striving to scoop all his fellow Richard Harding Davises in a cutthroat race for a beat. But Bill and Bruce did not seem to be trying to scoop each other, or me. They were kind and sweet to the greenhorn cub, and gave me all the dope they had.

I had a desk opposite Hamilton Peltz, the dean of the *Herald* staff. The day I went to work Ham was on the story of Theodore Roosevelt's death (or funeral?). Copy boys, re-write men, and editors buzzed about him. He was interrupted about once a minute but worked on unruffled. It was the first time I had seen a star reporter at work. I was awestruck.

The old *Herald* was a clannish paper. It did not take on many new men but once you got on you usually stayed. Two other cubs were hired that year, 1919. One was Cornelius Vanderbilt, Jr., and the day he went out on his first assignment the other papers assigned reporters to cover Vanderbilt covering his first assignment. Nowadays I believe millionaire reporters are a dime a dozen. The second cub that year was a laconic Texan by the name of Stanley Walker, who went on to make a jumbo-sized reputation for himself.

For a month or so I was homesick and almost—but not quite—wished I had stayed in the army. Then one night Ray McCabe, Jim Durkin, and Warren Leary asked me to join them at dinner. I felt I was in. Soon afterward the older newspapermen threw a shindig at the Commodore for the returned veteran buddies, each stay-at-home inviting a defender of democracy. Guess who invited me? Ham Peltz, and none other. I celebrated by accumulating a man-sized brannigan.

After that it was easy, and got easier as I came to know— let's see—Allen Eddy, Al Chandler, Martha Coman, Rachel MacDowell, Dick Conover, Al Copeland, George Van Slyke, Ray Doyle, Delt Edwards, Jane Dixon, Jim Hagerty (one G) and Mike Haggerty (two G's), Roland Harrison, Henley Hill, Wally Yerkes, Owen Oliver, Mary Watts, John Logan, Hughie Robertson, Tim Turner—and so many others.

I breakfasted around noontime at Child's on Times Square. Once a week or so, when feeling rich, I ate at Keen's, near the *Herald,* a tavern for which I still have a great affection. I dined often at the Waldorf, too, but on the house, as these were banquet assignments and you usually had to listen to a spate of after-dinner oratory. Along in the spring I made the first page for the first time with an interview (exclusive) with Charles M. Schwab.

When the 27th Division paraded, I walked the length of Fifth Avenue with them. Was I not a bronzed and recent veteran of Camps Devens, Meade, Gordon and Sherman, with the golden aura of a shavetail's bars lingering about my shoulders? It was on that assignment I first met two of nature's noblemen, Don Clarke and Gene Fowler. I covered the trial of Hardboiled Smith (who remembers him?) and the orgy at the Waldorf on the return of bewildered Sergeant York. Frank Ward O'Malley took one look at the Sarge, flanked by enough admirals and generals to make up a "Student Prince" chorus, then sank his head in his hands and sobbed, "Alas, poor York!"

At the end of 1919 things happened in quick succession. On December 23 I bought a new overcoat. On the same date it was purloined from a hook in Bristol's restaurant on Sixth Avenue, while I was eating dinner. On December 24 I borrowed Jack Donlon's spring overcoat and went home to Saratoga for Christmas. On December 25 I awoke with a roaring case of chicken pox that laid me up for a month.

And the end of January I reported back for work, to learn that the *Herald* had been sold to Frank Munsey!

—FRANK SULLIVAN, October 1965

LETTER WAS TO LIPPMANN,
BUT SWOPE CAME ACROSS

More than six of the most exciting years I have experienced as a journalist began early in December 1924 when I joined *The World* as a reporter. I had arrived in New York from Kansas a few days earlier with letters of introduction from Henry J. Allen, editor-publisher of the *Wichita Beacon* and former Governor, for whom I had worked nearly a year, also from William Allen White, editor-owner of the *Emporia Gazette,* who knew me only through Allen and my father.

One of White's letters was to Walter Lippmann, and it consisted of two sentences. The first gave my name and said I was the son of the Chancellor "of our University." The second, as I recall it, said only: "He has long legs and is willing to use them." That told all he knew about me, plus the hearsay about my willingness.

Lippmann received me pleasantly in his office on the 15th floor, explained that he chose only the editorial writers and asked if I was interested in being a reporter. A few years of reporting, he remarked, would do me no harm. He telephoned the executive editor, Herbert Bayard Swope, and then kindly escorted me to Swope's office off the city room on the 12th floor.

His first question was: "Do you want to be a reporter or an editorial writer?" I had no trouble in giving the right answer, which was also honest. "Then," said Swope with the air of a triumphant prosecutor, "why didn't Bill White write to me?" Swope continued to explore my ambitions, gave me an eloquent lecture on the supreme glory of being a reporter, and called in James W. Barrett, the city editor. As I recall, all that Swope said to Barrett after introducing me was: "Bill White sent him."

All that Barrett asked was what salary I had been receiving and whether I was willing to start for the same amount, which I think was $35 a week. I said "yes" and he told me to report for work the next day.

That is the way many young reporters were hired during my years on *The World*. If you were lucky enough to get to see Swope or Barrett and make a passable impression when there happened to be a vacancy, you got a job.

My first assignment was a story with human interest in Brooklyn. I don't remember what it was, but Joseph Canavan, night city editor, a warm-hearted man who became one of my best friends, liked what I wrote and put it on the lower part of the front page. The next day a thin man in shirtsleeves walked up to my desk, introduced himself as Frank Adams and complimented me—he had asked the City Desk who wrote the story. He was, of course, Franklin P. Adams, F.P.A. of The Conning Tower, so distinguished that he had a room all to himself in columnists' row.

Heywood Broun, another of *The World's* columnists, often went out of his way to encourage young reporters. In 1933 I had the pleasure of helping him to persuade Franklin D. Roosevelt to overrule Hugh Johnson, NRA Administrator, and institute the 5-day week on newspapers in the larger cities.

Others on the "op ed" page included: Laurence Stallings, literary critic, who soon, upon the success of *What Price Glory,* left for Hollywood and was replaced by Harry Hansen; Deems Taylor, music critic, succeeded by Samuel Chotzinoff; Alexander Woollcott, dramatic critic, succeeded by Robert Littell. Quinn Martin was movie critic; Alison Smith, assistant music critic. The assistant dramatic critic for some time was Jeffery Holmesdale (Viscount Holmesdale), who, after Eton and Sandhurst, had become a major in the Coldstream Guards and won the Military Cross in the First World War.

He succeeded his father as Earl of Amherst in 1927 but continued to work for *The World* far into 1929. A few years ago in London he reminisced to me about his wonderful days in New York.

Up in the Tower, writing editorials under Lippmann, were: Charles Merz, who became Editor of the Editorial Page of *The Times;* Allen Nevins, who, after leaving *The World,* devoted full time to his prolific career as an historian; sardonic James M. Cain, who became well known as a novelist; and two veterans from the days of Joseph Pulitzer, the Founder, John L. Heaton and L. R. E. Paulin. *The World* had also an incomparable cartoonist in Rollin Kirby.

Members of the local staff were proud of their association with these luminaries but took great pride also in their own contributions. I think most of them firmly believed that *The World* was the best-written, best-edited, newspaper of its time. I remember vividly:

—Alex Schlosser, genial and impeccably polite assistant city editor.

—Oliver H. P. Garrett, star crime reporter who moved to Hollywood.

—Dudley Nichols, another gifted writer who moved to Hollywood.

—Frank Sullivan, delightful as both friend and humorist.

—Henry F. Pringle, biographer of Al Smith, Theodore Roosevelt (Pulitzer Prize), and William Howard Taft.

—Charles J. V. Murphy, who wrote Admiral Richard E. Byrd's biography, accompanied him to Antarctica, was for many years with *Fortune* and *Life,* and is still producing.

—Herbert E. Gaston, night editor, whom I recommended to Henry Morgenthau, Jr., State Conservation Commissioner, when *The World* folded. He became an able Assistant Secretary of the Treasury.

—William L. Laurence, who was paid $25 a week by *The World* and for a time lived in the box office of the Cherry Lane Theatre. He later won two Pulitzer prizes and many other awards, including one from the Silurians.

—Ben Franklin, first-rate reporter, writer, and editor, also teacher at the Pulitzer School of Journalism.

—Robert Ginsburgh, army officer who did night rewrite while stationed on Governor's Island, and later became well known in Washington as probably the best writer in the armed services.

And so on. I'd like to call the entire roll.

When *The World* was sold and folded in February 1931, I think we all felt as Frank Sullivan wrote: "When I die I want to go wherever *The World* has gone, and work on it again."

—ERNEST K. LINDLEY, March 1972

YOUNG MAN FROM CHICAGO
SEES NEW YORK AND *THE WORLD*

It seems quite unlikely to me that those of you who grew up in New York and landed jobs on its newspapers ever felt the excitement and exhilaration of the man who comes to work in Manhattan from Chicago and points west.

To me the move from the *Chicago Daily News* to *The World* of New York in 1926 was a peak in the great adventure of life and no amount of pelf could have kept me from risking it. There was no great reason for my leaving Chicago —my roots were in the Midwest, I had covered the World War and the Peace Conference for my paper, and built a comfortable home on the North Shore. I had become part of that electric period that produced Carl Sandburg, Ben Hecht, Sherwood Anderson, Bob Casey, and John Gunther—and then the smell of books pulled me irresistibly on to New York.

The World was a great place to work. I used to drop in at midnight to make changes in my copy, and there would be Alexander Woollcott, all decked out with his opera cape, standing over the forms with a printer. I enjoyed Herbert Bayard Swope's heartiness, his determined camaraderie, and I missed him greatly when he left before the debacle, as did Woollcott and Heywood Broun.

I am convinced that the greatest thing in life is the interaction of individuals, one on another, the swiftly changing relationships, the play of personality, always new. We try to pin down a period and say "That is the way it was," but nothing that we remember was ever static. The still life that catches us in fixed attitudes is out of date the day after.

The World, I was told, was going downhill. This didn't unsettle me; the paper gave me a three-year contract and I was willing to risk its demise. (It survived four years after I got there.) It was an extraordinary place; a newspaper with terrific national prestige and no income at home. Department stores practically had deserted it; national copy was slight. Financial copy, the mainstay of *The New York Times,* had taken flight after *The World* investigated the bucketshops—for the reason that a great many legitimate brokers used bucketshop methods.

If *The World* could have lasted through 1933, it would have become the spokesman for the New Deal. But alas, Joe Pulitzer, who was making money in St. Louis, didn't see why the family should make up the deficits of *The World,* and Herbert Pulitzer, who had the deciding vote, was not a newspaperman. The man hurt most was Ralph Pulitzer, a kind boss who stood by his experts, paid them generously, and tried his best to avert the inevitable.

This didn't bother me a great deal. I had come with an ironclad contract to review books without interference from editors and I was determined to do so. We clicked, but I was under no illusions that this was solely my doing. F. P. A., Woollcott, Frank Sullivan, Samuel Chotzinoff, and Broun won an intelligent audience that read books, attended first nights, and fought over the issues of the day. Swope had packed them all into his famous "page opposite editorial." It was the best-read page in New York and it turned the publishers to advertising books every day. We led in lineage for four years, and Roy Howard made a big mistake when he failed to continue the page in *The World-Telegram.*

Laurence Stallings had preceded me, Harry Salpeter worked with him and me, and Louis Weitzenkorn was Sunday editor. John O'Hara Cosgrave had his office on our eleventh floor, and later Paul Palmer occupied it.

Irvin S. Cobb had worked years before on *The Evening World,* and I listened to his anecdotes about his beats while riding with him through Belgium in 1914 in the wake of Von Kluck's German hordes, marching to the Marne. Cobb knew Chapin and was the author of the famous quip, when informed that Chapin was ill: "I hope it's nothing trivial." Like other humorists Cobb loved to repeat his best lines; he would make a wisecrack and then look around to see us laugh. After three days of this my laughter became a dry cackle.

Wisecracking was the universal practice of columnists, but it was more subtle than the present punning of television comedians. Men like Woollcott also appealed to the imagination because their personalities were eccentric and entertaining. Today's newspapers tend to substitute twaddle from Hollywood for the more intelligent columns of the 1920s.

It is my observation, however, that columns such as that of F. P. A., which were a cross section of our culture, also developed a large following and had great influence. A newspaper is a mosaic of interests; if you can attract 10,000 readers to one small feature every day you can reach the 100,000. I saw it done on the *Chicago Daily News,* which, like *The New York Times,* was a habit-forming newspaper.

The World hired me to write three columns a week about books and authors, but that, to me, didn't seem sufficient, so I decided to write six a week. Laurence Stallings told me: "You killed a fine racket." But it paid, and after a time the other newspapers followed suit. Our Sunday book section, on the contrary, was neglected, as was the rest of the Sunday paper. I still don't know why the Pulitzers didn't scrap the *Sunday World* altogether, or why they didn't turn *The World* into an evening newspaper, since the *Evening* was paying moderately. I suspect they were tired of signing interminable checks, although some of the expense, such as rent for the Pulitzer building, came back to them.

—HARRY HANSEN, April 1965

TO THE *NEW YORK SUN*—
IN FOND REMEMBRANCE

Early on the morning of January 3, 1950, I was awakened at my Long Island home by a phone call from city editor Edmond Bartnett.

"Will you try to get in as early as you can this morning?" he asked. (It was characteristic that as a boss Bart always asked, and never ordered his men.) "Mr. Speed has a special assignment for you." There was a slight pause, then, in an undertone: "I can't tell you any more, but it's a tough one."

"Do I get any other kind?" I grumbled.

When I got to the office, Bartnett said: "Mr. Speed is waiting for you in his private office." I knew then that something unusual was afoot because Executive Editor Keats Speed rarely used his private office, preferring to sit at a desk in the northeast corner of the city room.

When I entered his office Mr. Speed looked at me with red-rimmed eyes and said in a distraught voice: "Mr. Johnson, I must take you into my confidence. We are being sold today and I am an absolute wreck."

He told me that *The World Telegram* had bought *The Sun*'s name, good will, and circulation list but not its physical equipment. The next day would be the final day of publication of *The Sun*.

Then Mr. Speed told me to get the necessary books and clips from the morgue, to lock myself in the office of the antiques editor and write the story of the sale and of *The Sun*'s 117-year history for the next day's editions. I was to work secretly and to talk to no one.

I had to write the obituary of the paper I had worked on for nearly 22 years and that others on the staff had served much longer. As I tried to work I could hear the boys in the sports department next door laughing and joking. It did not make my task any easier to feel that I had guilty knowledge of which they were blissfully unaware—that the next day would find their paper and their jobs gone.

Once Bartnett looked in and asked: "How are you coming?"

"I can't get started," I said miserably, staring at the blank paper in my typewriter. "I don't believe I can do it." "I know it's tough," Bart said, "and it's easier said than done, but try to tackle it as you would any other story—or any other disaster."

Somehow, I managed to hammer out a three-column story, giving some of the highlights of *The Sun's* history and mentioning some of its famous reporters. Then I took the obit to the publisher's office on the seventh floor. What took place there has never been published. Present were Thomas W. Dewart, the publisher, who had little to say; Edwin S. Friendly, vice-president and general manager, and Mr. Speed.

Friendly insisted on reading the story aloud and querying Mr. Speed at various points. When he came to a reference to "the death of a great newspaper," Friendly objected: "We shouldn't say that, should we? *The Sun* isn't dead. It's just being merged."

"Ed," I said angrily, "go down and tell the boys in the city room that and see if you can get away with your life."

As Friendly continued to nitpick, Mr. Speed raised his head wearily and said: "Whatever Mr. Johnson has written in that story is true as far as I am concerned. Change it if you like, but don't bother to read any more to me and don't ask me anything about it."

That broke up the conference. As I was leaving Friendly called: "Mike, what are you going to do now?"

"I'm going out and get stinking drunk, naturally," I said, still sore.

Friendly was genuinely concerned. "For God's sake don't do anything foolish like that," he said. "The top people at *The World-Telegram* want to see you tomorrow, I know."

I'm sure Friendly meant well. He had always been nice to me, but I was in no mood to be charitable that day.

Actually, I had no intention of getting drunk. My oldest son, Haynes (now a Pulitzer Prize-winning reporter for the *Washington Star* and my favorite newspaperman and author) was returning to college that night after the Christmas holidays. I was to see him off at the airport.

* * *

When I turned in my story, Bartnett asked: "Do you want your by-line on it?"

"No," I replied. "No *Sun* man would want a by-line on that story."

Bart nodded, tears in his eyes. "I understand," he said. And so the story ran without a by-line.

Bert Goss, chairman of the public relations firm of Hill and Knowlton, Inc., my present employer, has described my story as a "newspaper classic," but he was just being kind. I wish I had been able to tell how newspaper people feel—that a good newspaper has a heart and a soul and that to them the death of a newspaper is as grievous and personal as a death in the family. But I didn't, and I couldn't. The story was fairly straight-away, otherwise I might have come up with a weepy exercise in bathos. As it was, there was no pride of authorship and no apologies either. I felt then, and I still feel, that in the circumstances, I was lucky to get anything down on paper on that dreadful day.

For months Tom Dewart had denied rumors that *The Sun*

was about to be sold. *"The Sun* is for sale for five cents a copy on any newsstand—and in no other way," Dewart said.

The big lie was maintained to the very last—and we were foolish enough to believe it—until the brutal truth came out on the morning of January 4. At 8 A.M. that day a notice was posted on the bulletin board. This was *The Sun's* last day of publication and the end of all employment on the paper. That is how the employees got the word, without warning, in the cruel pattern that was followed in later years as other papers died.

When *The Sun's* first edition came up it carried the bold eight-column line: *THE SUN* IS SOLD. Other front page headlines that day: 'Truman Demands Fair Deal' . . . 'Britain to Recognize Red China This Week' . . . 'Mercury Hits 64 in Hottest Jan. 4'. The only staff by-line was that of Phelps Adams over the Truman story from Washington.

Soon the city room was swarming with outside reporters and photographers covering the story while dazed staff members began cleaning out their desks.

The knowledge that they had severance pay coming was poor consolation, as it turned out, especially for older employees with many years of service. "A lot of us are still holding those worthless I.O.U.'s, one *Sun* man told me recently. Severance was paid for several months, then we were told that there was no more money in the till.

Appropriately headed "Death in the Antiques Room," *Time Magazine* reported that negotiations for the sale of *The Sun* had been in progress for months. I have since learned that they were in progress for a full year. At one point an offer by *The Sun* to buy *The World-Telegram* was vigorously rejected. Most staff men refused to accept Dewart's explanation, which mainly blamed the union for the paper's failure. They felt that Dewart simply lacked the will to save the paper. In view of what has happened since then it is hard to say. I have no intention of attempting a postmortem, but I did learn that *The Sun*'s troubles actually began in 1947, when several big department stores cancelled their advertising. That started a trend never reversed, as *The Sun* tightened its penny-pinching and circulation dropped sharply from its 1947 all-time peak.

In a story in *Life Magazine* on the death of *The Sun,* W. C. Heinz, who under Bartnett's guidance had progressed from copy boy to reporter, war correspondent, and sports columnist, quoted Bartnett as saying:

"People think I am tough but I'm not tough. I cried when my mother died. I cried when my son went off to war. I have been crying now for two days."

On that last day at *The Sun* Mr. Speed's face was gray and haggard but he tried to smile as staff members, one by one, went over to his desk to shake his hand and say goodbye. Then we could understand, at last, why Mr. Speed had almost collapsed at the surprise pre-Christmas dinner party staff members gave for him. Tears streamed down his cheeks and he was visibly shaken when he entered the dining room. What was intended to be a happy evening for him became one of heartbreak instead as the staff demonstrated its respect and affection. For Mr. Speed knew then, but felt he could not break his silence, that the end of *The Sun* was near and that its employees were about to be sold out.

I derived a perverse satisfaction in not going to work for the merged papers, *The World-Telegram & Sun.* I was lucky enough to have a choice. On Mr. Speed's advice, I went with International News Service. In urging me to accept this offer, Mr. Speed paid me a flattering compliment, one that any reporter would appreciate. "You like to write the truth," he said, "so make them give you a contract and pay you a lot of money. Then you can write as you please."

Well, God knows *The Sun* management didn't believe in paying anybody a lot of money, although it could be generous and gracious about most other things. Years later when I joined Hill and Knowlton and received my first Christmas bonus, I told John W. Hill, the firm's founder, that it was the first time in my life that I had ever received such a bonus.

"You mean you didn't get one in all those years at *The Sun?*" he asked.

"The only Christmas gift I ever got from *The Sun*," I replied, "was a fancy reprint of that God-damn editorial, 'Yes, Virginia. There Is a Santa Claus.' The publisher sent it out one year to all the employees, infuriating everybody."

Hill hasn't stopped laughing yet.

In all fairness, I learned from Bartnett only recently that in its most prosperous days *The Sun* did hand out some handsome Christmas bonuses. They evidently went only to key executives and department heads. I am glad to know, even now, that somebody got bonuses. It makes me feel a little kinder towards the erstwhile publisher—but not much.

On impulse one day when I was in the neighborhood, many months after *The Sun* went down, I climbed the dark stairway to the City Room on the second floor. Only one light glowed and under that light Keats Speed sat at his desk in the corner where he had always sat. Dust was thick on the desks and the covered, silent typewriters.

It was the first of several visits I made to find Mr. Speed just sitting there, sometimes reading a paper, sometimes just staring across the gloom; in a room full of ghosts. He arrived at 8 o'clock every morning just as he always had done and he would leave shortly before 5 P.M. It wasn't until my last visit that I summoned enough courage to ask him why he came down every day. He smiled faintly.

"Well, I don't have anything else to do," he said. "But that is not the only reason. I feel that perhaps I can help *Sun* people by coming here, and if they know they can find me here every day. I have already helped some in getting jobs. I want to do as much as I can." If it ever occurred to him that he could perform the same service from home, he did not say so.

I never saw him again, although I know he continued to go to the *Sun* office every day until renovations were made for new tenants of the building. Keats Speed died on March 12, 1952, at age 72. Among the *Sun* alumni those of us who could attended his funeral.

Speaking for myself, I have no doubt that if *The Sun* could still function I would still be working there—assuming the management would let me—griping about the low pay and threatening to quit but staying on because I would be doing what I like most to do. And maybe it's just the difference between youth and age, but for me it is pleasant to remember when working in New York was an exciting adventure instead of an ordeal.

—MALCOLM JOHNSON, October 1969

IV.

TOUCHING ON HISTORY

Famous Events and Names—
Doubtless More Historic Than Most—
From the Personal Angle
Of Men on the Spot

THE
WEATHER:
Slightly
Damp

Silurian News

PRICE —
LESS
But Worth
Much More

VOL. I   NEW YORK CITY, SATURDAY, NOVEMBER 15, 1947   NO. 1

MACDONALD IS WINNER OF '47 SILURIAN AWARD

World - Telegram Writer Exposed Relief Abuses in Brilliant Series

The Silurian Award Committee has awarded the Silurian Scroll Award for the best editorial achievement by a New York City newspaperman in the year 1947, to Walter MacDonald of the New York World-Telegram, for his series of stories on the administration of New York City relief by the Welfare Department.

The submissions from the various newspaper editors were of uniformly high caliber and the committee feels that it should commend especially the Herald-Tribune's nomination of the series entitled "Behind the Iron Curtain" by Walter Kerr, Ned Russell, Russel Hill and William Attwood; the Times' nomination of its "Cost of Living" series by Charles Grutzner, and the Son's great series on "Jobs for Disabled Veterans", by Dan Anderson.

These, as well as other nominations, gave proof of the public service of our New York newspapers, and the continuation of the tradition of fine newspaper work of which our town is justly proud.

The winning reporter, Walter MacDonald, dug up his facts against a fortified bureaucratic opposition, and wrote a masterly series of exposures of inefficiency and an analysis of the basic causes. He found and described economic waste, and bared callous indifference in a City department which should be the most humane division of the city government. Then he climaxed his work by bringing on a State investigation followed by a City inquiry, which together forced the resignation of the department head. Through it all the World-Telegram supported and widened the force of his work by a magnificent display which never let his attack be sidetracked.

Our No.1 Silurian Allows Memory To Searchlight Distinguished Folk

By Charles M. Lincoln

Joseph Pulitzer — "You can print any damned thing in that paper if it is True. That is all I ask—that it be True. Bear in mind that nobody—NOBODY can keep anything out of that paper if you want to print it and it is True. My son Ralph has married into the Vanderbilt family, but if you ever want to raise hell with the New York Central Railroad you go ight ahead."

That was the old World!

James Gordon Bennett—"Never print anything about me unless it is something highly defamatory."

Again—"We publish that prominently this morning, a communication of some length from a

Charles M. Lincoln

gentleman who attacks the character of the editor of The Herald. The gentleman has wasted his time. The editor of The Herald lost all the reputation he ever had many years ago."

And again—Blank had made a bad error. Mr. Bennett, in Paris, spotted it. "Send Blank over." Blank was sent ten days later: "Blank returning. Just wanted to see what the damned fool looked like."

Adolph S. Ochs—"All I want is a paper of record. If any one can show or tell me of anything of real importance that happened yesterday of which there is not at least some mention in The Times of today I shall be greatly obliged to him." Mr. Ochs built The Times on an enduring foundation,

as has been said, "by brick upon brick," and in the capable hands to which he passed it his newspaper has long been a matter for pride, not only with Times men but with all American newspapermen. Of Mr. Ochs it might be said that, coming to New York, he found a small, struggling college "in extremis," but that he founded a great university.

William Jennings Bryan—"Col-onel, what's your opinion of Roosevelt?"

After reflection: "I think that if it were possible to open Theodore Roosevelt's head it would be seen that his brain consisted of two lobes, each distinct and separable from the other, neither of which having the slightest idea of what the other was doing."

I wonder if anybody ever heard Bryan laugh? He was the most deadly-serious man I have ever known. He was paid $7,500 for "covering" the two national conventions of 1912. He put the $7,500 into Miami real estate which he sold at the height of the boom for $200,000 or some such ungodly figure.

Nostalgic—Why are there no first class murders any more? What would not a city editor give for something even approaching the Harry Thaw-Evelyn Nesbit-Stanford White story? Or Herbert Swope's "Becker Case"? Or that Roland Molineux-Harry Cornish drama? Or that gradual assembling of the component parts of a human body which, in life, had constituted an obscure rubber in a Turkish bath named Guldensuppe? Or even what used to be the frequent result of a reporter's beating a path to Abe Hummel's door?

I'm sure none of us wish it any body any hard luck, but I'm also sure that if we found a top-notch murder mystery on our front pages tomorrow morning which would give us surcease from all the Vishinskys and such, even for a little while, we would all welcome it.

Menu --- It's on Page 7

YOUR SOCIETY HAS NEW NAME: SILURIANS, INC.

Victor House, Our Counsel, Outlines Benefits from New Legal Status

By Victor House

On July 21, 1947, the charter of the Society of the Silurians, Inc., under the New York membership corporations law, having passed the gamut of approval by our membership last spring and by a Justice of the Supreme Court during the summer, was filed with the Secretary of State in Albany. Thereby the members of the Society as heretofore constituted automatically became members of the new membership corporation.

Incorporation will qualify the Silurians to receive and administer bequests and other funds that may be entrusted to the Society for the benefit of New York newspaper men.

The Silurians having always prided themselves on the spirit of informal comaraderie of their organization, it is appropriate to record that incorporation will in no sense operate as a straitjacket or alter the congenial informality of the semi-annual reunions and other activities of the Society.

The incidents of incorporation that have caused concern in this regard in some quarters are chiefly the initiation and dues provisions and the new organizational set-up. Initiation fees and dues were the subject of considerable debate in the committee charged with the incorporation. No member of the Society of the Silurians as heretofore constituted will be required to pay an initiation fee under the new set-up. For new members hereafter, a $5 initiation fee was fixed.

As regards dues, there was a sharp division, some of the committee feeling that the dues should be substantial so as to put the Society on a solid financial footing. Others felt equally strong-

(Continued on Page 3)

THE SMOKE-FILLED ROOM AT CHICAGO, INCLUDING A FRESH VIEW BY "BELLBOY"

Part I

Jim Hagerty's Classic Preview

James A. ("Old Jim") Hagerty not only was the great reporter all Silurians knew him to be. He was also a fine story teller, eliminating the unnecessary while preserving the flavor of the yarn he was about to recount. One of his best was the background of how the phrase "smoke-filled room" came into everybody's political glossary.

In 1920 the old Waldorf, which had stood for decades on what is now the site of the Empire State Building, was the traditional headquarters for visiting political firemen. Anyone coming to New York to hold advertised or unadvertised political conferences stayed there. In the presidential election years it was worthwhile any day for political reporters just to hang around the lobby and the Men's Bar.

In the spring of 1920, one of the lesser lights who called a press conference at the Waldorf was Harry M. Daugherty, an Ohio Republican of no national repute, who was, however, attorney general of Ohio, and sponsor of a favorite son candidate, Senator Harding of Ohio.

Only three reporters showed up—Hagerty, who had just switched that year from the old *Herald* of Bennett to Och's *Times,* Charley White, a veteran *Tribune* man with distinct Republican partisan leanings, and Jasper ("Jap") Muma, New York correspondent for a Cincinnati paper, who was close enough to the then unsung Ohio gang to figure in later investigations of it.

Daugherty, after extolling Harding's virtues, confidently predicted his nomination. He was so confident in his language and manner that Hagerty said,

"Mr. Daugherty, what you have after all is just a favorite son candidate. What makes you so confident? Have you any special reason for it?"

Daugherty replied: "Well, it will happen about like this. Some time after the first three days of the convention, after Lowden and Leonard Wood have had their runs and missed, and the convention is deadlocked, a little group of bleary-eyed men will meet in some smoke-filled room in the hotel to pick the actual nominee. I will be there; I will present the name of Senator Harding, and he will be nominated."

Either Muma or White, not enthralled, asked: "Is that for quotes?"

"Well," Daugherty said with a grin, "well, I guess you could cut out the 'bleary-eyed,' but the rest of it stands."

Hagerty wrote a modest half-column or so on the story, which *The Times* printed well back in the paper. No other paper printed it.

Two or three months later, Jim was on *The Times* staff at the Chicago convention at which Harding was nominated, after a smoked-filled room conference of the convention leaders, breaking the deadlock the Wood and Lowden rivalry had created. He recalled the Daugherty incident to Joe Tebeau, in charge of *The Times* staff at the convention and of course then wrote it in the light of the new developments. *The Times* printed the story this time on Page One, along with its famous frontpage editorial denouncing the Harding nomination and the crowd behind him. So it entered into history.

The only thing wrong with the Daugherty prediction was

that Daugherty himself was never in the room. He wasn't invited nor was any other candidate's manager.

—WARREN MOSCOW, October 1964

Part II

Not Quite as Planned, but Harding Got It

Jim Hagerty's story of the smoke-filled room stands in our annals like the Rock of Gibraltar, far more than a legend. Trying to upset it would be sacrilege, no less. But I am glad of the invitation to add a supplementary personal footnote.

As a brash young intruder I was there myself at that smoke-filled room, at least on the threshold, and the candidate agreed on that night was Will H. Hays.

I attended the convention at Chicago in 1920 as one of a small group of Amherst College alumni who had organized a Calvin Coolidge for President Committee.

Senator Murray Crane was head of the faction in Massachusetts opposing the faction of Senator Henry Cabot Lodge. Coolidge was aligned with Crane, and the Senator was advising and helping the Coolidge group.

I was assigned the job of running Coolidge headquarters, which distributed buttons and literature. I had a list of the hotels of all the important delegates and convention officials. I was young and exuberant and had two young assistants: John Elwood, a nephew of Owen Young, and H. P. Davison, Jr., a senior at Yale.

The leading candidates were General Wood, Governor Lowden and Senator Johnson. In the early balloting Wood and Lowden had about 300 votes each, Johnson about 190.

After the delegates had stood pat for three ballots, Senator

Penrose from his sickbed in Philadelphia, made the suggestion by telephone of a Philander C. Knox and Hiram Johnson ticket, to be accomplished by a shift of Johnson delegates to Knox, with such others as influential senators could persuade. I learned of this from Raymond Robbins who was Johnson's campaign manager.

Robbins came to the Johnson hotel suite to put the proposal to Johnson, and just as he thought Johnson was prepared to give the go-ahead, the door from the bedroom flew open and an eavesdropping Mrs. Johnson burst into the room, pointing a finger at Robbins and shouting "When did you sell out?" Robbins beat a retreat and that was that. The convention went to six ballots with no indication of the deadlock changing.

Late Friday night, after the convention had recessed, Elwood, Davison, and I were in Dwight Morrow's suite in the Blackstone Hotel. All the big-wigs in the Coolidge group had gone to a social function. Elwood went to the lobby and returned with the information that something was going on two floors above us in the George Harvey suite—that most of the important senators had assembled there and that newsmen were milling around outside trying to pick up information.

We three joined the newspaper men. The emphatic consensus seemed to be that the convention leaders were secretly attempting to break the deadlock. No one either entered or left the suite after we joined the crowd except bellhops with trays of ice, bottles of soda, and sandwiches. We knew that Senator Crane, our only person of sufficient importance to participate in such a conference, was ill and had gone to bed.

Davison suggested that we ought to bribe one of the bellhops to be a fifth column for us. A few minutes later we got into a very crowded elevator just ahead of one of the bellboys. When it stopped two floors below, the boy had to step out of the elevator to let us out. Elwood jostled him and the bell-boy found himself alone with us in the hall outside the Mor-row suite. Davison unlocked the door and we pushed the boy in with us.

Agreeing that he might not be a reliable spy, we decided to borrow his uniform, telephone room service and have sent to our room the same order that our boy was supposedly getting for the Harvey suite. Both Elwood and Davison were taller than the bellboy, while I was about his size. So I put on the uniform and cap. We put the boy in the bathroom with El-wood as guard and when the second boy arrived with our or-der and had left, Davison and I returned to the upper floor. The newsmen paid no attention to me, and I had no difficulty getting in to the Harvey suite with my tray.

The conference was taking place in an inner room but the conferees were coming in and out of the outer rooms, dis-cussing what was going on. Actually, the suite was William Boyce Thompson's, and Col. Harvey was his guest. Neither Daugherty nor Harding was there. The plan arrived at was to stampede the convention the next day for Will Hays.

Hays was chairman of the Republican National Committee and had been nonpartisan as between the various candidates. William Boyce Thompson, a rich mining man, had a careful plan to nominate Hays which he had been working on for months.

The participants in the conference, most of whom were senators, felt assured that they could deliver 212 votes for Hays, from Wood, Lowden, and the others. The first state to switch from Wood was to be Connecticut. The representative of Connecticut at the conference was Senator Brandegee. He was not himself a delegate, the real power controlling the votes being the national committeeman, J. Henry Rohrbach, but Brandegee was sure he would go along.

It was long after midnight when the conference broke up, it being agreed that there should be no leak of the news. Within minutes the newsmen left the corridor. Davidson and I returned to the Morrow suite, released the captive bellhop, restored his clothes, and paid him an amount satisfactory to him.

Elwood, Davison, and I then decided to take a taxi to the La Salle Hotel where Harry Daugherty had his room. At the La Salle we happened to get into the same elevator with Rohrbach, the Connecticut boss, and we left the elevator at the same floor with him. He went to Daugherty's room as we watched and in a few minutes we saw him and Daugherty come out together. Neither of them knew me. We went down in the same elevator. They were evidently much concerned but said nothing that we could overhear. At the door of the hotel they took a cab, and we did not see them again.

Senator Harding's nomination came the next day. Of course our adventure the night before had nothing to do with the selection of Coolidge for vice-president.

After Connecticut had changed from Wood, not to Hays, but to Harding, I learned from one of the Connecticut delegates that Rohrbach had turned down Brandegee on Hays, had alerted Daugherty, and that they had spent most of the night undoing the Hays plan and switching the scheme to Harding. There was a story going the rounds that Rohrbach and Daugherty had organized another conference with some of those who had been in the Harvey suite, which may or may not have been true. The newsmen pinpointed the Harding decision as having been reached in the smoke-filled Harvey suite. Hagerty, of course, recalled the early Daugherty prediction.

I have never heard any account, or seen anything in print of the decision about Hays which miscarried. Certainly,

Daugherty, Rohrbach, and Hays—as well as those who actually participated in the smoke-filled room in the Harvey suite
of the Blackstone—knew what happened. Eventually some
scholar writing a Ph.D. thesis will probably dig up something
about it in the papers of some senator who is dead.

—RICHARD B. SCANDRETT, October 1964

NEW REPORTER IN TOWN CAUGHT
LATE: STORY OF HARDING'S DEATH

When President Harding died, on August 2, 1923, I was in the press room in the Palace Hotel, San Francisco. The official bulletin read as follows:

"The President died instantaneously and without warning and while conversing with members of his family at 7:30 P.M. Death was apparently due to some brain envolvement, probably an apoplexy. During the day he had been free from discomfort and there was every justification for anticipating a prompt recovery.

> *(Signed) C. E. Sawyer, M.D.,*
> *Ray M. Cooper, M.D., J. T.*
> *Boone, M.D., Hubert Work,*
> *M.D."*

I was the only reporter representing the *San Francisco Chronicle* in the press room when this was handed out, having relieved the day shift reporter at 6 P.M. Others had gone to dinner. I soon found myself alone in the press room. A Secret Service man sat in the hallway. He barred the way to reporters other than those accompanying the party. There was a quiet and relaxed atmosphere. The President was supposed to be recovering. At least, that was what Dr. Sawyer had told us the night before.

Before the death of President Harding the outlook was for several rather boring days—quite a letdown from the excitement following the sudden decision of the party to put into San Francisco when the President took sick on his return trip from Alaska.

Practically everybody was strange to me, for I had been in San Francisco and with the *Chronicle* less than three months, up from Los Angeles.

Suddenly an atmosphere of tension seized the place. Somebody, I think it was Dr. Boone, walked quickly past the Secret Service man. The reporter for the *San Francisco Examiner* exchanged words with the Secret Service man that I could not hear. Another reporter telephoned his office, or tried to. A few minutes later he left, saying he was going to his office.

I asked the Secret Service man what was happening. He gruffly ordered me to stand back. People came in without saying a word. Members of the party went by the hall guard. Others came to the press room or crowded into the hall. I still couldn't find out what was going on or what had happened. Nobody seemed to know.

Then Judson C. Welliver, the President's press secretary came in with the bulletin I quoted at the beginning. Half a dozen reporters rushed at him as he passed out the bulletin copies. I grabbed a telephone. The lines were jammed with calls coming in and going out. A sympathetic telephone operator said: "I'll try my best to put you through." She finally did, but the delay was minutes long. I was afraid to leave the telephone, to dash across the street, to the *Chronicle* office as I still was there alone for the *Chronicle*.

When the call got through, a sports writer named Smith was put on to take down the bulletin as I dictated. When I read, "The President died—," he said "What? Are you sure?" "I am reading an official bulletin," I answered, "handed to me personally by Jud Welliver, press secretary to the President."

"Go ahead," he said, but he seemed stunned. I had to keep repeating. Then he stopped to talk with somebody in the office. "We've already got it," came the reply, the next voice was that of Bill Bailey, the night city editor.

"The AP had the bulletin ahead of everybody," said Bill. "Don't worry. Stay there. I'm coming over with a staff. Keep the line open. Dictate any more bulletins you get." *The Examiner* was the first on the street with an extra. The *Chronicle* came out considerably later. I feared the worst—that I would be fired.

Bailey arrived. He was calm and clear-headed as usual. He took over a nearby room. While giving directions, he came to me and spoke reassuringly. By that time, the top rewrite man in the *Chronicle* office was at the other end of my wire. Billy told me to get a line open in the *Chronicle* press room at the hotel. I did. Then they passed bulletins and copy to me to dictate. In between, Bill told me everything would be all right. He said he had Ralph Cromwell, the city editor, in a position where he would listen to him.

Evidently, he had told Cromwell off for not having made better press arrangements for me at the hotel. The *Chronicle* did not have a direct telephone line over there, not even after the President's death. I had told Cromwell that I could not get through the Secret Service line to the President's party. But he had not had me cleared. Evidently no other local newspaper man had been cleared.

E. Ross Bartley, who represented the AP with the party, was smart enough to take advantage of the situation. He had sat with me at the door of the press room for a couple of evenings. Then he shifted his tactics. He sat inside the Secret Service line and around a corner in the hall across the way from the President's door and set up a death watch on him. He got a 12-minute beat and was presented with a gold watch by the AP for his ingenuity.

Later Bailey gave me a friendly hint. "The story was told in the first three words, 'The President died,' " Bill said "All the rest of this stuff is just dressing." He continued to come to me throughout the night and to speak with a calm confidence that convinced me I would be retained on the staff.

Early on the morning of August 3, 1923, I left the Palace Hotel to go home for a few hours of sleep. The lobby was vacant except for a few hotel employees. Out in front, the funereal festoons swung mournfully in the chill morning breeze.

Around noon I reported at the office. Cromwell, the city editor, greeted me pleasantly. He said the *Chronicle* showed that everyone had done a good job. He asked me if I had heard the rumor that the President had been poisoned. I had not. Later evidence makes me believe that he died of any but natural causes, but that is another story.

One incident of the evening of August 2, 1923, seemed to have helped me later to get a job on the editorial staff of *The New York Times*. It was the fact that I was the first to tell Richard V. Oulahan, then chief of the Washington Bureau of The Times, that President Harding had died.

—EARL O. EWAN, November 1961

HE SAW ABE LINCOLN AND WATCHED
AUTOPSY ON GARFIELD'S ASSASSIN

This reports a narrative that Dr. Lewi told the Silurians at their fall dinner in 1949. As a young doctor he had witnessed the autopsy and was prepared to meet the demands from the newspapers in Albany, his home town, expressing their partisanship as to the compulsive psychotic or criminal bent of the assassin. After this talking-to-himself debate, the doctor retained through the years his own sturdy neutrality.

"I was a haphazard reporter for several newspapers in my younger days, and never was on the payroll of any of them. I chased the old horse engines to fires many times, covered various events, and later became Fire Department Surgeon in my home town.

"As a medical witness, I was present at the execution of Charles Guiteau, the assassin of President Garfield. I had made all arrangements to send a special report to the *Albany Express* of happenings at the execution, but obligations to be present at the autopsy of the body of the assassin prevented me from filing a story in time to meet the deadline. Moreover, the everalert staff reporters of other newspapers were far ahead of me. By the time I was free the regular reporters had every wire in use and were burning them up with details that escaped my rather unskilled reporter's mind."

Before the autopsy, said Dr. Lewis, an issue arose as to who should perform it. A Dr. Sowers, who was then coroner's physician for the District of Columbia, and a Dr. Lamb of the Army Medical Corps, were both ready to perform the autopsy. They stood for some moments with instruments in hand, while a question was being debated to determine whether it was legally the task of the District's official or that of the Army's representative. Finally, Dr. Sowers waived his rights and the army doctor proceeded with the task.

"There were only seven persons present at that autopsy," Dr. Lewi recalls. "They included the two doctors mentioned above, myself, two other medical witnesses and two persons whose identity I never learned. Nevertheless, next morning the newspapers carried a report of the issue mentioned and depicted it as a quarrel between the two medical officials, declaring that 'even in death Guiteau caused friction.' Actually there was no quarrel. There was some embarrassment on the part of each of the officials mentioned, but the determination was made in a gentlemanly manner and without rancor.

"Subsequently, by request, I wrote an editorial for the *Albany Express* bearing upon the incident. On the following day, and again by request, I wrote an editorial for the *Albany Argus* controverting the argument of the former. Once again the *Express* requested an editorial justifying the original story. And so this one-man controversy continued for several days, without the public or the competing newspapers suspecting the truth. Two years later at a dinner, attended by editors Keyes and McKelway of the respective competitive newspapers, I told the true story of that mild feud to the great amusement and surprise of the men who had hired my elastic if somewhat erratic pen."

A great event in Dr. Lewi's life occurred when he was too young to realize its significance. As a boy of eight he saw President Lincoln in his coffin and vividly recalls his tearful amazement as he gazed upon the features of the worshipped President.

—MAURICE J. LEWI, May 1950

OUT OF THE TRENCHES BY CHRISTMAS; PRAYER AND JEST OF 1915 PEACE SHIP

Just 50 years ago I was a teen-age rookie reporter covering Police Headquarters and general assignments in Manhattan for the *Brooklyn Eagle*. One day, the assistant managing editor, one Hans von Kaltenborn, emitting a louder grunt than usual, asked me to find out what was happening in room 717 at the Biltmore Hotel. Henry Ford had set up "Peace Head-quarters" there and was about to tell the press what his plans were for ending the war in Europe.

Henry Ford, when I met him, was burning to stop "the silly killings going on abroad." He felt that America should step in and ask the warring nations to kiss and make up. He had no hope that President Woodrow Wilson would adopt the role of mediator. But, "If I can make automobiles run," he said, "why can't I steer those people clear of war?"

Unlike my colleagues, older and more cynical, I was inclined to take the Peace Expedition seriously. Ford's plan— the brainchild of journalist-pacifist Rosika Schwimmer of Hungary—was to corral a goodly number of pacifists, with the press, for a voyage to the neutral European countries. Object: to get these countries to persuade the nations at war to adopt Mme. Schwimmer's "Continuous Mediation" plan.

When I got to my typewriter, I treated the story with reverence. Very earnestly, I quoted Mr. Ford's happy thought of "getting the boys out of the trenches by Christmas." The hard-boiled Park Row fraternity took a different slant. To them, this was another Tin Lizzie joke. I favored Peace and Henry Ford.

Evidently, this enthusiasm attracted the Peace Ship orga-nizers, for they invited me to join the newspaper delegation on the Peace Ship, *Oscar II*, scheduled to depart from Hoboken, December 4.

"If this Expedition fails," Ford declared, "I'll start another." John Wanamaker, far from unsympathetic, evaluated the enterprise as, "a mission of generous heart, fat pocketbook, but no plan." Judge Alton B. Parker, on the other hand, called Ford a mountebank and clown. Theodore Roosevelt, one-time Nobel Peace Prize winner, was variously quoted as condemning the Expedition as "mischievous because ridiculous" or "not mischievous only because ridiculous." The London Spectator called the *Oscar II* "The Ship of Fools."

For the press at the Biltmore's "Stop the War Suite," there was "color" unlimited. Dr. Charles Pease, (Anti Smoking League), whose avocation was riding subways to snatch cigarettes from passengers' lips, received an authenticated invitation. An application for the papal blessing was addressed to the wrong Pope—one deceased for centuries. An herbalist, promising medication for all the wounds of the world, applied for passage. Cardinal Gibbons' routine "God bless you" was taken as formal approval.

For the men writing for a sensationalist press, all this still was not enough. Ford's press conferences unfortunately established a chaotic tone for his enterprise. When actually "on," especially before a large audience, Ford invariably floundered. He bewildered the reporters, who overwhelmed him, with generalizations about his particular anathema, "preparedness." He had an almost Franciscan affinity for birds, and he said now, "No boy would kill a bird if he didn't have a slingshot." The Peace Ship in fact was an ancestor of the modern protest march.

It sailed with some sixty-odd peace delegates, three newsreel men, 15 reporters and editors, Ford's personal staff of 20, and our own Louis P. Lochner.

The newsmen lost no time in founding the Ancient and Honorable Order of the Vacillating Sons of St. Vitus, with headquarters at the ship's bar.

The Expedition got under way with a bang, and another and another, from the "world's longest gun." (Marconi wireless, it was then.) The first message to go out was an additional farewell to "Ma" Clara Ford. The next was to be the longest ever sent, the first radio sermon. It was the Rev. Dr. Charles F. Aked's Sunday sermon in the dining saloon, more than two thousand words long, and it cost over a thousand dollars to send. No paper printed it. The total tab for "wireless" transmission was more than $10,000. To any comment on the expense, Ford's answer was, "I can make fifty million in a minute."

But it was not only sermons and delegates' speeches that kept the transmitter hot. The newsmen were continually hassling to beat the others with their messages, many of them in the form appropriate to the police reporting to which many had been accustomed. The atmospheric conditions were bad to start with, and the congestion jammed the wireless. This started the rumor that the top brass was censoring stories, although the reverse was true. Ford absolutely refused to inhibit the sending of any story, regardless of content.

A London newspaperman, whoses application to sail had been denied by Ford's lawyers, was discovered traveling steerage, outside of chartered territory. Not only was his ruse applauded by Ford, it was rewarded with an exclusive interview, which naturally did not dispose the American correspondents any more kindly toward their patron. The London reporter's gratitude showed in the headline over his story: "Ford a Prisoner in his Cabin, Chained to Bed by Secretary."

The *Oscar*'s Captain William Hempel, reading the messages to make sure his ship's neutrality was not violated, let Ford in on the scurrilous content of many accounts. Ford remained genial and unperturbed. "Let them send anything they please," he said. "I want the boys to feel perfectly at home. They are my guests. I wouldn't for the world censor them."

The press roster included John English, *Boston Traveler;* Herman Bernstein, editor of *The Day,* later minister to Czechoslovakia; John D. Barry, *San Francisco Bulletin;* Irving Caesar ("Tea for Two," the same who sang for us at last fall's Silurian dinner) then of the *Greenwich Times;* Thomas W. Seep, Associated Press; Helen B. Lowry, *N.Y. Post;* Miriam Teichner, *N.Y. Globe;* Charles P. Stewart of United Press.

Berton Braley and Marian Rubicam, both of *Collier's,* were married on the ship by the captain.

One early morning our patron emerged from his cabin to the sea-swept deck of our violently pitching vessel. Done up more as if for the Easter Parade than for a midwinter constitutional on deck, Ford was resplendent in a sable-collared coat and derby. But his gold-mounted walking stick did not steady his progress. He quickly went down and coasted through the inches-deep water of the slanting deck, straight for the opening between the lifeboat davits and the railing, wide enough in those days—before Coast Guard regulation—for a body to go through.

This writer, the youngest newsman aboard the *Oscar,* had also come up on deck at that stormy early hour, in solo celebration of his 19th birthday. I slip-raced across barely in time to grab the first part that came handy, the sable collar, and managed to get a flustered, soaked, and grateful Ford back on his feet. I was too modest, then, or too stupid, to dispatch this life-saving tale to my editor, but proudly told all in a letter to my mother. This is, in fact, the first time I've made the incident public, with due apology to a scornful Kaltenborn up there in Heaven.

In any case, Ford's near-drowning, a secret on and off ship, brought misfortunes. Ford was felled with la grippe (of course as a result of the dousing) and so he lay at the mercy of two forces combined in their destructive attitudes—gloomy Dean Marquis of Detroit's St. Paul Cathedral, dedicated to getting Ford back home, and the newshawks, dedicated to getting a story, preferably a scandal. And each was grist for the other's mill.

One delegation of newsmen succeeded in getting into the sick-cabin, and challenged their germ-ridden host with "Mr. Ford, J. Pierpont Morgan was dead six hours before any newspaper knew about it. We won't be scooped that way this time. So we've come to see for ourselves whether you are still alive." Ford was no doubt not inspired by this visitation, although probably thinking, already as he said in Stockholm, that "it was time to get home to mother."

The total cost of the Ford Peace adventure has never been established as a dollar and cents accounting sheet. Fantastic sums ranging from one to five million dollars have been mentioned. Such items as gifts of some twenty Ford cars to important European figures kept popping up and were neither confirmed nor denied.

Louis Lochner years ago did obtain figures which added up to some $400,000. Assume then, he said, that Ford's total worth at that time was no less than 150 million dollars, and that this bore 6 percent interest. Ford's money within 16 days after we started from New York had already "earned" the entire cost of the Expedition with all its extravagances, all its "extras."

After a strenuous tour in Scandinavia and a sleepless night on a sealed train through Germany to Holland, most of the newsmen felt the need of libation. We then found that our rooms were reserved in a vegetarian temperance hotel. The

Hague was so crowded with refugees that this hotel was the only recourse.

"I'm a sick man!" the protests went up. "We'll send out for a bottle," we reassured ourselves. But the manager courteously relieved our messengers of any long-necked parcels. It might have been easier to take the hostesses to their rooms, had we felt up to it in our parched state.

The Expedition ended the way it began—a sublimely screwy paragraph in history. The reporters were the only realists there. Their cynicisms, however, helped to wreck the peace chase with a cruelty and levity which was unique in the American press. Possibly a part of the world's scorn for the Peace Ship was because Ford had the dollars to buy a larger share than anyone else in the world-wide failure to "get the boys out of the trenches."

Having pitted the neutrals against each other, the pacifists cut for home. In some cases, they petitioned for a rest from Peace in the snowy Alps or sunny Spain, or with a newborn interest in organized war, for the means to look at the fronts, Western or Eastern.

Those of us who were invited by the Germans to junket down to Roumania to see Von Mackensen's victorious operations were permitted to detach from the Expedition provided we rejoined the *S.S. Rotterdam* in Holland. The passage home would be forfeited if the passenger failed to show up. The Ford paymaster had now pulled the pursestrings shut. The houseparty was over. Anybody who didn't have independent business in Europe, could go home.

December 4, 1940, in the old grad desire to "eat, drink and reminisce," newsmen who had sailed on the *Oscar* pitched a reunion to commemorate the Twenty-Fifth Anniversary. A handful of aging survivors showed up at this Overseas Press Club luncheon at the Gladstone Hotel. Elmer Davis, then ill, sent this message, ". . . This reunion seems to have but one purpose as far as I can see, namely—to get us out of our wheelchairs by Christmas in order that we can come and gloat over our ability to outlive the others. . . . If we still call ourselves the Vacillating Sons of St. Vitus, it may be due more to Parkinson's than to Park & Tilford. . . ."

Henry Ford sent this writer a lengthy telegram, ending: ". . . At least we who sailed in 1915 did not decrease the life or love that was in the world."

—BURNET HERSHEY, October 1965

WHEN BINNS'S HEROISM
AVERTED SEA TRAGEDY

Jack Binns in 1909 acquired instant fame. He was hailed, by force of custom, as a modest hero. All heroes, of course, were "modest." In Jack's case the term was refreshingly appropriate.

Marconi operator on the White Star steamship *Republic*, sinking after a collision, Binns stuck to his job and thus put wireless telegraphy on the world's front page —first time it was used in a major sea rescue.

Overnight, the story of Jack Binns transmuted in the public mind the mysterious experiments of Guglielmo Marconi into an exciting understanding of the marvels of radio. The generation coming on stage recognized better than its elders that a new era was dawning.

Uncounted thousands of teen-agers, thinking of Binns, haunted the hardware store, the electrician's shop—even the Five and Ten—seeking the wire, binding posts, lumps of silicon (a nickel here, a nickel there) which, along with an empty cardboard oatmeal container, would make a two-slide induction coil receiver. "Cat's whisker" entered the language as the young explorer of the new universe disappeared from normal society, Wearing the earphones borrowed from Uncle George, who worked for Telephone, he spent most of his waking hours in the attic fishing, at first, for the gritty chatter of the spark gap, later, for the high-pitched "do-do-dit-doo" which was radio before it found its tongue. What if he should pick up a distress signal?

But Binns took no bows, claimed no credit, made no complaints. The public forgot him for the next five decades, when he was a reporter for the *Tribune* and the *American,* then a successful businessman and cherished Silurian.

He didn't bother to shed his anonymity when history buffs protested that his name had been left off a stele in Battery Park erected in memory of radio heroes lost at sea. Others pointed out that Jack obviously was disqualified for a martyr's crown. He was vigorously-and silently alive.

Years later, an incident at a Silurian dinner disclosed that Jack Binns rarely mentioned, even to close friends, his onetime celebrity.

His good friend, George Sokolsky, was asked if Binns was indeed "the boy hero of the *Republic."* Surprised, Sokolsky said, "I really don't know. I've known Jack for years, and it just didn't occur to me. I'll ask him now."

Jack replied, softly, "George, that was a *long* time ago."

Here follows *Silurian News'* reminder of the hero in our midst.

The steamship *Republic,* with 1,600 passengers aboard, had left New York for the Mediterranean at five o'clock on the evening of Friday, January 22d, 1909. Jack Binns was the lone operator on the ship. By the time the *Republic* cleared Sandy Hook it ran into a thick fog bank. The automatic foghorn began its moanful blasts. Jack remained at his wireless instrument until midnight, exchanging location reports with other ships and shore stations—and sending various messages. He turned in at midnight, but rested rather than slept, listening to the fog signals.

Suddenly at four o'clock on the morning of the 23d, while the ship was some twenty-six miles off Nantucket lightship, there was a terrific crash. Binns rushed to the ship's deck. He saw that the *Republic* had been rammed badly by the Italian liner *Florida,* the bow of which had plowed through the engine-room compartment and had torn away part of the wireless cabin. Binns rushed to check his wireless equipment, soon had it working and sending CQD to Siasconsett station on Nantucket. Hours passed while both ships drifted about.

(The code in 1909 was CQD—popularly called "Come Quick Danger." The *Titanic* disaster introduced SOS in 1912.)

The *Republic* was helpless but the *Florida* was able to navigate, so Captain Sealby of the *Republic* ordered his 1,600 passengers placed aboard the *Florida,* a ship of much smaller capacity which already was carrying 2,000 passengers, chiefly steerage. The transfer, while hazardous in the bitter January weather, was made without mishap. Eight hours later the White Star Liner *Baltic* was reported eight miles away and rushing to the scene. More long hours of waiting and the *Republic* began listing. After 18 hours at his station Binns was still one of seven aboard the *Republic.*

Captain Sealby gave the order to abandon ship, with a request for volunteers. All volunteered, but the captain selected second officer Williams. While the *Republic* was in tow it was evident that she could remain afloat only a short time. It was dark when she sank. Then followed a long and heart-rending search for Captain Sealby and Williams, who could not remain alive long in the freezing waters of the Atlantic. A shot from Captain Sealby's gun brought ships to the rescue just in time. Both were clinging desperately to floating debris. Thus ended one of the truly great and successful adventures of the sea, with high credit to the efficacy of wireless and the heroism of seamen.

Jack Binns, who is now chairman of the Hazeltine Corporation, manufacturer of radio and radar equipment in Little Neck, N.Y., has also had many exploits as a reporter. At the time of the sinking of the *Titanic* he, Martin Dunn, and several others of the Hearst organization equipped a tug with wireless and lay off Nantucket to intercept the incoming *Carpathia* for interviews with survivors. On that occasion Binns intercepted the Yamsi messages which were sent by Bruce Ismay to Franklin, head of the International Mercantile Marine and which eventually were to lead to Ismay's being given the silent treatment by all his associates. He also covered the arrival of the German submarine *Deutschland* when it came over with a commercial cargo during World War I and was war correspondent in Mexico when the U.S. fleet took Vera Cruz.

—May 1957

WALL ST. WHODUNIT!
SO EVERYBODY FLED

Wall Street was enjoying warm sunshine on September 16, 1920. Brownie and I had stopped at Mannie's cigar stand in the lobby of 25 Broad Street, as we did each day on the way to lunch, to play his punch board. We were $47 to the good and working on velvet.

The boom of an explosion brought everyone in the crowded lobby to a freeze, with expressions of bewilderment. Glass could be heard falling in the street outside, in rising volume.

We raced out into Broad Street, avoiding the sidewalk and the falling glass. People were huddled against buildings or standing in the entrances. At the corner of Wall Street some activity was noted and we headed up Broad Street.

As we turned the corner at 23 Wall (Morgan Bank), we came upon a battlefield scene. Bodies lay motionless in grotesque positions against the Morgan building and across the street against the U.S. Assay Office. The few people who had arrived ahead of us were motionless, bereft of any power to act.

At the curb, on the Assay office side, was the splintered ruin of a flatbed wagon which had carried the explosive. The horse, blown apart, was lying at the curb, a straw hat to protect him from the sun, still on his head. The driver of the death wagon at least was kind to animals.

The crowd which had increased to a silent, awe-stricken ring around the scene started to get restless. Then a shout arose that "another bomb was coming." Panic set in and people started racing away.

I had felt that I could keep my head when those about me were losing theirs, but I failed the test. I joined the fleeing crowd.

The scream of sirens could be heard from several directions and within minutes police, fire, and ambulance cars converged on the spot and the area was roped off. The Wall Street explosion resulted in 30 deaths and over 100 injuries, mostly from falling glass.

It still remains a mystery, with who did it and why, unanswered.

—EDWARD P. TASTROM, March 1967

SUICIDE RECORD FROM 1929 CRASH?
WALL ST. VIEW: IT'S EXAGGERATED

The stock market panic of 1929 which contributed to the world-wide depression of the early 1930s, happened thirty-five years ago. That's far enough back so that even an organization such as ours, with no youngsters in its membership, has a dwindling number that were on the firing line covering Wall Street at the time. The editor of our *Silurian News* looked back over the records and, when he found that two months after the *Herald Tribune* appointed me financial editor, the whole economy went to pot, tapped me to tell all. Later, when I got out of newspaper work, the longest bull market in history and our greatest period of prosperity quickly followed.

On a Canadian program recently, patterned along the line of "I've Got a Secret," when the questioners eventually discovered that my secret was that I had covered the crash, one panel member asked seriously: "Is it true that people kept jumping out of windows?" I replied that no one person did it twice, and that while there were indeed many suicides, some by individuals who saw their dreams in ruins, I had yet to see convincing statistics that suicides were more prevalent than now. The story that people walked down the middle of the streets for fear of being hit by falling bodies, was a canard. Many used the sidewalks and did not once get hit. We have more jaywalkers today.

Tomes have been written on both panic and depression. They are erudite and well written, so the *Silurian News* will not attempt to compete. But one can find amusement, this long after an era that was at the opposite pole from amusement, by looking over headlines and stories of that day.

"Kreuger Backs $125 Million Loan to German Government," said one in October, when the panic was well on its way. "Bonds Guaranteed Personally by Ivar Kreuger," read the bank of the head. There was a suicide for you, and a spectacular one. Kreuger's machinations finally caught up with him. He took his dive from an airplane on a Saturday morning, when the stock market was open, as Wall Street traded for two hours on Saturdays in those days.

That was a few days after the chairman of the National Air Transport Association assured the public, according to the headline, that "Aviation Is a Safe Travel Means." His name was Coffin—a vice-president of the Hudson Motor Car Co.

That was about the time, "Mr. Hoover Promises to Make Washington Dry Enforcement Model." His confidence was no less than that which prevailed in the business world. Selected headlines of the time, with the stock market already falling, included "Metropolitan Life to Build 100-Story Home," "World's Tallest Skyscraper for National City Bank-Farmers Trust," to rise 925 feet and have 71 stories; "Cities Service Offers Rights to Buy Stock, Valued at $50,000,000"; "American & Foreign Power Pays 5 Quarterly Dividends on 2nd Pf.," and sees rapid growth; "Stock Frauds Curbed," says Investment Bankers Association official in Quebec; and "Big Gains in Railroad Earnings Expected." Those who are familiar with the New Haven Railroad's present financial condition will appreciate one in September, 1929, "New Haven Continues Its Gain in Earnings."

There was one severe jolt in the stock market early in August of that year but the list recovered, and as September opened, one headline read: "Heavy Buying Sends Stocks to New Highs," and another, "Shares on Curb Make New Highs in Active Trade." Another severe jolt followed, then on September 8 was a headline: "Brokers Scoff Dire Warnings of Economists," with the bank reading: "Resent Comparison with Bust in Florida Land Boom."

Even in October when the panic in stocks was evident, confidence in the country's business remained. One leading commercial bank, in its monthly letter, declared: "Trade Decline Not Alarming." Many in the Street professed to question whether we were actually in a bear market, even shortly before a session when leaders broke 5 to 70 points.

Such questions could be said to have ended on October 29, when a record of more than 16,000,000 shares changed hands on the big board. At times during the day specialists couldn't find any bids whatever for shares of many top grade companies. The ticker fell hours behind actual floor prices. It was so late that after the close, final bid and asked quotations were made available to newspapers even as the ticker was still recording sales. It would continue doing so until after 5 o'clock. *The New York Sun* that afternoon ran the complete bid and asked table on the front page, on six columns, right down the middle, because no one knew whether the market had ever closed.

It was a period of excitement, as much so in newspaper work as in the stock market itself, and while thousands saw their savings extinguished, there remained an undercurrent of optimism that only speculators in Wall Street had suffered, that business would right itself and that the economy was fundamentally sound. We know now how false was that hope, and while the panic took a severe toll, far greater losses were sustained in the years immediately following. After a comeback of about half of its loss in the panic break, a recovery that developed in the closing weeks of that year, the long depression started. There was very little joy in this land or any other in that period when it seemed all our economic machinery had stripped it gears.

—**C. NORMAN STABLER, October 1964**

VIEW FROM ROOM 9
WALKER TO WAGNER

Reviewing the years spent in covering City Hall is like peering through the big end of a telescope. Almost everything seems so small and far away, so lost in the shadows of years that have passed.

The things that seem clear in the mind's eye after thirty-six years of City Hall coverage, first for the old New York City News Association and later for *The New York Times,* are people rather than events. The doings at City Hall have constituted essentially the same play. The people have made up an ever-changing cast.

What newspaperman who ever worked in Room 9, the City Hall press room, could ever forget dapper, charming, gaily irresponsible Jimmy Walker, who became Mayor in 1926 and resigned under pressure in 1932? Who could possibly banish from his mind the swarthy, stocky, fiery, irrepressible Fiorello La Guardia?

Joseph V. McKee and John P. O'Brien had their brief stays at City Hall, leaving little behind except official notations of their service. William O'Dwyer, the charming Irishman whose chief fault was indecision, had a record of accomplishment, but left office with his reputation tarnished, however unjustly, by a Congressional investigation. Vincent R. Impellitteri, recently retired from the Criminal Court bench, will always be remembered as the Mayor who got himself elected on an insurgent ticket carrying his name alone.

Mayor O'Brien was handicapped by a shy disposition and complete loyalty to the political leadership which plucked him from the calm and serenity of the Surrogate's Court. He was elected to a short term highlighted by a financial crisis.

His outstanding contribution to the City Hall saga was

his reply to a reporter who asked whom he planned to appoint as Police Commissioner.

His reply—"I haven't got the word yet"—remains a classic City Hall utterance.

Room 9 was a busy place when Jimmy Walker became Mayor in 1926. About a dozen Manhattan daily newspapers were being published, to say nothing of dailies in Brooklyn, Queens, Staten Island and the Bronx. Many Silurians will remember such City Hall reporters as stately Hamilton Peltz of *The Times,* Ned McIntosh of the *Herald Tribune,* Irving Pinover of the *Journal,* Dan Breen of *The Evening World* and George Dobson of the *Post.* Most of the reporters assigned to Room 9 today are young, aggressive and eager to analyze and interpret what they see and hear. Gray heads are few.

Mayor Walker, a born showman, gave the press plenty of material. Radiating charm, he could talk an unimportant fact into a first page story. His press conferences were held on the run as he left City Hall to keep his social engagements.

"What do you want to know?" he would ask. "Make it fast, boys. I want to get out of this flea bag."

Mayor Walker was more popular with the "boys in Room 9" than any of his immediate predecessors and successors. City Hall men who asked him unpleasant questions when his official conduct was under scrutiny received courteous, if not informative, answers.

Mayor La Guardia, who is generally regarded as the city's "best" mayor, was not noted for courtesy to newspapermen. Many times he answered reasonable and pertinent questions with loud denunciation of the questioners and their queries. It was commonplace for him to charge that the questions were "not asked in good faith." It was also common practice for him to write to publishers and editors complaining about stories written by their City Hall men.

But even his severest critics among the City Hall reporters agreed that he was the kind of Mayor needed to drive corrupt and useless employees out of the city's service.

The boys in Room 9 found Mayor O'Dwyer a likeable man with the mind and vocabulary of a poet or historian. Although his relations with the press were almost always good and occasionally cordial he would sometimes resent questions he regarded as invasions of his personal privacy.

Television and radio coverage of City Hall has developed rapidly. The Wagner administration has been accused of giving these media preference over the newspapers on important stories.

The complete story of Mayor Wagner's stay at City Hall has yet to be written. He has made it clear that he intends to run for a fourth term. He is recognized as a good public servant, a resourceful politician and a man who has better than average luck in the clinches.

—PAUL CROWELL, April 1965

CITY HALL AFIRE, BUT—
NOT A REPORTER ON THE JOB

Back in the "good old days," just before we got into the First World War, I was working on the old *Globe,* serving my apprenticeship covering Police Headquarters.

At City Hall for the *Globe* at the time was Bill Graemer, affectionately known as "The Millionaire Reporter," because he lived in a four-story brownstone house on Thirty-sixth Street, just east of Fifth Avenue, with a butler and other hired help. Being a reporter, it seemed to me, was more an avocation with Bill since, mixed in with his coverage of the Hall, were extraneous enterprises that occupied more of his time in Room 9 than did the newspaper business.

At any rate, Bill probably was the first artisan anywhere to plump for the five-day week; he insisted on having Saturdays off. As a result, George Hughes, the city editor, switched me to City Hall on Saturdays.

John Purroy Mitchel was Mayor. The office of President of the Board of Aldermen at the other end of the Hall was occupied by "Al" Smith, recently elected after a stint as Sheriff.

In those days, City Hall was notably quiet on Saturdays. The Mayor rarely, if ever, came in. "Al" did, however, and to break the monotony of the day, he established the Saturday Bean Club. With "Al" as informal president, the members were the boys in Room 9, all of whom would stroll with him at noon each Saturday to Schmidt's, on Chambers Street, to partake of the free lunch, beef and beans, and something to wash them down.

This particular Saturday all of us were in Schmidt's in our usual convivial mood. Not even the distant clang of fire bells and sirens' wails disturbed our session. Leisurely, we ate and drank and talked. Just as leisurely, after several hours, we left Schmidt's and headed back to Room 9. And we found City Hall Plaza curb deep in fire apparatus. Hose lines stretched across the Plaza, up the steps and through the doors and windows of the Hall.

The cupola had been afire. And not a City Hall reporter on the job!

That was the last Saturday I covered City Hall for the *Globe*. But to this day I can't understand why I wasn't fired. I presume it was because all of us in Room 9 were in the same predicament.

I prefer to think, though, it was because I explained to the city editor that the Saturday Bean Club had been disbanded—in bad odor.

—MACK A. NOMBERG, May 1948

HITLER, THE TORRENTIAL TALKER, OR CUTTING IN TO GET AN ANSWER

In August of 1932, five months before the Nazi take-over of Germany, Harvard-bred Dr. Ernst F. (nicknamed Putzi) Hanfstaengl, then Adolf Hitler's Man Friday for international press affairs, rang me up to suggest that he could secure me an interview with the self-styled "Fuehrer" if I were to take the night train from Berlin to Munich. He would then drive me out to Berchtesgaden, Hitler's Bavarian mountain home.

Putzi was at the railway station in Berlin all right but three journalists—Karl von Wiegand, H. V. Kaltenborn and yours truly —looked at each other in surprise to find us all boarding the same sleeping car with F.D.R.'s Harvard fellow alumnus. Putzi had made each of us think that he was to have an "exclusive."

Karl, always a loner, objected violently and threatened to leave the train immediately unless he could see Hitler alone. Putzi tried to assuage him and assured him a satisfactory solution could be found. Karl remained adamant. H. V. and I exchanged meaningful glances and said we didn't mind seeing Der Fuehrer together.

Kaltenborn and I were not competitors. He was radio and I, Associated Press; we could therefore well share our findings. As soon as we were alone I told H. V., who had not before met the former Austrian corporal, that Hitler was a very talkative man. If the first question an interviewer asked suited his purpose, I explained, he might talk for half an hour on that one answer and then abruptly terminate his audience. (Putzi had informed us that our interview would be limited to 30 minutes.)

"Our strategy," I continued, "should be for you and me to agree in advance on six questions. While Hitler answers the first, the questioner takes full notes while the other keeps his eye on his wrist watch. As soon as five minutes are over, he must interrupt, rudely if necessary, and pose the next question. Our victim may not like this, but as he probably craves publicity, he won't object. If we alternate every five minutes with a new query, then with luck we can extract answers on six questions."

H. V. agreed. We made out a list of tentative questions which we rehearsed the next morning while Karl was having his "exclusive." Putzi accompanied him down the hill from a small Bavarian rustic inn to the Fuehrerhaus. Half an hour later Putzi waved to Hans and me sitting on the terrace, indicating we should come down.

Wiegand was mopping his brow. "Gosh," he said, "I didn't get to first base. That man never stops talking, once you throw a question at him. My half hour was over before I knew it. I had a whole bunch of questions up my sleeve, but never got beyond the first one."

Hans and I had entered the house, which in those days was a typical, unpretentious upper middle-class home. After Hitler seized power, he rebuilt and greatly enlarged it. The future dictator greeted us unsmiling but affably in his native peasant tongue which his enemies derisively called a "summer vacation dialect."

Since I have deposited all my papers covering 57 years in journalism with the Mass Communications History Center at my alma mater, the University of Wisconsin, I have no record of the questions. I distinctly remember, however, that H. V. posed the first one. That made me the fall guy for the first interruption.

Loquacious Adolf seemed bewildered that anybody should dare break into his soliloquy. He gave me the dirty look I anticipated, but then grudgingly discussed Question No. 2.

With our pattern thus established, Hans interrupted after the next five minutes. Again the non-too-gracious look, but no tempestuous blow-up of the kind which the underlings encountered when their leader was in a bad mood. Our strategy paid off beyond our hopes. We extracted six replies.

Putzi Hanfstaengl, incidentally, defected to England in 1937, and in 1942–43 was frequently consulted by President Roosevelt in Washington.

A little later I found myself in Munich again. When I learned that Hanfstaengl was in town also, I asked for a truly exclusive interview. This he did, on condition that I submit my story to his Fuehrer for approval. I agreed.

Many of my colleagues in the foreign service deemed it humiliating to submit copy for approval. On the other hand, a correspondent time and again is disavowed and charged with erroneous quotation or misrepresentation when an interviewee finds that his mouthings prove to be a big mistake. If, however, he has indicated his approval by his signature or initials, he cannot afterwards disavow the quotation. Submission for approval can thus become a boon for the interviewer.

One of the questions I asked was, "Herr Hitler, why are you so anti-semitic?" This was the only query of mine, the reply to which the "Fuehrer" eliminated. I distinctly recall his exact answer:—"Because we Germans cannot digest the Jews. The Italians, for instance, can. The British can. But not we. Since we cannot digest them, we must eliminate them." By "digest" he obviously meant "assimilate."

I could not but chuckle at this statement, for Hitler had only a few minutes previously extolled the superhuman qualities of the Nordic race, the Herrenvolk of which he was a most unrepresentative specimen. It seemed like a fatal confession of weakness for him to admit that a nation made up 99 percent of alleged supermen could not assimilate, or, if you please, co-exist with the one percent of its population that was non-Aryan!

The pseudo-Herrenmensch must himself have realized what a damaging admission he had made, for with an angry gesture he crossed the whole paragraph on the Jewish question out as he read my story. Incidentally, when I started him on anti-Semitism, saliva exuded from his mouth as he ranted.

When the Mass Communications History Center at Wisconsin was launched on January 25, 1958, I brought with me the script of this Hitler interview, with the passage about the Jews stricken out by the objecting apostle of supermanship, as part of my contribution to the new venture.

After the ceremony at which I told the story, two professors, one of history, the other of psychology, came to tell me that they considered the document very revealing. This concerned both the answers to my various questions and, even more, the passage through which the later dictator had angrily run his pencil and had forbidden publication.

"A man filled with inferiority complexes" was their joint verdict.

—LOUIS P. LOCHNER, March 1966

YES, HITLER COULD BLUSH,
AND DID FOR WILY REPORTER

When I took back upon the nightmarish, though to the newsmen tremendously interesting, Hitler years, I recall with special relish that on two occasions I had the rare experience of making the vain, self-assured, opinionated Fuehrer actually blush. The first time it was an embarrassed blush, the second, an angry, irascible one.

After Adolf Hitler came into power on January 30, 1933, he and his propaganda minister, Joseph Goebbels, disdainfully shunned the foreign press, although correspondents from twenty-six nations were accredited by the Nazis regime. Finally, in the spring of 1934, my efforts to see Hitler for a publishable interview bore fruit.

My first question dealt with his foreign policy aims. For a moment he looked at me, then his eyes turned toward the ceiling. He seemed to have forgotten me completely, but instead envisoned a mass meeting which he was addressing. His eyes roved back and forth along the ceiling, and as he pontificated his voice became so thunderous that the two bodyguards before his inner sanctum asked me, as I left, "Was the Fuehrer very angry with you? he sounded awfully mad."

He ranted about the Treaty of Versailles, condemned the Polish "steal" of the Corridor, demanded the cession of the German-speaking Sudetenland from Czechoslovakia, and vowed to end the reparations burden imposed by England, France, and Italy upon the defeated German people.

Several times he interjected, "Das muss alles anders werden" ("All that must be changed"). Without pausing for a breath, so that I could not even pose another question, he castigated the German Weimar Republic and its leaders for their

—to him—weak, ineffective, and vacillating foreign policies. At last he seemed to run out of steam. I quickly asked, "Why, sir, are you apparently paying so little attention to the United States as a factor in world politics?" That caught him off-guard. He was embarrassed. He blushed, hemmed and hawed (usually he was never at a loss for words), and finally blurted out, "I just haven't had time to pay much attention to America; domestic and European problems kept me more than busy."

To embarrass a man of Hitler's type is unforgivable. The interview came to a sudden end!

A few months later, in September, 1934, the annual pow-wow of the Nazi Party took place in Nuremberg. Hitler now seemed eager to present himself favorably to the foreign press. His handling of the rebellion in his own party and the execution of its alleged leader, Hitler's most intimate friend, Ernst Roehm, had elicited derogatory comment throughout the world.

The annual Nuremberg Parteitag of the National Socialist movement was one of the most spectacular shows of modern times. Though designated as Party Day (Tag), it lasted a full week as the various supporting organizations, the brown-shirted S.A., the black-shirted S.S., the women's auxiliaries, the youth movement, the labor front, etc., all in distinctive uniforms paraded with brass bands, flamboyant flags, and pennants to hear Hitler in the stadium.

All along the Fuehrer's triumphant ride through the narrow, winding streets of medieval Nuremberg out to the stadium and back to his hotel, frenzied supporters shouted themselves hoarse with Sieg Heils, or waved ecstatically from upper-story windows.

Surprisingly, a largest-size Mercedes car for the press was inserted between Hitler's and Deputy Fuehrer Rudolf Hess's cars in the long procession from the final stadium meeting on the seventh day, through the city and up to the 11th-century castle perched on the crest of a 1000-foot sandstone mound. The car was filled with about a dozen foreign newsmen, selected because of the importance of the media they represented: AP, UP, and INS from the U.S.A., Reuters of England, Agence Havas of France, Agenzia Stefani of Italy; *Times* of London and of New York, *Le Temps* of Paris, *Popolo d' Italia* of Rome, *Zürcher Zeitung* of Zurich.

If "Der Adolf" thought that the Heiling masses impressed us, he was mistaken. A cousin of mine, a resident of Nuremberg, had explained to me that no Nuremberger could invite a friend or relative from elsewhere to this annual show except with the permission of the Gestapo. Only party members or proven sympathizers of the Nazi regime were allowed to travel to the Parteitag. In other words, the Heil Hitlers were solely from members of the faith. I naturally shared this knowledge with my colleagues.

Hitler's own estimate of this organized cheering was revealed when we reached a particularly narrow lane in the old city. For once there were no howling masses on the sidewalk. The dictator turned furiously to his chief aide and commanded, "Get off and find out why nobody's here to greet us." The adjutant later rejoined the Fuehrer's car as it was driving on a winding road leading up to the castle, and we heard him report, "Mein Fuehrer, the lane is so narrow that anybody standing on the slender sidewalk would have been crushed to death by our cars."

Finally the hysterical screaming was behind us and our cavalcade reached the spacious courtyard of the castle. Adolf Hitler quickly stepped out of his car. I happened to sit next to the door of the first compartment of our Mercedes, which meant that he would probably reach me first.

I must confess that I had long felt bitter about historic Nuremberg, which one poet described as "the German Reich's Jewel Box," desecrated by the booted Nazi ruffians. So here, in the city of my paternal forbears, I could contain myself no longer.

I anticipated Hitler's greeting by saying, "Mr. Chancellor, may I welcome you here in the city of my ancestors?" Nonplussed, Hitler replied, "How come? You're an American, aren't you?" and motioned to Rudolf Hess and the unspeakable Julius Streicher to listen in.

"Yes indeed," I replied, "I am an American. But my family from 1468 on lived continuously in this city until my grandfather and my father emigrated to the United States. I therefore think I have the right to greet you here."

This time Hitler blushed in anger. He had fully grasped what I was aiming at, namely, to remind him that he was not even a born German. I had struck an exceedingly sensitive nerve.

Without replying he turned on his heel, left our correspondents' car, and stalked into the castle. He never received me again. I thoroughly enjoyed the luncheon that was served.

—LOUIS P. LOCHNER, October 1965

NO DOLCE VITA FOR IL DUCE
IN ROLE AS EDDA'S PAPA

Benito Mussolini, tough and rabble-rousing revolutionary and dictator of Italy, had trouble squaring his duties as a devoted paterfamilias with his avowed aim to rule.

He left the Socialist Party in 1915 to accept a French enticement of thousands of francs to start his own newspaper, *Il Popolo d'Italia,* with the definite purpose of inducing Italy into the First World War, even though he had prated about capitalism as the cause of war. Now, he conceived the idea of Fascism, a super-patriotic movement, and by 1922 this force made him prime minister. This had been his goal, attained at thirty-eight very much ahead of his own schedule.

Here he had to adopt a semblance of respectability, since he had accepted his post as a favor from the royal house. His marital relations were those recognized as a common law marriage. His wife and children lived in a six-room apartment in a moderate, middle-class section of Milan.

Now, within a year, he induced a Franciscan monk he knew to solemnize the wedding. This was done somewhat in camera, in the Grand Hotel in Rome. His wife now officially though covertly joined, returned to Milan to supervise the rearing of the children. She was a plain and simple woman who had been a barmaid at the bistro of his father in Predappio where the now thoroughly ensconced dictator was born.

At this time, there were three children. Edda, the eldest, was fifteen. There were two boys: Mario, twelve, and Romano, seven. Edda was the apple of the strongman's eye. But she was not born to Rachele. Her mother seems to be lost in the meanderings of the young revolutionary when free love was a tenet. But he loved Edda.

She was of medium height. Her face was sculptured rather

than painted. She was not unlike Greta Garbo. Her stance was arresting, like her father's.

At the height of the Fascist dominion, I was stationed in Rome as bureau chief for UP. There was good news, bad news, sad and even glad news. This was a time in 1930, when I had my picture taken with Hitler and Mussolini in Venice. Of course, my job was Mussolini. I ghostwrote his American articles for United Features. I was often a visitor at his house.

As Edda was growing up, from fifteen to sixteen, he conceived the idea that the Milan menage was not a worthy place for her. She had the wild spirit of an Arab steed. Rachele herself thought Edda was too much for her to handle with growing responsibilities in raising the boys too.

Il Duce, as the dictator now called himself, ordered Rachele to send Edda to Rome. She stayed with him in the spacious Villa Torlonia, his official residence. It was a new life for the turbulent child, of whom it was said her spirit came naturally from her father. Now he had a problem second only to the affairs of government. He was learning English, taught by an English lady, Lillian Gibson. He had been impressed by Miss Gibson because of her classical erudition and social dexterity. He now assigned to her the care of Edda, in the hope Miss Gibson could make a lady of her.

It was summer, and looking over the whole of Italy for a quiet place for Edda's tutelage, he chose the sleepy town of Courmayeur, back in the recesses of the Italian Alps, directly below Mont Blanc. There Edda was sent with Miss Gibson for her acquisition of the courtly manners which Il Duce prescribed. And there Edda received a letter from one of her Milanese boyfriends, the prize fighter, Monteverde. He was in the seaside resort of Rimini on the Adriatic. Edda now wanted to go there.

Miss Gibson of course, had to refer the problem to the Big

Man. He was disappointed, but said they could go, for at Rimini also were Rachele, Mario, and Romano. A limousine was put at Edda's disposal by the Prefect of Turin, and in a day or two Miss Gibson and Edda arrived at the Mussolini cottage.

But the strangeness of an English woman in the household led to talk. Rachele's neighbors and her closet friends insisted that this foreign female had been sent to spy on Rachele. The relations between Monteverde and Edda rose to a taboo. Miss Gibson was in the midst of it. She asked the Prefect of Ancona for a limousine. She was driven directly to the Villa Torlonia, and when she told Mussolini the story, he ordered Edda sent to Rome, leaving poor Monteverde with only a warm "arriverderci."

Now, the prime minister must conceive a new plan. He urged some of the men in government to have their friends or relatives give parties for Edda, intending that in this way the wildness might be put under control. This indeed was accomplished by the eager jostling of the ministerial wives to curry favor with Il Duce. Edda was introduced to a score of young men and girls in the echelon barely below royalty.

For Edda, this was a new and glamorous life. Her choice, in due time, was Galeazzo Ciano, son of the Minister of Communications, Costanzo Ciano, wearer of Italy's highest military decoration, the gold medal for valor. The selection filled Il Duce with joy. It was the solution.

The wedding was held in distinctly sub-royal exultation. It was celebrated in the parish church of Villa Torlonia, with the parish priest officiating, although Edda ranked a cardinal. The church was crowded but there were no royal princes or princesses. Since the church was almost on the land of the villa, there were no carriages or presidential limousines.

Now a reception was imperative for the Fascist chiefs and

their wives. Rachele was left in the north. Mussolini invited me, introduced me as (true or false) the most important foreign newsman in Rome. I was the only American correspondent there.

Edda was pleased indeed to meet any friends of Father, she said. She showed she had been strictly coached in the niceties of the highest Fascist manners. Then came Galeazzo whom I already knew because he was now press chief in the government. Speaking perfect English, he had been raised an aristocrat and showed it.

The couple lived quietly in one of the wealthy sections of Rome. Edda was happy because she was always in nimbuses of admiration as daughter of the supreme chief. Galeazzo, in his turn, was soon promoted to foreign minister. He worked agreeably with his father-in-law who admired Ciano's culture, a quality Il Duce inwardly envied.

But the Second World War came. Ciano, now a count, disagreed violently with his father-in-law. Ciano favored neutrality. Il Duce wanted to enter the conflict on Germany's side. But Ciano bravely stood his ground.

Mussolini fired his son-in-law on February 6, 1943. Later he accused Ciano of communicating with Churchill, charging him with "treason." Ciano was shot by a firing squad a few months later. The dictator thus made his own grandchildren the sons and daughter of a "traitor." Finally, by the hazards of war, Mussolini himself was executed by partisans and hung up in the square at Milan, upside down.

The last time I spoke to Edda was in 1960. She had become quite restored in that time from the deep tragedies of father and husband. I met her while having dinner at the Ambassadors Hotel. She was accompanied by a Roman baron. She may have been married again by now.

—TOM MORGAN, April 1968

SILURIAN SEMANTICS, TWO-WAY,
AND FIRST THE GEOLOGICAL SIDE

Like a child asking "Where did I come from?" the Silurians in the 1950s began seriously inquiring, "How did we get our name?"

The founders being then securely beyond questioning, a loyal son of a founder gave his testimony, *Silurian News,* November, 1957—Hugh Baillie:—

"The first I remember of the Silurians was a discussion of what the name of this new organization should be. My father brought forward the title of Silurian and stuck to it until it was adopted.

"In paleontology, the Silurian era was marked by the appearance of the great crustaceans. In its later stages, there appeared upon the earth vegetable growths, amphibians, and reptiles. It ran into the Devonian age, and since my father came to this country from Scotland on the Anchor Liner *Devonia* he considered this a happy augury.

"So the name was a gag. A bunch of fossils calling themselves Silurians were to assemble once or twice a year, when the spirit moved, usually at the Brevoort or Lafayette, and exchange yearns about the good old days. There were fewer than 50 in the original group."

The next issue of *Silurian News,* May, 1958, presented a discovery by Emmet Crozier, an article in *Harper's New Monthly Magazine,* May, 1867, which says:—

"Frederick Hudson, for many years the managing editor of the *New York Herald.* . . . used to allude to the papers which existed before and at the date I have mentioned (1827) as belonging to the 'Silurian period of journalism,' and to add laughingly that they formed a substratum of mud."

Crozier continues: "This quotation definitely links the term 'Silurian' to journalism and . . . associates it with the geology of prehistoric times rather than with the Anglo-Saxon tribe that fought the Romans."

The following year, February 1959, *Silurian News* returned to the subject with a letter from Chester Beecroft, the renowned "Sinbad," who recalls:—

"During World War I, I was sight-seeing in Glamorgan, just outside Cardiff, the home of the original Silurians. A violent air raid drove me down into one of the many coal mines thereabout. I got to chatting with the superintendent and asked him jokingly if they had yet reached the Silurian strata. 'Long ago,' he said, 'both the upper and the lower strata, would you care to see them?' He then guided me down a seemingly endless shaft to a high, cavelike excavation. He switched on a light and told me to look closely at a formation. I did so and was amazed to note that the lower stratum was studded with fossils, shells, crustacea, and other manifestations of ocean life.

"I obtained a piece of this authentic Silurian shale, brought it back to New York, had it framed and presented it to our Society, at one of the semiannual dinners at the New York Athletic Club. I made a short speech in which I outlined the history of the Silurians and, I believe, you will find a copy of this 'knavish piece of work' in the Silurian files—if they still exist."

The foregoing items are, in fact, pretty much of an introduction to the research report April, 1963, of Henry Senber, which comes next—a sketch of persistent, virile, hard-drinking ancients that any reporter might enjoy claiming as ancestors.

However, Hugh Baillie, March 1964, came back with a sturdy last word:—

"One more sentence on my rebuttal. If my father had been

selecting the name of an early British tribe who fought the Romans and all these interesting things that Henry dug up, it's a cinch they would not have been Welshmen. They would have been Scottish."

ANOTHER CHOICE AS TO "SILURIAN," THE ROMANS ENCOUNTERED THEM

I braced myself against the wall of the dimly lit entrance or porch of the small Welsh church in an attempt to steady my camera for a ten-second exposure. The only light came through the door which my wife held open.

My lens was focused on a stone tablet with a Latin inscription that had been carved on its surface seventeen centuries ago by the Respublica Civitas Silurum—the Commonwealth of the Silures. Discovered fifty years ago, it is one of the most significant artifacts of a four-century Roman occupation of Britain and one of the last links to a long-vanished civilization.

I was in the village of Caerwent, once known as Venta Silurum or Market Place of the Silures. For me it was the end of the trail, the last chapter in search for the tribe from which directly or indirectly, the Society of the Silurians derives its name.

*   *   *

Just who or what were the Silures? In common with most members of our Society, I suspect, I knew of them only vaguely as "an ancient British tribe." But where and when?

I found a clue in the *Encyclopaedia Brittanica,* but certainly not the full story. The local office of the British Information Service suggested I write to the South Wales and Monmouth Record Society whose secretary, Mr. A. J. Roderick, advised me to go to Dr. H. N. Savory, Keeper of Archaeology at the National Museum of Wales in Cardiff, an expert on pre-Roman Wales. I did—first by mail, then in person.

The complete story remains buried under farms and gardens in Southern Wales. As Dr. Savory wrote me:

"The fact of the matter is that there has still been quite in-sufficient excavations and chance discoveries to build up a reliable picture of the culture of the Silures and the stages of its development, although enough is known to suggest that like other ancient British tribes their origins were complex, no doubt with a subject population of Bronze Age origin ruled by a warrior class of Celtic origin but derived from more than one quarter in Western Europe, i.e., southern England and northern France on one hand and the Cornish peninsula and lands round the Bay of Biscay on the other."

The first written reference to the tribe is found in Tacitus, Roman war correspondent and historian. Commenting on the variety of racial types in Britain he wrote:

". . . the swarthy faces of the Silures, the tendency of their hair to curl and the fact that Spain lies opposite, all lead one to believe that Spaniards crossed in ancient times and occupied the land."

It is to Tacitus, too, that we are indebted for the story of the Silures' military operations against the Roman legions who began their invasion of Britain in A.D. 43. Their natural skill in the arts of war was heightened by the leadership of Caratacus, a Celtic prince from Essex whose father, Cuno-belinus, once had been the most powerful of early Britain's warrior kings and who was the prototype of Shakespeare's Cymbeline.

After discussing the fall of the other tribes, Tacitus says: "But neither sternness nor leniency prevented the Silures from fighting. To suppress them a brigade garrison had to be estab-lished . . . the natural ferocity of the inhabitants (the Silures) was intensified by their belief in the prowess of Cara-tacus, whose many undefeated battles—and even some vic-tories—had made him pre-eminent among British chieftains."

Unfortunately Caratacus risked an open battle. The superior

discipline and weaponry of the Romans won the day. Caratacus eventually was captured and taken to Rome to be marched in a triumphal parade prior to his execution.

Then came a switch which might have been invented by a Hollywood writer. Caratacus made a speech which charmed the emperor, Claudius, and the prisoner and his family were freed to reside in Rome for the rest of their days!

Meanwhile, back in the country along the Severn River the Silures were far from subdued. Again we quote Tacitus:

"In Silurian country, Roman troops left to build forts under a divisional chief of staff were surrounded and only saved from annihilation because neighboring forces learned of their siege and speedily sent help. They were mostly guerrilla fights, in woods and bogs. . . .

"The Silures were exceptionally stubborn. . . . Then they began by gifts of spoils and prisoners, to tempt other tribes to join their rebellion. At this point, exhausted by his anxious responsibilities, Ostorious (the Roman governor) died."

This was in 51 A.D. . . . Five succeeding Roman governors avoided reopening hostilities against the Silures, and it was not until the appointment of Sextus Julius Frontinus, a literary man as well as a soldier, that the issue was joined again and about 74 A.D. before fighting ceased.

What happened? Some historians say the Silures were defeated but there is another theory which brings us back to Venta Silurum. We quote from Dr. R. E. M. Wheeler's "Prehistoric and Roman Wales":

"It was at length realized by the Roman authorities that armed force was insufficient to break so obstinate a spirit of resistance unless supplemented by some more subtle and comprehensive policy . . . The insidious attractions of town life were dangled before the semi-barbarous native, who was thus lured gradually from his own tribal traditions and from the memories of his former independence.

"Roman dress, Roman customs, even Roman speech were gradually sought and adopted until by and by the tribesman had become, in all but name, a Roman citizen. Caerwent, therefore, may be regarded as the deliberate civil counterpart of Caerleon (the old Isca Silurum, Roman fortress, eight miles from Caerwent) . . . the ordinary citizen of Caerwent would be the native Silurian at last subjugated by the arts of the Roman peace."

It was a peace that lasted for three and a half centuries with only occasional interruption by Saxon and other raiders. In Venta Silurum, sometime in the Third Century a tablet was erected in honor of a Roman governor who had been friendly to the Silures in an earlier military assignment in their area. Its wording is valued by scholars for the information it gives regarding the political status and organization of the Silures— a kind of tribal commonwealth with limited local autonomy.

And just in case I didn't hold my camera steadily enough, here's a translation of the abbreviated inscription:

"To Tiberius Claudius Paulinus, formerly Commander of the Second Augustan Legion, later Senatorial Governor of the Province of Narbonensis, now Imperial Governor of the Province of Lugudunensis, the Body-Politic of the Commonwealth of the Silures in pursuance of a decree of its Senate erects this monument."

The most comprehensive collection of relics of the Iron Age of which the Silurian story is a part is to be found in the fascinating National Museum of Wales at Cardiff, a city well worth visiting. It was in the National Museum that we found one item which was particularly intriguing.

This was an enormous tankard made of fragments of pottery found in a nearby "dig." Some six inches in diameter and equally as deep, it held a vast quantity of whatever beverage the Silures favored. The precise nature of this beverage remains a mystery to archaeologists.

—HENRY SENBER, April 1963

Postscript, July 1973

Like most of us, I have no idea as to precisely what the Founding Fathers of the Society had in mind when they selected our name. But from later research (i.e., a more modern set of the *Encyclopedia Britannica*) I have learned that the Silurian Age was named after the Silures tribe, so I wasn't too far off base when I wrote in my story: "the tribe from which directly or indirectly the Society of Silurians derives its name."

V.
JUST SIT AND LISTEN

Remembered Hangouts
As the Papers Moved
Uptown from Park Row
—Oases After Work—
And Yarns You Heard There

PARK ROW IN THOSE DAYS, PARK ROW! ALAS FOR US WHO NEVER WORKED THERE

In the 1934 program of The New York Press Club Frolic, the late Martin Green of the *New York Journal* and *The Evening World,* tells how Park Row "busted right in his face," when he arrived and how he saw it fade and die as a newspaper center:

The highlight of my life as a newspaperman was undoubtedly flashed on August 28 (1897), a hot afternoon and my birthday, when, for the first time, I landed in New York to go to work on a New York newspaper. Unlike a great many men who came to New York at that time, from the west and south, I didn't have to sit in City Hall park, or call on unresponsive city editors.

I had landed a job before I left St. Louis with William Randolph Hearst's *New York Journal,* which he had bought a couple of years before from John R. McLean, who had purchased it from Albert Pulitzer. I hadn't a worry in the world.

As soon as I got to Beekman street and Park Row, I knew I was where I belonged. I had passed the old office of the *New York Evening Post* and the *New York Daily News.* I didn't know where they were, but I could smell them. The office of the *New York Press* was, I believe, in the Potter Building and *The New York Times* was at the north end of the triangle formed by Nassau Street and Park Row.

At Park Row and Spruce Street, Printing House Square

busted right in my face. I saw to my right, the combined offices of the *Journal* and the *Tribune* and a block farther on the measly little office of the *Sun* and the towering, gilt-domed, slaughterhouse of the *World*. At the far end of the square, I could see the home of the *Staats-Zeitung,* bolstered and flanked by saloons. The intangible odor of printers' ink, beer, whiskey, and delivery horses was overpowering and pleasant. The cries of newsboys were as music to my ears. I was sure I had found the spot where I was to spend the rest of my life.

Making my way to the city room of the *Journal,* on the second floor of the *Tribune* Building, I came upon some friends I had previously met at the Republican and Democratic Conventions, gave my grip into the custody of the office boy, and, attended by the aforesaid friends, walked out into the bright, smelly sunshine. Three days later I got back to Park Row, ready, of necessity, to take my first assignment.

A young man coming to New York to seek or fill a newspaper job today will not find the lush atmosphere I found on Park Row. All newspaper plants have gone and the only smell apparent is that of gasoline. Where there were thirteen morning and evening newspapers published in Manhattan thirty-seven years ago, there were only eight in 1934.

The population of the city has increased about three times in that period and the number of newspapers has decreased by almost one-half. The plants are scattered all over town and in no section is there such an authentic newspaper atmosphere as made Park Row what it was in its heyday.

Oh, well, newspaper publishers had guts in those days!

—MARTIN GREEN, May 1953

Postscript:—

. . . and then in 1909, around the corner at the *New York Journal,* when John R. Hastings was managing editor and Tom Dibble was city editor:

"The editorial rooms of the *Journal, American,* INS, and King Feature writers and artists all adjoined one another on the seventh floor. I well recall one night when fire sirens made such a noise down on William street that someone looked out of the window to see where the fire might be. Firemen were fighting a fire on the third floor. Fortunately it was of minor importance and quickly extinguished.

"Another incident which has carried over these fifty years and still clings vividly in memories was the service provided by the rattling open-cage elevator which had no operating call bell and served you only after repeated yells down the open shaft. One night our calls went unheeded so we decided that special action was necessary if we were to get down from the seventh floor. We dumped a fire bucket full of water down the shaft. From the cussing that came up the elevator shaft we knew we had awakened the operator but our scheme didn't bring service. That night we walked down the seven flights of stairs.

"There was a friendly atmosphere about that four-unit city room which you don't find in present day editorial rooms. You knew everybody. It was much like the old corner saloon, with its foot rail, sawdust floor, and cuspidors.

—CLYDE D. WAGONER, March 1964

A THRILL ON OLD PARK ROW
FOR CUB IN SEAGOING HACK

And now the mellowest memory of all is the old city room of the *Tribune,* in the attic under the tower at midnight.

The very babble of it gave peace. The cats continued their ungenerous warfare against the courtly old cockroaches who inhabited our desks. The incessant click of the telegraphers made music in our ears. The whisper of pencils on paper, the blended tapping of many typewriters, the calls of "Copy! Copy!", the hurrying, rushing errands under the old drop-lights, the sense of imminence of the high moment when a great paper goes to press, even the archaic tinkling of the one telephone on the wall—234 John—they all merged in a harmony of suppressed excitement that I can hear and feel to this day. The visits to the comps—aristocrats above the earth —and then the roar and crash of the great presses below helped to enshrine the sweetest scent in all the world, the smell of printers' ink. Once in the blood, it stays forever, even to 70 times 70.

And so, long life to all Silurians! For we are the elect. We know the smell of printers' ink.

(From the first issue of *Silurian News.*)

—HENRY H. CURRAN, November 1947

My greatest thrill as a newspaper man had nothing to do with life or death, scoops or beats. It had to do with a horse-drawn hack.

When Admiral Dewey, having satisfactorily sunk the Spanish fleet in Manila Bay, came back to the United States in 1899 on his flagship *Olympia,* the *Tribune* was caught short. Word came to the city desk, very suddenly, that a police launch would leave Pier A at the Battery in ten minutes, to take one reporter from each paper down the bay to interview Dewey, who had come into port unannounced a day ahead of time. I was the only reporter in the city room. I was a cub, unlicked and unwanted. The city editor called me over, gave me a sick look and a police line badge and said: "Get the hell out o' here—and make that launch!" I grabbed my hat and ran.

Now, in those young days, I could run fast and far, but could I dodge through the crowds, all the way from Spruce Street to the Battery, in ten minutes? It looked bad—and there seemed to be no other way. There were no subways, no taxicabs, in 1899. The cable cars were like mud. There were no traffic lights, no cops, nothing but a barrier of pedestrians, trucks, and drays, all mixed together like a dish of animated spaghetti, and all wanting their own way.

But, as I emerged from the *Tribune* Building, I saw a hack coming down Park Row, slowly. The horse looked as though he were about to die. I ran to the hack, hopped in, and addressed the driver, showing my tin badge. "Police," I exclaimed, "plain clothes, murder at Pier A, drive like hell, you bum!"

The driver took a close look and whipped up. The old horse leaped, sprang away, broke into a heavy up-and-down canter. We were off! He must have been a race horse when he was young. He went like hell, the driver whipping, still holding his segar in his teeth.

Down Park Row, into Broadway at old St. Paul's, down, down to the Bowling Green, scattering pedestrians, pushing drays aside, the driver lashing his whip at objectors, the cub reporter leaning out, flashing his badge, and yelling, "Get out o' the way, get out o' the way, get out!" We left a wake of cursing humanity. We skirted the Battery in a free sprint. It was the stretch. We were there!

I gave the driver all the money I had, which was very little. He took a long puff at his segar, saying nothing. The old horse lifted his head high. I dashed into Pier A and, just as the police launch shoved off leaped aboard, missing a fall into the water by inches.

So I covered the arrival of Admiral Dewey . . . and went straight to the front page—whew! Ah, yes, that felt good.

—HENRY H. CURRAN, November 1948

PERRY'S DRUGSTORE? BAR?
WHERE FRIENDSHIP RIPENED

How many newsmen of the past generation remember Perry's three-cornered bar on the left side of the lobby as you walked into the old Pulitzer (or *World*) building on Park Row?

To the writer that is a hallowed spot. Or was. Real truths came out there after a couple of "shots" with an orange juice chaser. That was all there was to drink.

Actually it wasn't a bar. It was a three-sided room lined with shelves. On these shelves stood bottles of every kind of whiskey imaginable. Old "Doc" would pour you a shot, then reach over and pick up a large bottle from which he poured orange juice into your shot glass after you had drained it of whiskey.

What memories! After I had been with the United Press in 1914 about two or three months World War I broke and Roy Howard put me on the emergency night news desk. The UP then brought the brilliant John Edwin Nevin, better known as Jack, up to New York to write the war.

As I sat opposite Nevin on the desk memories of my first political campaign came back. I was on the *St. Joe Gazette* in 1908. Bryan was finishing his campaign tour in St. Joe before proceeding to his home in Lincoln for election day. The *Gazette* sent me to St. Louis to ride on the Bryan special train through the state en route to St. Joe.

The train would stop at small towns and Bryan would come out on the platform, wave to the crowds and make a brief speech. He was the first presidential candidate I had watched perform and I ate up every minute of it.

Finally, as the train neared Kansas City I knew I had to

file an early story to the *Gazette* or the late Harold Hall, then city editor, would scalp me. We had an early country run and Hall wanted to show the *Gazette* was an up and coming paper and would send its own staffer as far away as St. Louis—at least 300 miles.

I didn't have a typewriter so I made my way thru the cars looking for an idle one. I spotted one in a compartment that I knew was occupied because it was full of bags and clothes. A table was up and the typewriter was sitting on it. I ducked into the room and started to pound out a story. What a chore it was. I tore up sheet after sheet. I just couldn't get going and I had visions of Hall telling me I wouldn't do.

Just then, a rosy-cheeked, hefty man with a smiling countenance came into the room. He was John Edwin Nevin.

"Hiya, son," he greeted me, "having trouble?"

"Plenty," I told him.

He asked me who I was with. I told him. He pulled out of his pocket a list of newspapers and quickly scanned it.

"St. Joe, eh?" he said. "I'm Jack Nevin of the Publishers' Press. We have no client in St. Joe, so you can use a copy of a story I just filed."

With that he handed me a thousand-word story.

"Scratch off the Nevin by-line," he said, "and put your own on it. No one will ever know the difference."

The heck they wouldn't. But wait and let me tell it. I did as Nevin said and scratched out his name. But I didn't have the nerve to put my own on it. I just signed "Faris" at the bottom of the story.

We reached St. Joe late and I rushed to the office before heading for the Tootle Opera House to cover Bryan's last speech of the campaign. Hall greeted me brusquely.

"Who the hell wrote that story you filed from Kansas City?" he demanded. "I know damned well you didn't."

The first night Nevin sat opposite me on the UP desk I immediately recognized him as the good samaritan of six years before. But he didn't have the faintest idea, I know, of who I was. He stuck his hand across the desk and said, "I'm Jack Nevin. Glad to meet you. I know we'll get along." And how we did. Nevin suggested that when we knocked off we stop by Perry's so-called bar. I agreed. After the second drink I told him my story. At first he was incredulous but finally believed me when I quoted from the story he had written.

When I told him what Hall had said he slapped his leg and shouted: "I want to meet that fellow Hall. He must be good."

Hall was good. He was one of the best. But he switched to the money side, the business end, early and when he died, all too soon, he was the business manager of *The New York Times*.

—BARRY FARIS, October 1962

THAT SNAKECHARMER'S MISERABLE
SNAKE, JUST HAUNTING CHUMLEY'S

It happened so many years ago that probably, by now, even the smoke is dead, and so there really isn't any reason not to tell the story. The basic locale was Chumley's, the speakeasy cum restaurant in the Village, which was for decades the home away from home for literary pretenders, part-time artists, newspapermen, and others who drank. Since newspapermen in the early thirties ate more regularly than other Villagers, Chumley's then clientele was weighted heavily in the direction of newspaperdom.

The Times, with the most reporters, naturally furnished the largest contingent: Paul Crowell, Bill Laurence before the atom, Bill Conklin, Jim Kieran, Bob Bird, the writer of this piece, and countless others whose names memory has dimmed —or else they were comers-in by the Bedford St. door, which meant they weren't regulars. *The Telegram* contributed Lou Wedemar and Carl Randau, *the Trib,* Eddie Lanham and Ned McIntosh; Jack Iams from the *News,* Bud Disney from the *City News,* Lew Levick from the *Journal.*

Lee Chumley, the tall fidgety ex-Wobbly, ex-bouncer turned host, dominated the place he started in 1928 until he died suddenly in 1935. And even later, with Nick Saluzzi running the joint for Lee's widow who appeared, after his death, from nowhere (Boston), the policy continued of letting guests while away the hours at bridge, chess, or conversation without molestation from waiters or management whether they bought or not. For the regulars, who entered by protocol through the garden entrance at 58 Barrow St., it was the place one ate and drank and played and while one didn't sleep there, most had slept sometimes with people they met there.

The only real hazard to peaceful bohemianism—and we now reach the point of this tale—came on the occasional evening when Lee would get restless, and insist on going what he called 'night-clubbing.' He would take two hundred dollars or so—big money in the early depression years—from the cash drawer and insist on any regulars present accompanying him on a tour of third-rate downtown saloons—any one that had a floor-show. Lee would buy everything, get introduced from ringside between fourth-rate acts, and charge the night off to 'promotion,' as a business expense. The regulars would go innocently the first time, and try and escape thereafter. We preferred Chumley's.

On one of these evenings out, Lee picked up Sonya, a snake-charmer by trade, in a particularly dismal East Side joint. The atmosphere made even Sonya look good by comparison. She accompanied us to various other dives after 2 A.M., when her 'act' was over, and she and Lee and I finally shared a cab to 58 Barrow, where Lee had a tiny apartment off the court. I lived around the corner on Grove. When last seen, Lee and Sonya, enamored more than ever, were disappearing into the courtyard, at 4 A.M. The plot seemed obvious.

The next afternoon, Lee was pacing the floor, wearing a sheepish grin. He had a long succession of girls, but never talked except in the concept of the Tennessee gentleman that he was. This time he had to tell someone, or bust. He sat down at my table, bought a drink—the invariable sign that he had something to get off his chest—and told it.

It seemed that he and Sonya had reached the point of bringing their new-found love to a climax—at least they were stripped and primed—when Sonya screamed—"My

: **217** :

snake! My snake!" Lee hated snakes. Sonya told him that the little case she had been carrying around with her since she left the 'night club' contained not her make-up, but her snake, and it was now loose in the apartment, someplace. Romance vanished.

As Lee told the story, he and Sonya had spent from 4 to 8 A.M. on hands and knees searching for the vanished serpent, and finally he gave her cab fare home plus $15, to buy a new snake. As for Lee, he had already moved out of the garden court apartment to one upstairs on the Bedford St. side, and he never set foot in the courtyard Eden again. Nor did anyone find the snake.

All this was sometime in 1932 or 1933. Lee died, as noted, in 1935. About 1953, after I had left *The Times,* and Chumley's was but a memory for me, I picked up *The Times* one morning, and read with interest—and rapid recollection—a news item about a snake.

Someone had started to remodel a brownstone, two doors down from Chumley's at some number like 54 Barrow street, and found a contented snake, fat on Village mice, living beneath the flooring. It saddened me even then to think that no one else in New York knew where it had come from.

—WARREN MOSCOW, October 1965

FOND SURVIVORS KEEP RETURNING
FOR ANOTHER AT ARTIST & WRITERS

A couple of hundred or so former employees of the *New York Herald Tribune* gathered in Bleeck's for their annual reunion on the evening of December 10, 1971. On the shaky theory that nothing of this nature is news until reported in the *Silurian News,* and also on the remote chance that *Herald Tribune* exes are still unaware of those periodical shebangs, let us examine the facts.

The chief generator of these parties—there have been four so far—is Dick Wald, vice-president of NBC News, who was the *Herald Tribune*'s managing editor when the paper appeared for the last time on April 24, 1966. With a certain ironic fitness that final issue contained a superb story (by John G. Rogers) on the retirement of Emma Bugbee after 18,911 days in the newspaper business.

Miss Bugbee had first walked into the *New York Tribune* city room at 154 Nassau Street on July 23, 1910, fresh from Barnard College, and was hired on the spot. She had covered practically every sort of news (Eleanor Roosevelt, not least), but Emma was absolutely not going down to the three-way merger in Barclay Street.

The annual get-together in Bleeck's is strictly informal—no speeches, no songs, no dances, and not even any unusual number of funny sayings. But the mixture of alumni has been invariably good, with somebody for everybody.

The old *Herald Tribune* building is still there, but is owned and occupied by Group Health Insurance, Inc. The new owners are said to have spent again as much as the purchase price on reconstructing the inside, filling the pressroom pits, lifting the dismantled machinery through the roof and by crane to trucks in the street, and in general transformation to elegance. Yet the old raised letters of *New York Tribune* over the back door at No. 225 West 40th St. (dating back to before the merger of *Herald* and *Tribune*) were sanded off only about a year ago. On a misty day a keen eye can still discern the faint tracery beneath the surface, as the name insists on shimmering through.

The reunion in Bleeck's comes at no fixed time. Dick Wald arranges to have it about the time that Buddy Weiss, editor of *The International Herald Tribune* in Paris and a former managing editor in New York, comes over for a board meeting. On these occasions Dick buys a small advertisement in *The New York Times,* for he is known as a poet with a pocketbook, and Jock Whitney's secretary starts calling, and smoke signals rise from the tall towers. The word gets around.

By 7 o'clock of lodge night, the *Herald Tribune* clan has practically pre-empted the establishment. Among the first celebrants will likely be Walter Wellesley Smith, the genius who has always contended that sports writing beats shucking oysters. Red Smith is furthermore the oldest and greatest catch ever made by *The New York Times.*

Bleeck's has changed, but not much. The customers are largely a different crowd. But the middle and back rooms look much the same as when Jack Bleeck moved to No. 213 in 1925 from the previous premises at the northeast corner of Seventh Avenue and 40th Street. True, the $1 inch-and-a-half-thick steak sandwich has disappeared. This was the fodder that nourished Joe Alsop, John Lardner, Joe Mitchell, Tom Sugrue, Sanderson Vanderbilt and the endless bright young men of depression days on their standard $18 a week pay. However, French fries and ice cream have never been tolerated, then or now.

And yet Jack Bleeck had to yield on one fundamental, and that was the woman question. With the repeal of prohibition in 1933, the "store" went legitimate and a 45-foot bar stretched out in front to replace the coffeepot lunch counter that shielded the goings-on behind. (A lot of the wags always spoke of Bleeck's "store," because the Sani Drug Store used to be a front at the Seventh Avenue corner.) But Bleeck had never admitted women during prohibition, and he wasn't proposing to change now. For many months he resorted to a sort of club operation with membership cards, but finally—in 1935 —he broke down and accepted the inevitable.

The big swinging sign out front says Artist and Writers (formerly Club) Restaurant. The signpainter didn't make any mistake. Bleeck vociferated that plenty of writers, but only one artist, had ever entered the place. He insisted this was Langdon McCormick, a prolific creator of stage melodramas and designer of spectacular scenic effects who was supposedly responsible for the murky olde Englishe decor (if that's the word) of the Artist and Writers. Another version has it that the one artist was Clare Briggs, the cartoonist ("When a Feller Needs a Friend," etc.) who also knew Bleeck's well. But not true—Bleeck said it was Langdon McCormick.

By 1953 Jack Bleeck was perhaps weary. At any rate he was often indignant about taxes, unions, and itchy-palmed inspectors. He seemed to reminisce less about old speakeasy days. And so in that year he sold the Artist and Writers to Tom Fitzpatrick, a longtime sales executive for the Trommery brewery, and Ernest Hitz, manager of the Savarin restaurants. Bleeck may well have regretted his decision the very next day; under him the Artist and Writers often seemed to be conducted almost as much for pleasure as for business. He occasionally talked about a book—"I'm going to hire me a good writer"—and certainly he had material, but nothing came of it. He died in 1963, age 83, truly a man with a heart as big as a watermelon.

The new owners, the genial Fitz and Hitz (as they are known to all and as the brass plaque at the door proclaims) have intelligently avoided changes, except for the vanished newspaper next door. Still on hand is that nonpareil bartender, Leo Corcoran, who began chauffeuring for Bleeck in 1919 and has nobly functioned behind the Artist and Writers bar since 1940. The veteran at the tables is Ernst Zorn, who began in 1937. And the maitre d' is Dick Walsh, nephew of Gene Winter, the reformed wrestler, who preceded him. Maybe a good saloon and restaurant possesses more staying power than a good newspaper.

For the record, however, let us note that *The International Herald Tribune,* published in Paris, is decidedly a going business. With a daily circulation of 120,000, this English-language newspaper of 14 to 16 pages is distributed in some 50 countries. It contains more national and international news than many an American newspaper. *The International Herald Tribune,* which greatly resembles its New York parent, is owned by John Hay Whitney (37 percent), *New York Times* (33 percent) and *Washington Post* (30 percent). The story goes that the paper is like the French tricolor; when the flag flutters in the breeze all three shares look equal.

John Hay Whitney, the last editor-in-chief and publisher of the *New York Herald Tribune,* is chairman of the *International.* The co-chairmen are Arthur Ochs Sulzberger and Katharine Graham. The editorial staff is headed by three *New York Herald Tribune* veterans—Murray M. Weiss, editor; George Bates, managing editor; and Roy Yerger, assistant managing editor. And back in the United States it's Harry W. Baehr, the iron man of the old editorial page, at his typewriter in *The New York Times* office firing off leading editorials for *The International Herald Tribune.*

And down at 693 Broadway, on the twelfth floor of a dingy loft building, Mrs. Mae Nyquist Bowler presides over the John Hay Whitney Herald Tribune Library, an adjunct of the New York University Library. Mae Bowler is of course remembered by all as the ever-cheerful source of all knowledge in the old *Herald Tribune* library uptown. In her N.Y.U. library are the clippings and bound volumes as they once existed at 230 West 41st Street, the complete source for everything printed to 1966, and Mae is always happy to help.*

At least one survivor endlessly hears people say how they miss the good old *Herald Tribune,* and why doesn't somebody start a new newspaper, and so on and on. Well, the lamentations are obviously sincere, but if their numbers are laid end to end and all these mourners were actually buying the *Herald Tribune* in those days, there wouldn't have been any demise.

—L. L. ENGELKING, March 1972

* N.Y.U. closed this service later in 1972.

BLEECK'S COULD MATCH PERRY'S IN LORE ABOUT ITS CHARACTERS

Ned McIntosh was great for jokes, you know, as well as for political stories.

Bleeck's was going full blast because, if for no other reason, it was very cold outside. Ned and others from upstairs were well along in their cups as was a mounted cop who had tethered his horse outside while gathering warmth outside and inside.

Ned quietly went out and led the horse into the big freight elevator that carried newsprint to the *Trib,* took him to an upper floor, then returned to Bleeck's.

When the cop went out for his horse that wasn't, he got scared. He tried to find out where his horse had gone but no one knew. The cop started down the street looking for him.

When the cop got out of sight, Ned returned the horse to where he had stood outside. The cop returned, couldn't figure out what had happened but, to mull over the problem, went back into Bleeck's and had a few more. He kept shaking his head.

Ned left, took the horse back into the elevator and the whole thing was repeated, with the cop again rushing down the street.

When the cop returned and found his horse, he lost no time climbing aboard and getting out of there.

—MURRAY DAVIS, March 1967

HOW FAR DOES ETHICS GO?
ANY LIMIT WITHIN REASON?

The writer was nineteen years old when he became apprentice reporter on John Kelly's newspaper, *The Star*. "Honest John" Kelly had become leader of Tammany Hall following the exposure of Tweed and his associates. He had convinced his district leaders in the reorganization of the shattered party that a daily newspaper to appeal for the return of voters to the wigwam was essential—hence *The Star* which he directed from 1876 until 1884.

But this story centers on the history of that newspaper under managing editor George Sandison, and city editor, Caleb Dunn. No such two men before or since ever graced a newspaper office. George Sandison was a top-alive man in energy and knowledge of news, but the ethical standard set by him for the gathering and use of information never had its equal in the newspaper world. He set his strong Presbyterian conscience on training his staff to high moral standards and when John Kelly sold the *Star* in 1884 Sandison quit to become managing editor of a powerful denominational Christian weekly which he graced for twenty years.

Two illustrations follow of George Sandison's stringent, ethical code regarding news gathering. A woman named Amey was found bruised and dead in a Chatham Street hotel one evening about three blocks from the *Star* office. Billy Cowan the top sleuth of the *Star*, who knew 90 percent of the police of every grade below 14th street, learned that the captain of the Elizabeth station had carried away a small bag from the scene. The captain had returned to the hotel so Cowan planned to get a peep at the bag in the police station. He had a young reporter with him.

In those days an accredited newspaperman covering police stations had much freedom among the uniformed force, especially one as well known as was Cowan.

Cowan after asking if the captain was in, and knowing he wasn't, said he would go into his room and wait for him. He soon had the little bag which he handed out the window to the waiting young reporter who hastened with it to Sweeney's Hotel about a block from *The Star* office. Cowan, on arrival, acquired a room and began a clinical examination of a batch of florid love letters. He kept the young reporter running with pages of copy to Caleb Dunn at the city desk.

Mr. Sandison, informed of a lively and exclusive story, asked how it had been obtained. When he learned just the surface facts he killed the "exclusive" material and the expanding-heart joy of Billy Cowan. He would have no such method of producing news for *The Star!*

Another ethical crises—Mrs. Astor's first big ball about this time. Town gossip centered on the possible preferred guests, the adornments of the mansion, and the general arrangements for this woman's adventure in claiming the leadership of the "society" of that period.

Ralph King, young graduate of the University of Virginia, turf and sports writer for *The Star,* tall, lean, and personable, informed city editor Caleb Dunn that he had a cousin in the store which was supplying the floral decorations. He said he might get on one of the wagons as a helper, gain entry to the mansion on the morning of the great ball and thus pick up some colorful news as well as data with respect to the guests. Dunn blessed him and told him to be on his way.

So Ralph King, who carried flowers into the Astor home, was soon on good terms with the head butler and became his first assistant in suggestions for floral arrangements. The excited butler, at intervals rehearsing with King their respective doings of the night, and King, working smoothly with the top menials! So King got possession of a copy of the guest list, and learned where Mrs. Astor would stand in greeting guests, how the arrivals would be announced, etc. Shortly afterward King departed and headed for the *Star* office.

As King was reciting his success in his soft, Virginia drawl, to the amusement of the City staff, managing editor Sandison asked what all the merriment was about. Informed, he delivered a short lecture, incisive in its basis, of the moral obligations of the newspaper craft and vetoed the use of any information obtained by King in what he called his "ill-advised adventure" into the Astor precincts. Only news honorably obtained of the Astor affair was used in *The Star* next morning!

—JOHN A. HENNESSY, May 1950

MOB WITH VIOLIN CASES AT WEDDING
NOT A MACHINE GUN IN THE SWARM

Joe Moss, the society orchestra maestro, is hero of this story, which tells of the wedding reception some 35 years ago for John D. Rockefeller III and his bride. If the editor of *Silurian News* had not been asleep, he'd have assigned publication for last spring, to coincide with the marriage of that young couple's son, John D. IV, and the daughter of Senator Percy.

Anyway:—That long-ago wedding was not unnaturally an event of its year, socially, and the first big do in the new and shiny Riverside Church, of Rockefeller bounty. The papers were agog over it. However, all Rockefeller publicity was handled by Ivy Lee, a man oddly distrustful of the press. He sent around a sheaf of mimeographs detailing every item about the wedding arrangements. Period. Press tickets were refused, and there were plenty of cops to exclude from the church anyone without a ticket. It was an infuriating challenge, but what could the papers do?

That afternoon at the *World-Telegram,* Bo McAnney called me over. "You've got on a dark suit," he said, "so I think you'll do. I've fixed it up with Joe Moss. Just pick up a violin case at this address and go into the Colony Club reception as one of his band."

It worked perfectly. The club doorman waved me in and pointed upstairs, and did I feel good putting it over on that Ivy Lee! But Joe Moss played no favorites, had given nothing exclusive. The music gallery was overflowing with journalistic fiddlers, sort of a two-platoon system bumping the real bandsmen's elbows, a convention of old friends from every paper in town.

Each paper's story the next day, naturally, was different, although discreet. One theme, however, ran through them all. Every reporter was entranced by the music. As we described it, Moss playing the Blue Danube made Toscanini sound tinny.

—GEORGE BRITT, October 1967

A Scatteration of Short Takes

Luck for Frank O'Malley, Free Lesson in His Trade

My first job out of college was reporting for the *Republican-Herald* in Binghamton, N.Y. After about a year I was doing fine, covering local politics and also selling a story now and then as a stringer to papers in New York City. One evening after some sort of political meeting in Binghamton I wrote my three paragraphs for New York and rushed to the Postal Telegraph office.

And there I encountered a stranger who had just sent off a message of his own. When I mentioned that I was a correspondent for the big city papers, he showed a flattering interest. So I told him more, and as he kept asking questions, I blossomed forth. I explained to him just how to get a story and how to write it and how you hit the big papers. I greatly enjoyed talking to him, telling him all about it.

Next day I asked the postal operator if he knew who the man was. "Yes, he was sending off a press story too," he said, "to *The New York Sun*. He signed it Frank Ward O'Malley." So I guess that makes me the one who taught O'Malley how to be a newspaperman.

—GEORGE H. LYON, October 1966

As Viewed by Sports Editor,
Give Me a Break, Can't You?

It is well established that all newspaper departmental editors—society, financial, sports, marine, food, theater—regard their own pages as the real package, and everything else as rather unattractive gift wrapping. (The same is true, I have discovered during the last five years, of encyclopedia departmental editors—but that is another story.)

My favorite memory along these lines has to do with Stanley Woodward, the *Herald Tribune*'s sports editor, who went down to interview Fiorello LaGuardia. The Mayor had been in one of his rows with the press. He said he was sick of political reporters and wished the papers would send sensible sports writers to cover his activities.

Stanley Woodward volunteered, set up an interview and, as usual, came back with a magnificent story. In fact, it was so good that I told him I was going to put it on the front page. Was Stanley pleased? Not at all. He said with a scowl:

"You don't think, do you, that I'm going to let you *bury* me on the front page?"

—GEORGE A. CORNISH, October 1966

That 3. a.m. Lobster Trick,
Place Where the Action Was

On the lobster trick of the old *Telegram* about 1930, Asa Bordages, now an oil millionaire, was so frequently late that George Lyon, the city editor, warned him that the next time he did not show at 3 a.m., he would be fired.

There was an air of excitement in the old car barn office at Greenwich and Dey Streets the next morning. Speed Denlinger and Bill Doyle manned the copy desk—early. Jack Boyle and Roessner were at their rewrite desks—early. Wes Price, the lobster city editor, was nervous lest he might have to fire another human being.

The clock stood precisely at 3 when Asa dashed in. He was wearing a long topcoat down to his ankles, and carrying a bundle under each arm, followed by a taxi driver loudly demanding that he be paid $1.75. Somebody paid him and he left. Asa then threw off the coat and stood there in the middle of the city room stark naked. He opened one bundle, took out and donned his underwear; then from the other he got his shirt, suit, and shoes. Then turning to Wes Price, he shouted: "Well, I made it, didn't I?"

Years later Asa confessed he had stayed up until 2:30 a.m. to make sure he would make his entrance exactly at 3.

—ELMER ROESSNER, April 1965

Political Secrets Will Out
If Reporter Has His Pipeline

David Davidson, a Silurian, who now writes TV scripts, and is a former president of the TV Writers Union, used to be a reporter on the *Post*. In 1937, we were both doing politics in the city campaign. David came back from a closed meeting of the 9th AD regular Republican organization which was addressed by Ken Simpson, the county leader.

Everybody wondered what secret sources David had to find out that Simpson had shouted: "I know LaGuardia calls us clubhouse bums and loafers but we have to support him anyway," and much more of the same.

Simpson had ordered all reporters out of the clubhouse. The others left, but David stood disconsolately on the sidewalk, wondering what to do. He was under an open window and suddenly the bellicose tones of Simpson almost deafened him. It seems that Simpson's wife was deaf and so he talked habitually at hurricane force.

—OLIVER PILAT, October 1966

Somehow, He Didn't
Burn McKinley's Ears

As political news editor of the *New York Herald,* beginning there in 1894 I was assigned to the story of President McKinley's assassination in Buffalo in September, 1901. I was in Buffalo with Louis Seibold and Byron Newton, and was on the funeral train that went to Washington and later to Canton, Ohio, for the burial. Following is an anecdote told on the train:

Senator Arthur Pue Gorman of Maryland was one of the leaders in the Upper House. He could not get what he wanted from McKinley, and losing patience, stopped calling at the White House.

"I'm saving up a string of grievances, and when I call on McKinley the next time he's going to hear something from the Senator from Maryland that will make his ears burn," Gorman had said.

Finally he got a date to see McKinley, and was shown in to the President's office. There was no one but McKinley and Gorman there. The Maryland senator no sooner stepped into the office before McKinley strode across the room with out-stretched hand.

"Senator," said McKinley, beaming, "I have been missing you. I hear that Mrs. Gorman has been sick, but that she is convalescent."

Stepping to a stand surmounted with a huge bunch of American Beauty roses, McKinley added: "Senator, I want you to take these roses to Mrs. Gorman, and say to her that I am sorry she has been ill and that I am glad she is making a good recovery." With that he wrapped up the roses and pressed them on the Senator, blandly inquiring: "Is there anything special you wished to see me about?"

"Nothing important—it can wait," said the Senator, overwhelmed.

—CHARLES T. WHITE, May 1949

Puzzlers Very Put Out, Where to Get Answers?

When *The World-Journal-Tribune* stopped publication, some of the tidying up and putting away fell to Bob Grayson, the librarian, also for a long time before, librarian at the *Herald Tribune*. The paper's last edition came out on Friday. Now it was Monday, and a Blue Monday if ever one dawned.

"Where can I get the answers to Friday's Cryptogram?" said a voice on the telephone.

"Madam, I'm sorry," said Grayson, "but I can't tell you. The paper has stopped. There won't be any answers."

"But the Cryptogram was in Friday. It's got to have an answer somewhere."

"I'm awfully sorry," said Grayson. "But with all the people out of work down here, I'm afraid there won't be any chance for a while . . ."

"But . . . but . . . but," said the voice. "Why not? Irresponsible! Disgusting! Fine way to run a newspaper!" Grayson finally got the call transferred to the office of the publisher.

Before long the crossworders began. The Sunday magazine with other feature sections had been run through the presses before the stoppage. Some of them got out to the stands. So where was the answer to Sunday's Crossword Puzzle? Same Q & A. Same response—Dismay! Outrage! Unbelief!

Then again, a day or two later, a lawyer on the phone:—

"It has just been called to my attention . . . My client, a night club artist, libelled by your columnist, called vulgar and unfunny. We demand instant retraction, Page One, and in addition, a Sunday interview, promptly, setting him right before his public."

"Makes no difference, we demand retraction!"

Next on the phone is the office of the publisher. "Bob," says the voice, plaintively, "can't you send these nuts to somebody else beside me?"

October 1967

Traps For the Unwary
Betray Straying Steps

The New York Daily News, beginning publication in 1919, shared the office and plant of the *Evening Mail* at 25 City Hall Place. An agreement gave each city room exclusive use of the wire service stories that came in during its own hours.

When I came on the staff a month or two after the start, Merton Burke had just succeeded Arthur Clark as managing editor, with Sumner Blossom as his assistant. Phil Payne was city editor; Frank Hause, assistant.

The boys on the *Evening Mail* got the idea that certain items appearing in the *Daily News* had been arriving during hours that belonged to the *Mail.* They were wily lads. So, on the regular wire flimsy they tapped out and left on the City Desk one night the following story:

"Ekafasti, Greece.—Burglars today broke into the village bank and stole one million drachma, about $7.38."

Sure enough, next morning in the *Daily News,* the item appeared.

That afternoon, the *Evening Mail,* on the front page, had this to say:—

Our esteemed contemporary, the *Daily News,* has printed a news item with a date-line, "Ekafasti." It's astounding that when this word is spelled backwards, it says, "It's a fake."

—ED RANDALL, April 1965

Note:—The stunt is not strictly unique. Samuel Hopkins Adams, *Silurian News,* May 1958, refers to "the famous anagram whereby Hearst trapped *The World* into an unwitting confession, "Reflipe W. Thenuz—We pilfer the news!"

Bit of Advice to Beginner, From Which All May Profit

In the palmy days of Park Row, if you skidded one short block down Spruce street you came to the *Press* Building, with its vaulted and ornate corridors, and it was there that I got my first job as a reporter. Irving Wardman, one of the ablest editors and most genial gentlemen who ever blessed a city room hired me, and later . . . .

Wardman was tall, red-headed, quiet and very learned. He lived in Pelham Manor, and was a loyal supporter of the local baseball team, of which my brother Bill was the captain and I a pitcher. "Wardy" bought the uniforms, and was always on hand to see the games.

Brother Bill was then dramatic editor of the *Press,* so for a while everything was milk and honey for me. My assignments, of course, came from the desk, but one day Mr. Wardman sent for me. "A man named Ignatz Roth," said he, "has bought Glen Island, the big day summer resort off New Rochelle. Go up and find out what he is going to do with it. Roth is in the business of making felt covers for pool tables. Go get a story."

I looked up Ignatz Roth in the phone book, went up to his place, and sure enough, he was in the felt-cover business. But, unfortunately, Mr. Roth had never heard of Glen Island, nor had he bought any real estate of any kind. "But you ARE Ignatz Roth who makes felt tops for pool tables, aren't you?" I asked. "Sure I'm Ignatz Roth, and I make covers for billiard tables too—any orders?"

S-o-o-o—it being then about theatre time, I used a pass brother Bill had given me, and went to a show. (Thim wuz the days!) Next day the chief sent for me again. "What happened to that Glen Island story?" he asked, without even glancing up from his desk.

"I saw Ignatz Roth, Mr. Wardman, and he said he had never heard of Glen Island. Evidently that was a wrong lead you had," I answered, just like that.

"Damn funny all the other papers have the story," Wardman replied. "Ignatz Roth bought Glen Island."

"Good God!" I gasped, "Is it possible there can be two different men with a name like that?" "Yes, there are," he snapped. "Now look here, Beecroft, I hardly ever give advice, especially *good* advice, but I'm going to tell *you* this: never let anything throw you off a story you are sent out to get. If Ignatz Roth number one won't do, find out Ignatz Roth number two. Go down a coal hole if necessary, and up the back stairs, or up a dumbwaiter shaft if you have to, but GET THE STORY. Now you're fired!"

—CHESTER BEECROFT ("SINBAD"), May 1949

He Played Cupid
To Get a Scoop

Jules Nielsen, brother of Kathleen Nielsen, who married Reggy Vanderbilt was trying to win a girl living on Madison avenue, but her parents objected. I was on the *Evening Journal* then. The papers were full of this romance, but never could get anything definite. The late Clinton Fisk was my city editor.

One day Fisk, who was full of "pep" to say the least, shouted to me that Nielsen had gone down to the Battery to see the girl's father, who was a ship chandler. He told me to get Charlie Nesensohn, the photographer, a couple of hansom cabs, and rush down there, which I did.

I had to go through a rather dark areaway to reach the office of the girl's father and while groping through there I ran into a chap whom I mistook for Paul Beatie, another *Journal* reporter. So I stopped him and asked: "What did the old man say?" He replied: "He threw me out." I then asked: "Have you seen young Nielsen?"

"I'm Nielsen," came the surprising answer. "Why?" He was a dead ringer for Paul Beatie, even to the derby hat and clothes. Well, I tumbled and set to work. I advised him that if the old man had turned him down, the thing to do was to go to the girl's home. He said they had thrown him out there.

"All right," I replied, "William the Conqueror kidnapped the girl he loved and rode away with her on horseback. They were married and when the father raised hell, Bill asked: "So what?"

I then added that if he had guts enough to go to the house, beat on the door with feet and fists after ringing the bell, he could probably win her. He thought the idea great. So I put him into my hansom, while Nesensohn got some shots and we proceeded uptown. We stopped at the old Waldorf-Astoria, where I ordered two King William high-balls, which were the real thing then and did cost only 45 cents each.

Meantime, I kept pepping up Nielsen. When we got to the house he rang the bell. No answer. Then he began kicking on the door. A flock of reporters was waiting near the house and they didn't know what the hell to make of it. Finally, the door was opened a bit and Nielsen was yanked in by a sturdy hand. Meantime, I phoned the office and was told to await results.

Late in the afternoon, about 5:30, a carriage drove up to the house and out walked Nielsen and the girl, arm-in-arm. I ran over. He said they were going to Philadelphia and asked me to accompany them. Not having any expense money, I politely refused. They were married, all right, and were happy. Nielsen, who is dead, left a couple of kids.

P.S. Fisk gave me hell for not accompanying them.

—JIM LOUGHBOROUGH, May 1950

News Wires Set Off
Search for Quake

Covering earthquakes became fairly routine for me when I was with the United Press in Mexico (1935–40), but actually my first quake was in New York, soon after I got my job at the UP bureau in the *World* Building.

Many people in New York on the night of February 28, 1925, did not feel it, but, some of us have vivid memories of it. And the earthquake historians credit it with having shaken 2,000,000 square miles in Canada and the northeastern United States. Our center, apparently, was the Hotel Theresa in Harlem, which reported guests shaken out of bed.

On the evening of February 28 the telegraphers had lots of copy about General Billy Mitchell, Mayor Hylan, the death of President Frederick Ebert of Germany, etc. All of a sudden at 9:19 we felt the room moving up and down. We didn't pay much attention, but soon the Morse operators began to get word from Chicago, Buffalo, Cleveland, and other points saying they had felt something.

When the observatories confirmed that it was an earthquake, Miles W. "Peg" Vaughn, the bureau manager, sent me out to interview the man at the top of the highest building in the world, the Woolworth Building, across City Hall Park.

The observation tower, which did a flourishing business in those days, was already closed. When I told the guards what I wanted, they simply would not believe that there had been an earthquake. They thought I was being a wise guy. In any case, they said, there was nobody upstairs, and they sent me back to the *World* Building empty-handed.

When I quit work at 2 a.m. the papers all had big headlines about the quake. I bought two papers. When I got to my apartment in 14th Street, the elevator man wouldn't believe

: 239 :

me about the quake, so I gave him my papers. My roommates were equally incredulous—but I had no more papers to prove my story.

—WILLIAM H. LANDER, October 1966

Note:—Bill Brady confirms the earthquake story. "I got blamed for it," he recalls. "My wife said, 'I wish you'd stop rocking back in your chair, you've got the dishes rattling.' "

What Could Anxious Brass Do About It?

The late Henry M. Paynter was a man of presence; he bulked large, he wore an impressive moustache, and he had an air of command. His obituary in *The Times,* October 31, 1960, notes that after the *Chicago American,* he worked on the *New York American, Evening Journal, Sun, Post, Mirror,* on the Associated Press and on *PM.*

Henry was also smart, shrewd and intelligent. When covering Washington for *Newsweek,* he scored some remarkable beats in the field of atomic weaponry. He would take release fact A and release fact B, add conjecture C, hypothesis D and come up with assumption E.

These assumptions were so uncannily accurate that government intelligence agents became alarmed. Finally a high intelligence authority called Henry and asked if he would meet secretly with an important Army and an important Navy officer. Paynter refused, but offered to meet them for lunch in the bar at the National Press Club.

On the day of the lunch, Henry's pals did not overlook the meeting. In consequence, there came over the loud speaker a message asking Mr. Paynter to call the Polish Embassy.

Paynter ignored it. Then came a message asking him to call the Soviet Embassy. Paynter continued with his conversation. Then a club member walked in, with coat collar, hat, and dark glasses concealing his features, and threw an envelope in front of Henry. In a simulated but heavy Russian accent, he said, "Mr. Paynter, you robber, here is your check. But this is the last five thousand dollars you get from us."

The Army officer turned to Paynter and suspecting him of having arranged the whole affair, said, with a note of rue in his voice, "Mr. Paynter, you don't seem to be taking this meeting seriously!"

—ELMER ROESSNER, October 1966

Watch Your Words;
Wolf at the Door

I once cost the *World-Telegram* $500, plus legal expenses, and I admit I was worth it. However, if the paper had paid the full bill of $150,000 as originally presented, I might have my doubts. It was all a matter of the simple word "rickety."

In his campaign against so-called Wildcat Buses, operating on certificates of public convenience and necessity instead of proper franchise, Mayor La Guardia got around to certain routes in Queens. Abruptly he banned the streets to the old company and announced that a new simon-pure franchised line would immediately take over. This clicked with *World-Telegram* policy, and I wrote an editorial cheering for the replacement of "the rickety old buses."

In came the lawyer, the very next day. What did I mean, "Rickety"?

"We've just filed suit for $150,000," he said, "which says

how rickety they were. You ought to know that every bus on the street every month carries a Public Service Commission stamp on its windshield, saying it has been inspected and found safe. So you say they're rickety and unsafe! The libel on the company's good name is worth far more than this $150,000."

"Unsafe?" I floundered. "Here's a dictionary. Look it up. Rickety is shaky, tottery, lots of things. But not unsafe."

"Webster disagrees," said the lawyer. "See the Unabridged. Rickety is weak, unsound. We'd never have been permitted to run rickety buses."

So began the conferences and the depositions, the getting set and the postponements. Meanwhile, our fine reporter MacGregor Bond went over and learned that when the specified routes were closed, the company had sold the buses now out of service to a junk dealer, twenty-two of them in a single deal for $1050, or $47.73 apiece. (After sweating my way through that business, I thought I'd like to keep a memo of the figures.) Yes, $47.73 per bus, but not rickety. The paper settled the case out of court. It seemed that the lawyer had filed the suit on a contingent fee basis, the company being little interested, and he agreed to drop the matter for a cash payment of $500.

—GEORGE BRITT, October 1966

How Could It Ever Happen?

"This, of course, is not suitable for a family publication like the *Silurian News*," writes an eminent member—but nameless.

Since, however, the situation has a certain touch of universality, it seems worth a "To-Whom-It-May-Concern." It happened this way:

"One night, as I was leaving City Hall for home and dinner, having phoned my wife that I was coming home, and she having put a steak on the broiler or whatever, Barney and Charley asked me to stop over at the white-tiled Childs' on Park Row for a cocktail.

"When we got there, somebody suggested that since I was in a hurry to get home for dinner we order one round of Martinis all at once, so we each got three and split the check. The next I knew, it was 10 o'clock p.m., and we had been earnestly talking about something. I hurried home, and I did not again ever go out for a quick cocktail on the way home. That must have been about 1936."

If the shoe fits—Anyone—you may wear it.

October 1966

Swim for Your Story
if That's What It Takes

In the summer of 1934, among his many jobs, Bob Moses was Chairman of the Long Island Park Commission which added to other activities, had completed the first segment of a place known as Jones Beach. Bob invited all the newspaper reporters in Room Nine, City Hall, New York, to come out to Jones Beach, take a dip in the Atlantic Ocean, and have luncheon at his expense. It was a glorious summer's day and I phoned my boss, Amster Spiro, city editor of the *New York Evening Journal*.

He acquiesced, but he added one thing. He had a tip on a

hot news story in which Moses was involved and he wanted me to interview Bob Moses privately and get his reaction. It was not connected with the Jones Beach story. Anyhow here I was with the assignment and thirty aggressive, eager and smart competitive newspaper reporters surrounding Bob Moses.

In his college days at Yale University Bob Moses was said to be the best water polo player that the college ever had and was known as a first-class swimmer. When we all got into bathing suits at Jones Beach, having been transported by special bus, Bob Moses ran to the beach, dived into the ocean, and began swimming straight out in the high waves to Europe, or so it seemed.

But, it just happened that this humble writer had been brought up in the Hudson River (when it was clean and you could catch fish and crabs as well as swim in it) and had also been a life guard. So this reporter also dived into the ocean and swam out after Bob Moses. The other reporters saw it but apparently, were not good swimmers. I found Bob way out in the high waves. I interviewed him (without note paper or pencil) and we both swam back to shore. Next day, the *New York Evening Journal* carried an exclusive story (about something or other!) and the reporters, all friends of mine, wondered how I got it.

—MAURICE G. POSTLEY, October 1970

Composing Room Foreman— ## Still the Man in Authority

For years I had played with the thought that it might be interesting, entertaining and enlightening to run something from the King James version of the Bible in a newspaper. The splendid, sonorous, dignified language, the drama of some of the stories, it seemed to me, certainly would make interesting reading, might even be read by some who had never before even dipped into the Bible.

Then, one Easter-tide, while working on the *East St. Louis* (Illinois) *Journal,* my opportunity arrived. On the *Journal,* the newsroom had to keep a steady flow of copy into the composing room or, at make-up time, there would be a shortage of type and holes would have to be plugged with house ads. This was particularly true when we were getting out the Sunday paper.

This Easter Saturday nothing was happening, either locally or on the wires, and copy was quite short. It looked as though I, in my role as news editor and make-up man, would have to resort to not only a full page of house ads, but several quarter and half pages as well.

Then, I remembered my Biblical idea. I dispatched two reporters to the local hotel, each assigned to steal a Gideon Bible. Meanwhile, I called a minister and asked where, in the Bible, the story of the Crucifixion was to be found. He said the 22nd and 23rd Chapters of the Book of Luke.

When the thieving reporters returned, I ripped those chapters from both volumes, pasted it up on one long sheet of copy paper, wrote an eight-column banner head "The Story of the Crucifixion as told in the Book of Luke" and dispatched it to the composing room.

Harry Hamshire was the composing room foreman—a fat, calm, unruffled guy who was one of the best craftsmen in Illinois. Harry knew his trade better than any printer with whom I ever worked. Within five minutes of the time I shot my Biblical copy to the composing room, Harry came waddling into the City Room, clutching one end of the two chapters of the Book of Luke, with the rest dragging out behind.

He placed a firm fist on my desk, glared at me for a split moment and then, lifting his clenched fist, shook it dramatically at the clock.

He bellowed:

"They crucified Jesus Christ 2,000 years ago, but you, you lead-footed son-of-a-bitch, you can't get the copy in before 3 o'clock."

—KARL PRETSHOLD, April 1973

The Silurian Tradition— Memories We Like To Recall

This Society is a great leveler. Here the old legman, the reporters, the copyreaders, the by-liners, the editors, the cartoonists, and the literary lights meet on common ground to swap experiences, offer encouragement, and recall happy memories of earlier days. We gather at the festive table twice a year to extend the glad hand of friendship, to enjoy each other's company and to live over the days of Park Row, Herald and Times Squares—and to have fun. Men of modest earnings are as important and as welcome as those whom kind fate may have showered with riches or placed in positions of responsibility. See you at the dinner!

—WILLIAM J. BREDE, April 1960

No Prosaic Crowd, This;
On Your Feet, Everybody

SILURIAN SONG

Oh, we are the boys from a long way back!
    We never once let our steps grow slack!
We're the newspaper boys who EARNED
    their jack!
    For we come from an era before any shellac!

So here's a picnic: come, hire a bus:
    ALL Silurians are victor-i-ous!
Here's a toast to you and toast to me,
    And it's time for another whoop-de-de!

So here's to you, and here's to me,
    And a toast to each, and a three cheers
    three!
We will stick by each other, till hell freezes
    over,
    And be sure that we all will end up in
    clover!
We are Silurians, here to stay
    Till we all get together on Judgment Day!

—SAM MC COY, March 1964

VI.
NEWSPAPERMEN

A Random Picture Gallery,
Inkstained Personalities.
And Never Ask a Silurian
To Be Objective About Them

MR. NEW YORK, HIMSELF, RECALLS
NEW YORK WAS YOUNG

New York—where everyone mutinies, but no one deserts. And when, through a lapsing moment he finds himself away from his self-imposed confinement, he cannot be converted to his new surroundings. His mind and marrow, New York. Exemplified by the yarn of the two Manhattanites who went to Hollywood, went into a spree of spending, with and without reason. Finally one made a wild suggestion: "Let's do something real crazy. Let's take a taxicab to New York!" Agreed, they hailed a cab. As they were getting in, one said: "Let me get in first—I get out at Seventy-second Street!"

In my almost 60 years of toiling in the newspaper vineyards of New York, there have been a few imprints in my memory, good, bad, or indifferent. Sixty years of living it cannot be relived in speed-up, camera-like. It is running counter to Nature's gear. Reverse isn't made to move so fast, unless in drowning, your past is supposed to appear before you fast, in chronological order. But not this article. Here in montage, is my touch-and-go of my New York.

Preparatory years of Chicago and San Francisco seemed like kindergarten stuff, when I found myself in New York, when thrown into the den of lions in their fields—Tad, Bud Fisher, Bob Carter, Hype Igoe, George Herriman (the saintliest human I ever knew), Cliff Sterrett, Tom McNamara, Walter Hoban, Jimmy Swinnerton and Rudy Dirks. On their heels, Damon Runyon.

* * *

Coming into focus: Dinner honoring Marcus Loew for his pioneering the movies and an editor, Arthur Brisbane, as speaker, panning the life out of films—said it was for "children and morons." When reminded by the big boss afterward about the ads the *Journal* was getting from the Loew Theaters, another banquet was quickly arranged and again Brisbane was a speaker. This time "Double-Dome" got up and said: "The movies are great, adult entertainment, in the hands of such superb artists as Mary Pickford, Douglas Fairbanks, and others." Not many years later, this powerful editor, so opposed to competing movies, play-acted himself, with yours truly helping put on his make-up, for a honkey-tonk film called "The Gay White Way."

New York, a modern Babylon, with not enough room to fall in. Dreams and hopes crowding into Park Row, with every form of newpaper specialization. In New York, I kept bumping into specialists, as against the more or less utility newspapermen of Chicago and San Francisco. Irvin S. Cobb was selling "Irvin S. Cobb"—Franklin P. Adams, Roy K. Moulton and Rube Goldberg were already personal institutions. By-lines were the vogue in the major cities, though one powerful editor tried his darnedest to eliminate cartoonists' signatures off their art, so great then was their growing identification and salaries. That started the first cartoonist strike. Who won? The cartoons are still signed.

Trying my best to keep this article a generalization, thereby easier to finish at any given point. Tossing a few memories into the air: My first meeting with Mark Twain, in City Hall Park, nearly burning his moustache with the stub of a cigar . . . Sharing a table with William R. Hearst in a "poison-dish" eatery in the building, both ordering a steak—and the awed waiter yelling loud: "Two steaks—one especially good for Mister Hearst!" . . . Shared oysters with Diamond Jim Brady at Shanley's . . . Sipped a glass with Lillian Russell, at the Astor, at banquet to Weber and Fields . . . Lunched with them at the Lambs Club the day that ticket broker Joe Leblang died. Lew Fields, in tears, and Weber asking him:

"Was he so dear to you?" "Yes," moaned the great Fields, "I owe him a lot of money and he always delayed it for me—his estate now maybe won't be so generous!"

* * *

The sidemouthed George M. Cohan and his memorable viewpoint: "It doesn't matter what you are, so long as you ARE!" . . . And Will Rogers giving his advice: "The minute you ain't yourself, you're in trouble!" . . . My walking behind Will Rogers on Fifth Avenue and hearing him talking to himself and my passing him and cracking: "Oh, getting your ad libs ready?" . . . My singing with Enrico Caruso, in a maudlin quartet, in the original Friars Club, at 3 a.m.—something to hear is "Sweet Adeline" with an Italian overtone . . . Dancing to the tune of "East Side, West Side" with Al Smith and Jimmy Walker, in a minstrel show, in the Met Opera House . . . La Guardia doublecrossing the script, to embarrass the "end men"—and their ganging up on him, to chase him off the stage.

Riding with Franklin D. Roosevelt to Sea Girt, N.J. for his first speech for the Presidency. Being averse to fast driving, our saying to him: "Governor, do you have to travel so fast?" His reply: "Aw, they all know who's in the car!" "I know it, but do you mind slowing up so they can see who's with you!" . . . William R. Hearst Jr. and your writer, meeting King George of Greece, in private audience, at the Waldorf. And the look on his face, after 3 minutes of talk and his shocked laugh when we said to him: "We're busy men, Your Majesty —so we're dismissing YOU!" And his replying: "Only in a democracy can this happen, and I'm glad you're dismissing me—I'm tired and would like to take a nap!"

* * *

Accidentally breaking the colored, precious meerschaum

pipe of David Warfield, in his dressing room. And rushed out before he could regain his speech . . . First person to meet socially, was De Wolfe Hopper, in the famous Albany Hotel oyster bar—and his giving me a one-man-audience recital of his immortal "Casey at the Bat."

The unbelievable Bartholdi Inn (now the State Theater) of which there was no other such theatrical boarding house— housing such names of that day as Mary Pickford, Mack Sennett, Mable Norman, Barney Bernard, King Baggott. Most of them on the cuff till the next engagement. And hosted by the good Mme. Bartholdi, making the rounds of the Inn, with her tremendous chain of keys—and the guests calling her "Henry the Eighth." . . . Then the early days of the meteoric Walter Winchell, who reminded one of a firecracker, about to be exploded while you're trying to keep your dentures in.

New York, itself, the story of stories. Any newspaperman wanting more than such an assignment is downright gluttonous. This is generalization enough and a good place to mark my period.

—HARRY HERSHFIELD, October 1966

IN PRE-ABE-KABIBBLE DAYS,
LIFE WAS A LUSTY SONG

Advantage of "living in the past"—you cannot be dispossessed. Wars create history. History creates historians. Historians create wars again. Biographers start vicious circles also. But Silurians are entitled to the facts. Till I'm asked to make an affidavit regarding the truth of these memories, here are a few of them . . . pertaining to the Fourth Estate. I have basked in its aura since 1899. How much I have been part of it, was best answered by Arthur Brisbane, of the old *N.Y. Journal*. Being a cartoonist at the time, I asked Brisbane if he considered a cartoonist a newspaperman? His deflator, "Would you call a barnacle a ship?"

First smell of the traditional "printers' ink" came to this 14-year-older on the *Chicago Daily News,* published by Victor Lawson. And presided over by the vinegary Charles Fay, the prototype of what editors are like on TV today.

Reporters and camera men were supposed to be "boozers" in those days—and were. I was then in the "mixing with the boys" stage, in Chicago. Had a sandwich-bringing acquaintance with George Ade, James Whitcomb Riley. Cartoonists T. E. Powers, H. T. Webster, Will B. Johnstone and the top newspaper illustrator of his day, Frank Holme.

There was a code of honor, in Chicago, where murder was simply considered "disorderly conduct." Knew Al Capone, where in later years I did a "command performance" in Cicero, Ill. It was a "black tie" affair. The hall was filled with many of Chicago's "society" who were just as afraid NOT to attend as I was. Made drawing of my comic strip "Abe Kabibble" —a "character," who definitely was no competition to the gunslingers.

Chicago of that era, was the newspaper reporters' paradise.

If he went to only one shindig in those days, it was a lifetime story. That event had need only be the unbelievable First Ward Ball; the domain run by Aldermen Hinky Dinky and Bathhouse John. It was the lowest high event of the season. Every brothel was forced to buy tickets. And showed up.

Big Jim Colosimo, with a big red sash across his portly front, would get up in his box at the witching hour and have champagne given freely to the milling characters on the floor. But instead of having battling beasts tearing at each other, he had a more refined form for this Chicago Coliseum. With some one arranged to start it off, at exactly midnight, every brothel madame and gal and pimp would start to swing at one another in a free-for-all. Just so many minutes was allowed to settle the year's grudges.

Our present college protest battles are "beanies" compared to the big "cleansing" scene at the First Ward Ball. One famous writer at the time, covering the story, had this for his last line: "As I lay in the gutter, outside of the Coliseum, I looked up and felt right again, when I saw the stars in the heavens."

* * *

Chicago politics at the time, was no better or worse than in other major cities. They all had the same angles and the right technique. A "boodler" then was considered just that. Fact, a yarn at that time. One office holder, the books showed, had robbed the city of one million dollars. They faced him with the facts, but not to embarrass his family, decided just to let him resign and leave office. He put up this plea: "Our City accountants are not very efficient. I really stole four million dollars. I now own a country as well as a town house. I have yachts, automobiles, and jewelry for my wife and kids. Why do you want to elect somebody else and have him start from scratch?"

Chicago was far from being all sordid. In the early 1900s she had some of America's finest theaters—at one time, more plays running than going on in New York. It was a field day for us illustrators, covering the shows—line drawings in the main were used instead of photographs. Some of the best art schools in the country, producing some of America's finest painters and sculptors. Top opera. Developing one of the world's greatest park systems. Certain boulevards at present can match the best of Europe. Yet, Chicago was marked for scorn, a place to avoid. It was the political aspect the rest of the world wanted to damn her with. Remember discussing one Chicago politician, saying: "He's a pain in the neck!" The reply, "I've got a much lower opinion of him."

Visited our second-largest city, few weeks ago. Tried hard to recapture my youth there. Just couldn't. Walked through the old West Side slum district—not there any more. Walked down renowned Halsted Street—no more Hull House, where yours truly, studied art with the famous sculptor, Jo Davidson. Colorful Greek neighborhood, no more—ran out of partners to start restaurants. Halsted Street, Bijou, Academy and Haymarket Theaters, where I rushed to shake the hands of Terry McGovern, Robert Fitzsimmons—and back stage of the Haymarket, to meet George M. Cohan, then with the "Four Cohans," in vaudeville.

Yes, I shook the mitt of the great John L. Sullivan, he visiting the sports department of the *Daily News*. He roared out a lecture to me, the youngster, against the evils of drink. He was genuinely reeling, himself, while giving me that valuable advice. He had his sense of humor. I put up my dukes as if I was going to take a smash at him. He looked at me, waved a cautioning finger and bellowed: "If you hit me and I find it out. . . ."

* * *

In my 80 years, there's been more to my living than Chicago. There is yet San Francisco and New York. First impressions, however, grip me most. Some, surely, have carried over into the later years. As I think of it, the toast of America at the time, Fritzi Scheff, in "Mlle. Modste." Fell in love with her, when she played the Illinois Theater, even sent her terrible love poems, finally met her backstage. Her sensational song being "Kiss Me Again," I asked her for a kiss and received it. I was burning with desire, and as a desperate young shmo, I proclaimed for the whole stage to hear: "Like your song, 'I'll Kiss You Again' some day!" And by God, if I didn't, fifty years later in Yorkville, New York. At that time I was down to only an academic interest.

—HARRY HERSHFIELD, March 1966

HOW HE BECAME A NEWSPAPERMAN—
ADVICE OF GREELEY, DANA, BENNETT

Horace Greeley told Charles A. Dana that the real news-paper man was the boy who slept on newspapers and ate printers' ink. Dana added these recommendations: constant reading of the Bible for its simplicity of style, its solemn re-counting of great events; and familiarity with Shakespeare whom he called "the chief master of the English language."

Dana shocked the journalism class of Union College by telling them bluntly a good general education with Greek and Latin was far more valuable for the making of a newspaper-man than schooling in journalism; that he never found a journalism class graduate "of any great avail as a practical newspaper worker."

James Gordon Bennett completed a sturdy curriculum by insisting on an assiduous reading of Noah Webster's best seller. And he issued an 8-page pamphlet for the guidance of his editors, which, for its meticulous detail would be an excellent thing for some of the editing today.

Around the corner from me lived Alfred Henry Lewis, editorial writer of the *Washington Post* and foremost columnist of the day. Across the street, Allie Lyon, executive editor of the *Washington Star*. Each of these, as he strolled leisurely to his office, seemed to me the embodiment of a useful life, confident, independent, and something of an oracle to the thousands of persons who avidly read his writings and his preachments from day to day.

When fourteen, I received a small hand printing press for Christmas. I published the smallest newspaper ever in the U.S. —the *Eagle;* weekly, 5 cents a month; 350 subscribers; no free copies; advertising 1 cent a line. Type all handset; presswork new to me; I got printers' ink all over me and on my sandwiches, eating while running the press.

Here I was with six of the Greeley-Dana-Bennett formula. I surely was eating printers' ink. I had a Bible. We kids put on a crazy pound-of-flesh scene. We had one of those enormous Webster's around the house. Soon after I divided Gaul into more parts than a dog has fleas. All I needed now was to make my bed on a pile of newspapers.

The panic of 1893 extended into '94. Hundreds of printers were out of work. Frank Hatton and Beriah Wilkins, owners of the *Washington Post* had just moved into their fine new building. They told the unemployed printers to take the old *Post* building and do what they wished. They decided to start a newspaper, the *Washington Times.* I had been selling bits to the *Post* and *Star* on space. Emory Foster, city editor of the *Post,* was made managing editor of the new paper. "How'd you like to go along with me?" "Fine!" "As my first reporter; my star reporter?" "Fine!" "At seven dollars a week?" he smiled. "At that or anything." Seven dollars was money in those days for men were getting only a dollar a day when they could get work.

First copy of the *Washington Times* came out March 18, 1894. It has been published continuously ever since, and is now the *Times Herald.* My first "big story" was the Coxey Army descent on Washington. Had to cover it alone, as we had only three city reporters. The Associated Press attracted me, and after four months I transferred to the New York office. Became assistant night city editor—beating the typewriter from dictation through the week and sitting in as night city editor on Saturdays—twenty dollars a week.

While working nights at the AP I took on a day job with the *Woman's Home Companion* in the old *Tribune* Building —ten dollars a week. Went to the *Companion* at 9 a.m.;

worked till 5 p.m.; slept on newspapers on the floor till the
postman woke me at 5:30 p.m.; freshened up; got 30 cents
worth of ham an' beans, sinkers and coffee at Dolan's famous
emporium; then went to the AP at 6 p.m. and beat the typewriter till 2 in the morning. Slept on newspapers in the AP
delivery room till 8 a.m.; cleaned up, retraced my steps to
Dolan's sinkers and the *Companion* day job. Worked these
two jobs steadily for nine months—combined salary, $30 a
week. I caught up on sleep on Sundays.

Yes, I slept on newspapers aplenty, thus completing the
hard Greeley-Dana-Bennett course. So, with this background,
I loaded up with thick notebooks, a bushel or two of lead
pencils, and went out after those journalistic rainbows which
beamed now on all sides; and I found many a pot of gold.

From New York to the Tropics, to the Arctic, to the Pacific, to the middle of Austria; into War and out again with
army and navy. So, on my reincarnation, I'll be back in New
York in the newspaper game, reflecting on my fifty years of it.
I think a full newspaper life is the most fascinating, most
glorious of all vocations, with its admixture of adventure,
peril, and charm. Selah!

—DELT EDWARDS, May 1951

Footnote from Edwards (*Silurian News*, May 1954):

"It is possible that I have the only copy extant of the book that
Bennett got out, telling us how to write stories and giving instruction
to reporters and editors. In it is a list of 133 'don'ts' which writers of
today might study with profit. For violation of those don'ts we received
a bawling out the first time and a fine if it occurred again. . . . There
was also an unpublished list of twenty names of prominent persons
who were never to be mentioned in *Herald* columns. Woe to the person
who violated that rule!

"The *Herald* started the first information bureau. It wasn't really
a bureau, we just answered, or tried to answer, questions on all subjects imaginable. The questions became so numerous and varied that I

began scribbling them, with the answers, inside the old electric light shades. There were about six shades hanging over the assistant night city editor's desk—and before long there were several hundred of the questions and answers written inside of them—many of them duplicated year after year. There were questions about local history, famous stories, landmarks, where to dine, places of interest, and many very stupid ones. But the order was to be cooperative and we did so to the best of our ability.

James Gordon Bennett, Jr., issued an edict that under no circumstances should the name "Herald" appear except in italics.

One printer really showed his unflinching obedience to the order, when, during the holiday season, he set up a Christmas program announcement with the following item "Hark the *Herald* Angels Sing."

"SKIPPER'S" NEWS FROM NOWHERE
PEOPLED *TIMES* WITH PRODOGIES

I went down the bay at 4:30 one morning to meet the *Queen Mary,* and as we saw her moving in slowly under the Verrazzano Bridge, her thousand lights aglow, old Skipper Williams, the justly honored ship news reporter for *The New York Times,* came to mind.

It was simply a matter of remembering that the big ships were the meat of a long-gone journalistic fare that would give today's metropolitan editors the fantods, particularly the fantodprone metropolitan editors of the paper which Skipper served, shall we say? so many years on the ship news beat.

The stories he dredged up from the cabins and corridors of the great ships had a quality that would be quickly spurned by the paper of today, so preoccupied are its editors with a journalism that Skipper could not possibly have understood.

We are priviledged to use the word fantod because it was in Skipper's lexicon, a rich reservoir as one might expect from an unlikely Englishman who had sailed in sail and steam, sold lightning rods, roamed the Nile Valley, knew Cecil Rhodes, went up the Amazon, inordinately loved Scotch whisky, told the biggest damned tales you ever heard. He spent some forty years as a loving son of a great newspaper peopled nowadays by a passel of bright lads who missed knowing him and his kind, and do not know what they missed.

It is undeniably true that Skipper had a special affinity for British ships, and specially for the *Queen Mary,* on which he had made the maiden voyage in 1936. Those of us who got to know her later realized that one did not have to be born in England to feel there was something special about this stately liner. It is too bad he could not have seen her safely home, with her 300-foot "homeward-bound" pennant flying, on September 22, 1967.

If there were any truth in the old gag about the receptionist announcing, "Six reporters, Sir, and a gentleman from *The Times*," the seventh was surely Skipper Williams. He would have carried an umbrella or a cane. He would have taken off his high crown derby hat and straightened his tie, centering it suitably on the wing collar. And he would have presented his card: T. Walter Williams, *The New York Times.*

He looked like Stanley Baldwin, only a little more so. He was the very body of dignity. But in spirit he was a swinger long before the idea was thought up. He wouldn't go home as long as any of his cronies would belly up with him at the nearest bar. He was the kind of man who would peer around a protecting pillar at a mean night city editor in a particularly bad mood and bellow "God Almighty, the wind's in the East."

He was the kind who would go home halfway to dawn, 70 years old, roly-poly, twinkling with Scotch, and lie down by Mrs. Williams's grand piano, stilling her wifely protestations with "I'm a sailor, and a sailor can sleep anywhere." There are not very many of us left, but the few there are—we are glad we were his cronies, with all his crochets and light-hearted chicaneries. We remember how, as the night waned—and us with it—he could painfully prolong two ounces of Scotch, pacing himself, knowing the night would be long, he fondly hoped.

Don't get the idea he was an alcoholic. He just liked to talk, and he did have an uneasy fear of not having enough Scotch around. One of the last things he did, the eve of his final illness, was to order a case of it from Macy's and then get into a long-winded telephone colloquy with one of the top Straus people about not getting the sale price advertised earlier that summer. (Lucius Beebe and some others had unkind things to say about Skipper in their public writings, but it was not true that he drank only as long as someone else was buying. Beebe and Skipper were, one might say, at opposite ends of the bar.)

The first years of World War II took a heavy toll of his spirit. When England stood alone enduring blow after blow, he really suffered. What a pity he could not have stuck it out a little longer, because not long after his death the tide began to turn in North Africa. And he still had some of that Macy whisky left. It was November, 1942, just 25 years ago.

There weren't always enough interesting people around to satisfy Mr. Williams. He solved this by inventing a few. And he wrote straight stories about them under regular *Times* headlines, quoting from interviews and from their letters mailed along the Ramganga River, or somewhere in Upper Burma—probably the only fiction *The Times* ever printed, knowingly, that is.

There were Imbolega, the sable Amazon, who was given to capturing and carrying off Marvyn T. Winglefoot, the mendacious Mincing Lane teataster. Winglefoot's later descriptive chronicles to Marmaduke Mizzle, the London caraway seed merchant, detailing his escape from the rough care of Imbolega, were a caution. He alienated, Skipper did, a nice chap on the liner *Majestic,* the ship's chief surgeon, by using him as the lead character in stories about Dogface Jones of the Rangoon Rangers. And there were Chota Peg (a small but virile lad who sometimes ran Winglefoot's letters out from the bush to post them) and Ben Fidd, the New York waterfront philosopher.

One day another New York newspaper sent reporters and photographers roaming the port in search of the remarkable Fidd who had told of a clever tom cat who spent his life traveling by ship between Singapore and London. Skipper knew the cat personally, a knowing feline who would walk ashore majestically tail in air, as soon as his ship tied up in Singapore, and go directly to a London-bound ship ready to cast off.

In *The Times* morgue there are still index cards attesting to the existence of a Ben Fidd, waterfront philosopher, and of a Mizzle and a Winglefoot. But the folders are missing.

Skipper had a fierce curiosity. He was a frequent traveler and was always looking for stories and running into famous people. He was fond of telling how the late Samuel Untermyer owed him $2 which the wealthy Untermyer had borrowed in a moment of crisis in some lonely Indian venue. Once on a visit to Egypt he ran into an archeologist at the bar in Shepherd's Hotel, and filed a sensational beat on a discovery of some Pharaoh's tomb, with funerary boat and all.

In the later years as a ship news man he stopped going down the bay, but would mosey up to the ship at the pier and stay most of the day, having a drink with the purser and getting the gossip.

This was a source of considerable grief for other ship news men. In those days the *American,* the *World,* the *Evening World,* the *Herald Tribune,* the *Telegram*—all the papers— covered ships on speculation, not simply because some known notable was arriving. They would have a man aboard, but he would have to leave after the liner docked. Skipper would come in late to the office, push aside the City News copy and pound out his own story, poking with one finger at the ancient typewriter, which had an upper bank for capitals.

One day he stayed long enough on shipboard to ferret out a major story about a diamond smuggling caper in which the liner's chief steward starred.

Covering the old *Mauretania* returning from a cruise, he heard that Mr. Thompson, the chief officer, had entered in the logbook an item about the sighting of a sea serpent. Skipper got Mr. Thompson to draw the beast, as he saw it. *The Times* art department improved the drawing and it appeared the next day. Some of the other ship news men did not speak to Skipper for a while.

—GEORGE HORNE, October 1967

Sunk, on Literalist's Reef!

Herbert M. French, retired from *The Times*'s old national-foreign news desk, was moved by George Horne's story last fall about the vagaries of Skipper Williams, to contribute this postscript:

It was in 1929 or '30, as I remember, that Williams vanished for five weeks. He had been up the Yangtze, he said. And had *The Times* had word of a devastating but localized earthquake, a thousand or two miles inland, which had wiped out a town and killed all its 1,200 people?

It sounded like news. At Birchall's urging and close to first edition deadline, the Skipper wrote a brief account with geographical details, put his copy on the desk; and then went off to a nearby speakeasy.

The Chinese earthquake story was so good (and so different in style from the Skipper's Marmaduke Mizzle tales that George Horne notes) that Birchall found a place for it on Page 1, bylined.

A pressman brought the Skipper, while he was having his drink, a copy of the first run of the paper. Probably the rotund T. Walter Williams moved faster then than anyone on the *Times* had ever seen him go. He erupted into the news room, waving the paper, shouting for Birchall and almost weeping: "Take it out! Take it out! Fools! Fools!—I made it up!"

It took some convincing on the Skipper's part. But Page 1 of *The New York Times* was replated before many bundles had got into the delivery trucks.

—April 1968

GOLD MINE OF MIDNIGHT SAILINGS
PAYS OFF MORTGAGE MANOR DEBTS

When I went to work on the lively old *Morning Tele-graph* in 1923, the people in general and the newspapermen in particular were just getting used to Prohibition which was inflicted upon us, January 17, 1920.

My assignment at the time was to write a column on the front page as successor to Joe Van Raalte whose by-line was Beau Broadway and the title of the column, "Around The Town." It was later written by Walter Winchell when I asked for the waterfront after Harry Acton went to the *New York American.*

Be it said to his everlasting memory, Harry Acton was in a class by himself. He lost more pairs of kid gloves and walking canes than all the others owned, he referred to his Flushing home as "Mortgage Manor," he was a good but unlucky gambler, a good loser, and a sucker for a joke.

The group who composed the shipnews brigade in my day included Walter "Skipper" Williams for *The New York Times,* John Regan for the *City News,* Jim Duffy for the *Telegram,* Harry Acton for the *American,* Louis Hynes for the *Journal,* Dick Regan succeeding Percy Stone for the *Tribune* and various representatives from the *Wall Street Journal.*

In 1928 Mayor Jimmy Walker addressed the sportswriters' dinner at the Astor at which O. O. McIntyre, Gene Buck, and myself were invited. While leveling quips at the various reporters he happened to look squarely at our table and then said, "and here sits the grave of 1000 highballs, Ned Welch."

Harry Acton read it the next day and subsequently asked

me how I could drink as much as I did and look as fresh at night as though I just got up. Facetiously, I told him that as evening approached and we had a midnight sailing, I always ate a small sponge-cake which acted in the stomach as a blotter. Sad to relate, but nevertheless a fact, he believed me. A couple of nights later when the *Berengaria* was departing, he tried my remedy, and they had to carry him to the customs booth on the dock in a deck-chair.

When the steamship lines decided to have midnight sailings, wild bon voyage parties were thrown before departure which became social events at which dress designers and fashion editors were sure to make an appearance.

One of the outstanding affairs of this sort occurred at a midnight sailing of the *Paris* when "the Poor Little Rich Girl," Barbara Hutton, was about to go on her first trans-Atlantic trip. Her father, Franklyn D. Hutton had all the character assassins invited, even Peggy Hopkins Joyce who looked like a Lexington Avenue express coming into the Grand Central with her ruby earrings. This suite had the smell of brandy, gin, bourbon, so potent that you sort of got the idea they got it out of the pumps.

Society of that era was very like a fever patient in a delirium. The main difference was, that whereas a man in a fever had a nurse, society had none.

One morning when the *Aquitania* was due to arrive at quarantine at 7 o'clock, the shipnews reporters were all at South Ferry to ride the cutter down to Rosebank, the Staten Island anchorage for the quarantine inspections, but a heavy fog delayed it until the afternoon. We decided to partake in that quaint old American pastime of stud poker.

Harry Acton, as was his wont, hit the boneyard first and while wandering around the room mentioned the fact that he wished he had some idea for his Sunday column. Old John McIntyre who represented the Cunard press department stated offhand that maybe I could help him out of his dilemma.

With three aces and a lonely queen I had a dilemma of my own at the moment but I told Harry to get in touch with Clay Morgan of the French Line and suggest that he and the other lines charge all visitors to the midnight sailings 25 cents each and donate it to the Seaman's Fund. Acton stated derisively that it never would happen, so I forgot it. But, when his Sunday column appeared there it was in great detail and shortly thereafter all of the lines having midnight sailings put the whammy on the visitors for two bits per head.

The ironic conclusion of this memo is that Harry Acton was one of the shipnews reporters invited in 1935 to go to Cherbourg and return on the maiden voyage of the *Normandie*. But as the *Ile de France* approached Plymouth, going over with the newsmen, Harry passed away.

His return on the *Normandie* was in his coffin. The Seaman's Fund with over two million dollars now from the donations received, paid his funeral expenses, cleared the mortgage on his home, and gave his wife a secretarial job for life. His story returned a dividend, and it couldn't have happened to a nicer guy.

—NED WELCH, October 1972

From the *Morning Telegraph* the author went on to the *Daily Mirror,* the *Washington Times-Herald* and to editorship of *Who's Who in Thoroughbred Racing.* At the time this story was published he was doing a regular weekly column for the *Sun City Sun Citizen* of Phoenix, Ariz. On August 16, 1972 he celebrated his 90th birthday. The recommendation for himself that he quotes with most satisfaction is that of his old friend, "Skipper" Williams, (see story just preceding):—

"Welch, God spare my days, if you aren't the most arnery, cantankerius, insulting barstard it was ever my misfortune to know."

IN PARIS FOR FARIS IN 1920s, VARIED LIFE OF AN I.N.S. MAN

Barry Faris, International News Service editor-in-chief for over 40 years, was a genius in managing his relatively small staff to extract from them a maximum of news beats and exclusives. He did it without sacrificing spot news coverage in the hot competition with AP and UP.

Faris was on the job 24 hours a day and never took a vacation. He was always quick and generous with praise when it was deserved. During the post-war depression in the early twenties, when wire service bureau managers were earning forty dollars a week, Barry sent me a thousand-dollar bonus for my scoop on the top-secret log of the German U-boat that sank the *Lusitania*.

But Barry was even quicker with scorching cables that singed his foreign staff and kept them nervously on their toes. INS correspondents had many Faris stories, but their favorite was the three messages he sent to the London bureau. The first day, Barry messaged:

"CONGRATULATIONS CLEAN BEAT REGARDS FARIS."

The second day:

"YOUR EXCLUSIVE UPPLAYED BIGGEST UP-FOLLOW HARDEST REGARDS FARIS."

And the third day:

"YOUR STILL EXCLUSIVE STOP WHY STOP RUSH EXPLANATION FASTEST FARIS."

Karl Bickel, when he was President of UP, used to tell me that luck for a newsman simply meant that he was there when it happened.

Once, my good luck was the opposite. I wasn't there, when,

as Paris bureau manager, I was on the train to Rome when my staff killed Pope Benedict XV for American Saturday afternoon and Sunday papers more than 15 hours before the Pontiff died.

Two months later when I returned to Paris after covering the election and coronation of Pius XI, the inevitable Faris order for an explanation was cabled confidentially to my apartment and not to the office.

I explained, but discreetly. New to Paris, I had learned that the correspondents were very different from those I had known when I was manager of the Berlin and London bureaus. When Barry Faris reads this, now, 44 years later, he will learn that the false flash on the Pope's death was just another Paris tale of our newsmen's game called: *"Cherchez la femme!"*

The story of the premature papal death started with my INS predecessor in Paris clinking cognac glasses with a special correspondent of *The New York Times* in Harry's New York Bar in the rue Daunou. A few more cognacs, and they became confidential about their troubles. None of the accepted, traditional methods of padding expense accounts was providing sufficient francs to meet the increasingly nagging demands of both a wife and a mistress in Paris. The cost of living was rising rapidly.

A few more cognacs, and the two newsmen toyed with the idea of putting their mistresses on the office payroll as employees. Then one of them had a better idea. Each would put the other fellow's mistress on his payroll. Surely, Mr. Ochs could not complain if one of the girls in the office just happened to be carrying on a secret love affair with a newspaperman who worked for Hearst.

So when I reported at 38 rue des Petits Champs to take over the INS Paris bureau, I was introduced to a breathtakingly beautiful young blonde and told she was my secretary.

She knew no shorthand, and her typing was terrible. My friend, Guy Hickok of the *Brooklyn Eagle,* told me the payroll deal between *The New York Times* and INS men amused the other correspondents as in the spirit of Murger's *Vie Boheme.* Guy warned me not to fire her without having a good case, as American newsmen in Paris were jealous of their Bohemian traditions. He didn't want me, as a new man, to get off on the wrong foot.

Several days later, while I was pondering Hickok's advice, I received an urgent cable from Barry Faris to rush to Rome to take charge. Barry, who had ways of his own of keeping his finger on most of his bureaus, had learned that the Rome correspondent was covering the death watch on Pope Benedict XV from a Frascati Wine Tavern. Later, Barry told me that he was receiving more Frascati than fact in the dispatches from Rome.

In those days before the use of teletypes, foreign correspondents in Paris, Rome, and Berlin were required to file all messages at the main telegraph office, where only one window with a single clerk was assigned to handle their dispatches. The clerk would deliberately count the words in a message, figure the price, and affix the necessary rubber stamps before considering the next message. Consequently, when big international stories broke, the long press line-up at the telegraph window might delay transmission an hour or more. So it was standard practice for all of the large European news bureaus to backstop each other on important news breaks.

Before leaving for Rome, I arranged for our Paris bureau to backstop Rome on the flash of the Pope's death, in case the news should reach our Paris newspaper editor tipsters, before we were able to clear the dispatch from Rome.

Bill Cook of my staff and I wrote four identical news flashes that the Pope was dead, to hold for release. They were to be sent by each of the four cable and radio companies that had service between France and New York. We also wrote flashes to go to our London bureau in Fleet Street to be relayed to New York.

Bill Cook's weakness was the Longchamps and Auteuil horse races. With his new boss off on the train to Rome, Bill decided to go to the races. He handed the sheaf of hold-for-release flashes on the Pope's death to the office secretary and said:

"I have to go out for a few hours. If any of the Paris paper tipsters phones that the French press had a flash the Pope is dead, give these to the office boy and tell him to rush them to the Bourse telegraph office."

Shortly after Cook left, Kathleen Brennan, an Irish newspaperwoman, came in looking for Cook. She engaged our *New York Times* Beauty Queen in a desultory conversation, during which she casually asked:

"Have you heard the Pope died?"

"Oh that reminds me," said Beautiful-but-Dumb. She called the office boy, handed him the hold-for-release flashes and sent him to the telegraph office. She was totally oblivious that she was detonating an explosion in newspaper offices in the United States which would result in some 500 papers remaking their front pages or getting out special editions.

The INS report on the Pope's death remained exclusive. AP and UP sent denials from Rome. In New York turmoil engulfed Barry Faris. His urgent queries to the Paris bureau brought no replies. INS stuck to its story. Fifteen hours later, Benedict XV quietly died.

* * *

Three months later, Bill Cook, who, *in absentia* had killed the Pope, was succeeded by Fred Abbott as assistant bureau manager. Abbott had come from Boston to France in 1916 as a volunteer ambulance driver. He married a French girl and settled down. A smiling, collar-ad blond American, Fred Abbott walked the Paris boulevards and literally turned the Parisiennes' heads for a second look at him. In his affairs with French women he was always the pursued and not the pursuer. He became proficient in the seductive subjunctives of Bedroom French. And he was the bait that landed a series of INS Paris exclusive stories for Barry Faris.

One of Fred Abbott's exclusive beats, with the help of the close friendship of a Paris woman, backfired badly. Again it was a death watch. And again, Barry Faris had to cable us: "PLEASE EXPLAIN."

Sarah Bernhardt was old and feeble. She had been a sensation during the gay nineties, when, on her worldwide theatrical tours, she boasted that she had accompanied her lover aloft to be the first woman to *faire l'amour* in a balloon. She had made repeated "farewell tours" of American theaters. Her death would be a big story.

Fred Abbott and I talked it over to lay our lines for a beat. We planned that Fred should get acquainted with some one inside Bernhardt's home. Very soon, Fred was regularly entertaining Madame Normand, who, for many years, had been Bernhardt's secretary and companion.

The day came when, as Fred had arranged, Madame Normand telephoned him to come at once as Bernhardt was in a coma and death was near. So Fred scored a world-wide beat on the dying Bernhardt.

As we waited we continued to cable exclusive hourly bulletins from Bernhardt's home, where Fred was comfortably settled and using the actress's telephone. Then Fred telephoned me that Madame Normand had stormed into the salon, and grabbing him by the arm, pulled him to the window. Screaming invective, she pointed toward the street, where twenty to thirty newsmen and photographers had assembled in response to our bulletins.

Madame Normand said it was a disgrace that the press wouldn't let the old lady die in peace and that the press was like a pack of hungry dogs attracted by a bitch in heat. She ordered Fred to go out and make them leave. Fred didn't think Madame Normand's simile was exactly loyal to her mistress, but he tried to soothe her. He stayed where he was.

An hour later, he telephoned me that Bernhardt's physician demanded that he should not tie up the telephone wire. So Fred had promised not to telephone again until he called me with the death flash.

The hours wore on. No further calls came from Fred. Suddenly, our beat, for which Fred and I had planned so carefully, was shattered. A cable from Faris in New York said that Apathy, our code name for Associated Press, was featuring a story that Bernhardt had momentarily emerged from her coma, had motioned her secretary to her bedside, and in a scarcely audible voice had whispered a final, farewell message for her dear American public. UP also carried the Bernhardt quotes.

I had cabled Faris that Fred Abbott was the only newsman inside the Bernhardt home. He ordered me to rush an explanation, fastest.

I could not call Fred at the Bernhardt home. After our first bulletins, the phone had rung incessantly as French, American, and British newsmen called. Fred helpfully answered for Madame Normand, who remained in Bernhardt's bedroom. When he suggested that the jangling telephone might disturb the dying woman, Madame Normand had quickly approved his idea of disconnecting the bells to silence it.

Faris's second peremptory cabled demand for an explanation of our being beaten by both AP and UP arrived about 8:00 p.m. It was 3:00 p.m. in New York and noon on the West Coast. I quickly typed a note to Fred to telephone me immediately. If he could not use the Bernhardt phone, he was to leave the house and go to the nearest coin telephone. I told him what Faris had said about the opposition's beat.

Fred had happily told me that Madame Normand had followed his suggestion to order the servants not to open the door or talk to the crowd of newsmen on the street. How would I get the message through? I grabbed a bottle from the office medicine cabinet, and around it wrapped my message. I instructed our French office boy to take a taxi to the Bernhardt home and to tell the servants it was important to get the bottle of medicine to the *Monsieur Americain* immediately.

Half an hour later, Fred phoned from a tobacco shop. He branded the AP and UP stories as outright fakes. Bernhardt had hovered, scarcely breathing, between life and death all day and had never emerged from her coma.

I asked Fred if he could get through the crowd of newsmen on the death watch and back into the Bernhardt house. He assured me he had tipped a servant handsomely to wait at the door until he got back.

The street was empty when he returned to the Bernhardt home. The servant let him in and told Fred he had scarcely left the house when the physician descended the stairs, went out into the street, and made the death announcement to the waiting press.

Fred Abbott rushed to the Bernhardt telephone. I released the previously prepared death flashes. No more than five minutes later, it seemed, Faris' third cable arrived that the opposition was carrying the death flash. We were beaten over half an hour.

The next day, when they met at the Foreign Office press

conference, Abbott challenged Tom Topping of the Associated Press with the fake Bernhardt farewell message. Topping was a lusty, boastful, earthy hulk of a man who was built like a piano mover. He gloried in being the most adroit and notorious faker in the foreign press corps.

Topping offered no apology or excuse. Instead he warned Fred that this should teach him a lesson never to try to sew up a story and exclude Topping. The UP correspondent did apologize to Fred. He said Topping had worked out the text and handed it to him with the suggestion that if both AP and UP carried it, any INS denial would carry no weight. The UP man told Fred that they were so badly beaten on the early bulletins, he could not risk another beating by AP on the text. So he sent it.

* * *

Yes, competition was keen. And competition was increased by the clustering of colony of American correspondents in a single apartment house, opposite the Paris fortifications, at 8 Square Desnouettes.

My wife and I were on the second floor. Webb Miller, the UP bureau manager, Wilbur Forrest, *New York Herald-Tribune* correspondent, Harold Hall, later business manager of *The New York Times,* John Chapman of the *New York Daily News,* Bob Curry of the *Christian Science Monitor,* Herbie Davidson of my INS staff, Herbert Brucker, for the last 20 years editor of the *Hartford Courant,* Rose Wilder Lane the novelist, and two Chicago artists, Jamie and Dorothy Dulin all lived in the house.

Our wives visited back and forth. They shopped together. One morning my office telephone rang, and the voice of my wife anxiously asked:

"Where is the big story breaking? Do you want me to pack your bag and bring it to the office?"

"What big story?" I countered. "Everything is quiet here. What are you driving at?"

"Well," she replied, "when I walked to the garage this morning with Bill Forrest to get our cars, Bill was carrying his traveling bag. I asked him where he was going. He told me he was going to the American Hospital for a check-up. I told Bill he didn't look sick to me and asked what's troubling him. Bill gave me a funny, evasive answer. He said he's off his golf game and he's going into the hospital for a couple of days to find out what is wrong with him."

I was worried. We again combed the Paris press. Not a thing! We called our tipsters on French newspaper desks. Nothing! Finally, Fred Abbott telephoned the American Hospital. He asked if they had admitted a patient named Wilbur Forrest.

"Just a minute," replied the voice. "Yes, he registered in this morning."

We relaxed.

To our present jet age of telestar TV and quick trans-Atlantic telephone calls, the American correspondents of 1920 must look curiously stuffy. We wore spats and carried canes.

With only two hours to pack for herself and me, before she met me at the Paris PLM Railroad Station in February 1922 to rush to Rome to cover the Vatican story, my wife did not forget to take my white tie and tails and to bring my high silk hat in its own oval leather hat box. And I wore that regalia, too, for it was obligatory at the funeral of Benedict XV and the coronation of Pius XI.

And perhaps also, I was being a bit self-consciously stuffy when I signed the name of Herbie Davidson of our INS staff to my Quatz Arts Ball story, instead of using my own by-line.

Newspapermen were taboo at this bohemian event of the year. I persuaded my neighbor, Jamie Dulin, a bona fide and successful American artist, to let me go with him. First we went to the Julien Academie Atelier in the rue de Dragon to undress, to leave all our clothes and to smear our almost nude bodies with yellow ochre and stale beer. For the theme of the Ball was Egypt one thousand years before Christ. Our costume was limited to dancing pumps, a loin cloth, strings of wooden beads and a helmet. The helmets were tin kitchen colanders, upside down over which we had clamped inverted tin funnels from which stuck gaily colored feather dusters.

When we reached Luna Park for the Ball, we had to pass the inspection and scrutiny of a committee at the door. As we gave up our admission tickets and were greeted with nods of approval on our costumes, one of the committee members perfunctorily asked Jamie Dulin a tricky question on how to mix certain colors. Jamie was tongue-tied and his French answer came in a stutter. Impatiently, the doorman swished a couple of strokes of red housepaint over Jamie's nude back with a wide brush. Branded with paint, Jamie couldn't get in. In the confusion I evaporated through the door and lost myself among the semi-nude art students and models on the floor.

By 6 a.m., I was back at the Julien Academie to work off the yellow ochre and beer—and to dress and go to the INS office. In those prudish days of Prohibition, before bikinis and Playboy clubs, it seemed a trifle daring to cable a feature story about dancing the night away with nude artists' models. I had a lot of fun writing my story. But I hesitated about adding my signatures. After all, I was cabling weekly think-pieces on financial and economic trends. And would Barry Faris get the idea that I was spending my nights in Montmartre?

When Herbie Davidson arrived at the office and read the file—with his name on the Quatz Arts Ball story, he anxiously asked:

"What will my mother say when she reads this?"

Six months later, responding to urgent pleas from his parents to return to the United States, Herbie wrote personal letters to 100 American editors applying for a job.

By return mail he received three offers which were based on his feature story on the Quatz Arts Ball. One of the editors wrote that his paper could always use a reporter who could coin a phrase like "dancing with a living Venus clad only in dancing pumps and a string of beads of perspiration."

—FRANK E. MASON, March 1968

GREAT SILURIANS OF PAST,
RECALLED IN APPRECIATION

A very important part of the history of the Silurian Society is on the masthead, which reminds us that we exist for Good Fellowship and Happy Memories and were founded in 1924.

We meet semiannually to fraternize, spread good fellowship and discuss newspaper adventures that leave happy memories of the long association with reporters, editors, cartoonists, and others in editorial branches of newspapers.

While the *Silurian News* is only seventeen years old, it has published stories about great reporters who worked on our dailies before the turn of the century, and among our members were such famous departed writers as Herbert Bayard Swope, Richard M. Clarke, Gene Fowler, Meyer Berger, Poultney Bigelow, George E. Sokolsky, William Orr, Martin Green, James Hagerty, Martin Dunn, Charles S. Hand, Joseph and Eugene E. Early, John A. Heffernan, Fulton Oursler, Jack Binns, Ross Duff Whytock, Chester Beecroft, Rupert Hughes, and Jim Loughborough.

The originator of the *Silurian News* was our revered friend and former president of the Silurian Socity, Eugene E. Early, who died in 1956. Gene, while a star reporter on the *Globe,* operated with his brother, Joe, a newspaper in Jamaica, Long Island, called the *Queens Evening News.* I had been on the *Globe* with Gene, so I was elected fall guy, or associate editor, at the beginning.

The hardiness of Silurians is manifest in the great number of members who were famous in their eighties and even nineties. They made newspaper history before and after the turn of the century, after years of constant competition, starting with salaries as low as $10 per week but always competing for the exclusive stories that would make them notable figures in the newspaper field and, eventually, star reporters, writers, and editors.

Our records do not show that any of the great Silurians who achieved fame as leaders in their profession reached the century mark, but many came close to doing so. For instance, there was Dr. Maurice J. Lewi, who died in 1957, just a few weeks before his 100th birthday. About ten years before he died he had been named an Honorary Member of the Society because of his amazing ability as a speaker. In his late nineties he received a standing ovation at many Silurian dinners for his keen wit and interest in the Society's battles to preserve free speech.

Dr. Lewi once admitted that, although he had practiced medicine for almost 75 years, his earliest ambition was to become a journalist. "Oh, how I did want to be a scribe," he said to the writer. "I was a correspondent in my youth for an Albany newspaper. My association with you Silurians has made me realize how much pleasure I missed while my brother, Isaac Lewi, spent most of his life as a reporter and editor on the old *New York Tribune*—and as a Silurian before my time. Isaac experienced newspaper thrills to the last days of his life —as shall I."

He had been ill a good part of 1957. But Dr. Lewi had said he would speak at the dinner. He was too weak to get out of bed that night, but the New York Telephone Company set up a special wire from his bedside in an apartment on Amsterdam Avenue to the Silurian banquet hall in the Waldorf Astoria. At the appropriate time George Sokolsky telephoned him to wish him a happy forthcoming birthday in behalf of all Silurians. "I thank you and the Silurians who are listening in," he said. "Tell them I shall fight to be with them for another hundred years!" Three weeks later Dr. Lewi passed away in his sleep.

We must also not forget Poultney Bigelow. Although incapacitated through a fall during the last six of his 99 years, Bigelow kept himself in condition by wielding an axe and crosscut saw, building a wood pile. He was one of the truly great Silurians and journalists. Lawyer, newspaperman, lecturer, and author, he had crossed the Atlantic Ocean more than one hundred times; had traveled around the world in a sailboat; knew all of Asia and Africa and always fought pugnaciously for the things he belived in. He was a member of the French Legion of Honor, and was expelled from Russia for his capitalistic views.

There are ever so many more old-timers that I should like to write about, but I shall just name a few, with final ages: Charles A. White, 92; John A. Hennesy, 91; William O. Inglis, 88; Walter Scott Meriwether, 87; Moses Hyman, 87; Post Wheeler, 84; Samuel Blythe, 82; Deltus Edwards, 85; Edward D'Oench Tittman, 82.

—WILLIAM J. BREDE, October 1964

HIS PEERS AND CONTEMPORARIES; STAR REPORTER LOOKS THEM OVER

The greatest leg man I ever knew was Mike Claffey, who worked on the *New York Journal-American* for sixteen years until he died in December 1942, at the age of 45.

Mike had personality plus. The infectious Claffey grin, his curly reddish hair and brash manner opened all doors. He could get the news. Once, in the 1930s, while covering a trial in Foley Square, the judge was about to hand down an important decision. Several of us left the press table and eased our way to the police-guarded courtroom door.

When the judge announced his decision, we tried to get out. The cops said, "Oh, no, you don't." Mike spoke up: "Say, Officer, my coat is caught in the door!" A cop opened the door a bit and Mike pranced out with the flash. The rest of us were stymied and couldn't get out.

In those Park Row days there was an abundance of journalistic talent writing for the New York newspapers and press associations. There was the incomparable Damon Runyon and his good friend Gene Fowler.

And other stars such as Westbrook Pegler, Bill Corum, Charlie Hand, George Buchanan Fife, Martin Green, Edwin C. Hill, Heywood Broun, Jim Hagerty, John O'Donnell, Meyer Berger, Russell Porter, Bruce Rae, Alva Johnston, Frank Ward O'Malley.

Those fellows could write.

One of the best all-round tabloid reporters of the 1930s was the colorful Frank (Red) Dolan of the *New York Daily News*. Walter Winchell, Louis Sobol, Ed Sullivan and Mark Hellinger were making reputations for themselves as tabloid columnists.

On International News Service was a real star—George R.

Holmes our Washington bureau manager and one of the most brilliant writers in the business. Holmes's ability in covering a breaking story or a national political convention has never been surpassed.

William K. Hutchinson and George Durno were also stars of the Washington staff. Durno traveled with FDR. "Hutch" became noted for his scoop on the judge's decision in the famous "monkey" trial at Dayton, Tenn.

I worked out of the INS New York office, covering major news events all over the country and abroad. I went to work for Faris in Chicago in 1920. My first big assignment was covering the Herrin (Ill.) Massacre of June 22, 1922.

Later, when I was transferred to New York in 1923, Faris assigned me to one big story after another right up to the day INS folded in 1958. Beginning with the Hall-Mills trial, I covered dozens of courtroom dramas, including the trial of Bruno Richard Hauptmann for the kidnap-killing of the Lindbergh baby.

I also covered disasters, executions, sit-down strikes, the Dionne quintuplets, murder mysteries, and World War II in the Pacific, Africa, Italy and ETO. Over the years I interviewed people in the news such as Bernard M. Baruch, Henry Ford, Thomas A. Edison, John D. Rockefeller, Peaches Browning, Peggy Hopkins Joyce, Al Capone—and many others.

My two biggest stories, I guess, were (1) covering the six weeks trial of Hauptmann in Flemington, N.J. and his subsequent execution, and (2) being one of the three American reporters to witness the signing of the German surrender at Gen. Eisenhower's headquarters in Rheims in 1945.

Memories of fine newspapermen we had in INS at one time or other come back to me. Years ago we had Floyd Gibbons. Later we had Paul Gallico, Quentin Reynolds, and Malcolm

Johnson. Pierre J. Huss was one of our best war correspondents, and subsequently head of our United Nations staff. Richard Tregaskis of Guadalcanal fame was another of our war correspondents.

J. Kingsbury Smith, later publisher of the *New York Journal-American,* turned in one of the greatest journalistic scoops I have ever heard about. As European general manager of INS, stationed at the time in Paris, he managed to engage in correspondence with Premier Joseph Stalin of Russia.

In January 1949, Stalin sent Smith an exclusive written reply to four questions the correspondent had submitted to him. Among other things, Stalin declared he was willing to meet President Truman to achieve a "pact of peace," banning war between the U.S. and the Soviet Union.

In the last fifteen years of its existence, INS had a great reporter-columnist, Bob Considine. There isn't anything in the writing line, news or sports, that the highly productive and capable Considine can't do.

Under the editorship of Barry Faris, the slogan of International News Service was "Get it first, but first get it right." INS had a magnificent record for accuracy and speed.

He ran the service for more than 40 years.

BF, incidentally, was mighty nice about expense accounts, too. Years ago I covered the Samuel Insull story which took me all the way to Turkey. Insull was being extradited by the U.S. and I became friends with him on the way back to New York on the *S.S. Exilona.*

On deck one day while I was typing out my expense account, Insull came along glanced over my shoulder and exclaimed:

"And they indicted me!"

—April 1962

Jim Bishop, who has authored 14 books, including *The Day Lincoln was Shot,* once told me:—

"I write fast. I write once. I never rewrite, polish, revise, or kill. As a matter of discipline, I permit myself one swing, and one only. In this way I am forced to do my best.

"This goes for books, magazine articles, and columns. I never read a book I have written. It is enough to see it as a book, and heft it. To read it would invite nausea, not because I am ashamed of anything I've written, but because I know, without reading it, that I could have done a little better."

Bishop started his career as a $12-a-week copy boy on the *New York Daily News* and soon caught on as a cub reporter. He became a protegé of the late Mark Hellinger, who taught him "the ABC's of Writing." When Hellinger was lured to the *Daily Mirror,* Bishop went along. Bishop now writes a column for King Features Syndicate.

Bishop was 46 when he wrote his best seller, *The Day Lincoln was Shot,* which sold 3,000,000 copies and is available in many languages. He is now 62. Speaking of the Lincoln book, he said:—

"When I decided to write it, I quit everything, took my research home (24 years' off-and-on work on Lincoln), and wrote the book in 31 days."

—JAMES L. KILGALLEN, October 1970

Footnote on Kilgallen

In the late twenties, when I was president of INS, Barry Faris and I looked over our stable to pick a top man to build up as a star, roving reporter. Jimmie Kilgallen was the obvious choice.

This was before TV had made shootings, mayhem, and murder the steady diet of the American people enthralled before the picture tubes in their parlors. Sorry, we don't have parlors any more. But Jimmie and I can remember when we held hands with our best girls in the front parlor.

So in those simple days, gangsters, gun molls, and bootleggers were the stories to be covered by our roving star reporter. When Jimmie returned from Cincinnati, where he covered the murder trial of Bootlegger George Remus for shooting his wife, he dropped into my office and said:

"Frank, I had a funny experience with Remus. Of course I took a room in the same hotel where he was staying. When I stopped at the desk one evening, the clerk handed me a note. It was from Remus and asked me to drop by his room—he had something for me. I expected an exclusive story.

"Remus yelled 'Come in!' when I knocked. He was sitting at a table in the center of the room. On the table were stacks of ten- and twenty-dollar bills with rubber bands around them. Remus made a gesture of pushing the money toward me and said:

" 'Here, Jimmie. You can use this. I don't need it.' I tried in a nice way to thank Remus and tell him I didn't want it. He kept insisting. Finally, I told Remus I had never seen so much cash money outside of a bank teller's cage, and asked how much there was there. Remus said seventy-five hundred dollars. Well, Frank, I just turned and walked out. There was no use arguing with Remus. With the depression on, Remus couldn't understand why anyone would turn down money."

—FRANK E. MASON, October 1968

WHEN DIGNITY WAS IN FLOWER, AND $5 MORE WAS IRRESISTIBLE

My first newspaper job was on the financial staff of the old *Evening Telegram* just before Frank Munsey bought it.

In those days you could just walk into a newspaper office and ask for a job, but it was considered better strategy, especially for somebody who had never worked on a paper, to be more formally introduced. I had been freshly fired by a New York bank for putting one of the vice-president's Merry Christmas letters into the wrong envelope and since my grandfather had got me the bank job my father bounced me back to him.

Grandpa, as a member of the Union League Club, had a lot of acquaintances in the right circles, and these included an editor of the *New York Tribune*. Grandpa recalled that I had edited a paper in school and therefore conceivably might do the same for a newspaper. He thought newspapers were less respectable than banks but if a bank wouldn't have me a newspaper might.

So I went to grandpa's office in downtown New York and the old gentleman took his cane and put on his square derby and we strolled up Nassau Street to the *Tribune* offices in a strong wind which blew grandpa's white beard over his shoulder. A *Tribune* junior editor said he was sorry, but they had no jobs, but he understood the financial editor of the *Evening Telegram* did want somebody.

Out of courtesy to grandpa the *Tribune* man, whose name I don't recall, gave me a letter of introduction to Arthur M. Chapman, financial editor of the *Telegram*. Grandpa said that since he didn't know Chapman socially I had better go down there myself. The *Telegram*'s financial news office was at 44 Broad Street.

Chapman, short, stout and balding, received me with old-fashioned courtesy. Yes, he did need a reporter, but he wasn't sure I had the qualifications. For three weeks I brought in to him everything I had ever written, which he studied with care. On the sixth interview he said I was hired; he would take a chance, but I couldn't expect more than $50 a week. I was elated; that was fabulous pay and 50 percent more than the bank had paid.

Arthur M. Chapman was British, with courtly manners, who knew finance and Wall Street. He always worked in shirt-sleeves with a derby hat, perched at a rakish angle, which he never took off. To J. P. Morgan and other financiers he was Chappie; to all others Mr. Chapman. He was a stickler for decorum in the office; if anybody made an ungentlemanly noise, sneezed, uttered an indelicate expression, or interrupted him in a conversation he would turn around and say sternly: "Excuse yourself." He wrote all his copy in bold and beautiful penciled script, a paragraph to a page of copy paper, and one of my first chores was to type these paragraphs for him before they went to the composing room up on Herald Square. The typewriters were those Remingtons where you had to lift up the platen and look on the underside to see what you had written. I did pretty well.

With my most aulic (I learned that word from Mr. Chapman) manners and as a good typist I got along nicely and in due course I was sent out on my first interview. "Always ask to see the president or the senior partner," said Chapman, and it is still good advice. I had to see on this occasion the head of the then famous firm of Lee, Higginson & Co., Mr. Frederic W. Allen, about a Swiss loan they were floating.

Mr. Allen's secretary said he wouldn't see me and I guess I looked pretty woebegone. "How long have you been a reporter?" she asked. "Two weeks," I said, adding that "it's awfully important to see him." She said: "Important to whom?" I murmured "To me." She said: "Wait a minute; I'll see what I can do." In a few seconds I was in the presence of the Great Man himself. He was kind and encouraging. Then he gave me all the details. I rushed back so fast I almost knocked over a horse on Broad Street. Mr. Chapman said it was a real exclusive and put a great big head on the story. He frowned on by-lines so I had to be content with the big head.

Chapman would put on his coat, take his cane, straighten his derby, and go and call on J. P. Morgan once a week. He used six of us small fry reporters to call on less important financiers and corporation presidents. His training of reporters was long remembered with gratitude and affection by all who worked for him; once every two months he would go up to the publisher on Herald Square and try to get us $2.50 a week raises. I got two of them. Finally another newspaper lured me away with an offer of a whole $5 a week more.

Years later I called on Mr. Chapman in his retirement at Coral Gables, Florida, a short time before he died, and he was overjoyed that I had looked him up. He had learned to drive a Ford automobile and showed me how well he could do it. He went to the garage, put his cane on the back seat, put his derby hat firmly on his head and got in the driver's seat. He started the motor, raced it, set it in reverse and in one swoop shot down the driveway and across the street, coming against the opposite curb with a resounding bump.

His neighbors said he always did it that way, which accounted for the two "STOP" signs that the Coral Gables police had thoughtfully erected on both sides of the Chapman driveway.

Chapman was always reticent about his early career, but he once did admit that he had served long in the Royal Navy, in the course of which he did some boxing and inadvertently became the heavyweight champion of Australia. Wasn't particularly proud of it. Made quite a bit of money buying the "wrong" stocks at the right time and thereby got interested in finance.

He took me to lunch once at Harry & Gus's cafe on New Street, where he had whiskey and I had coffee. At that time I didn't drink and rather proudly said I was a teetotaler. He was greatly pleased to hear it and told me to stay that way. When I got lost in admiration of the paintings of nude females for which Harry & Gus's place was famous, Chapman was disapproving. "After you get married, boy," he said, "you'll think all these things are third rate."

—ED TYNG, March 1954

JEMAIL INQUIRES OF JEMAIL, GETS HUMAN INTEREST AS USUAL

(This rich and sparkling account was dug out of the subject by the most experienced interrogator in the business, the Inquiring Fotographer himself. With this story, the author enclosed a note indicating his sentiments toward his fellow Silurians:—"I have consistently refused to do this for other publications, some for a fee. Too much work. But here it is.")

In 1921, Jimmy Jemail, in a Navy senior lieutenant's uniform, answered an ad in the *Daily News,* "Man wanted to work Sundays. $8.00." Mr. Noble, the employment manager, took one look at Jimmy in his uniform and said: "The job isn't for you. We need a Sunday watchman." (In those days there was no *Sunday News.* Only the daily.) Jimmy replied: "I'm not too proud. It pays eight bucks. I'll spend the other six days looking for a steady job" . . . and jobs were tough to find in the depression of 1921.

The next day, Jimmy was the Sunday watchman at the *News* building, 25 Park Place, still in his Lieut.'s uniform. (He had just been placed in the Fleet Reserve and had no civvies.)

At 10 a.m., a man came into the building and without looking at Jimmy, said: "Watchman, get me copies of all the Sunday papers." It was the city editor, Phil Payne. Jimmy got the papers, put them on the desk and said: "Here are your Sunday papers, Mr. Payne." Payne, seeing Jimmy in a lieut.'s uniform, replied: "Who are you?" And Jimmy said: "Jimmy Jemail."

"Any relation to the Brown University football player?" asked Payne. And Jimmy replied: "I played football at Brown, Mr. Payne."

A half-hour later, Payne sent for him and said: "We have a column in this paper which no one likes. It's a tough assignment. The reporter must stop people at random and interview them on any given question. Jack Chapman has had it for a week and says he would resign rather than continue with it. Would you like to try it?"

On May 1, 1921, Jimmy became the Inquiring Fotographer and started a fabulous career which has spanned 47 years. The *News* itself started only on June 26, 1919.

He has been mauled, has gotten into street fist fights, been threatened and even hauled away to a psychiatric ward. Once, he was almost shot by the secret service men when he forced his way through their ranks and asked President Truman: "Why do you like parades?" But he got his answer. Said the President: "I like parades because they make me feel like a big kid again."

Early in his career Jimmy asked a group of middle-aged Jersey City women: "Do you remember your first kiss and did you enjoy it?" The *Daily News* was then unknown in Jersey. Before the day was over, Jimmy was forcibly taken to the Medical Center. In the psychiatric ward, he kept on insisting that he was Jimmy Jemail, the Inquiring Fotographer of the *Daily News.* "Call the *News,* if you don't believe me. The number is Barclay 0400." A doctor finally called.

Harry Nichols, then Phil Payne's assistant at the city desk, got the call. He shouted to the City Room: "They've picked up Jemail as a nut in Jersey City." Then he barked into the telephone: "Doctor, we never heard of the guy."

Carton (forgot his first name, maybe Frank?) once called Jimmy and asked him if he could help the police get a raise in pay. Carton was the head of the Police Benevolent Association. Jimmy asked him to get six young married cops together, in uniform, cops with kids. He asked the six: "How much money do you take home to your wife and kids each week?" Their answers and head shots, in uniform, appeared during a session of the Board of Estimate. The highest amount taken home each week was $56 and the lowest, $32. As a direct result of the column, the Board of Estimate voted to pay 75% of the pension costs. Each cop got a raise of $9 a week.

Jimmy once asked France's President deGaulle: "Is the size of a man's nose an indication of character?"

Jimmy was born in Lebanon and came here when he was five. His tough, hard-working boyhood was the ideal background for his job. He was the first American of Lebanese ancestry to win an appointment to the U.S. Naval Academy. Jimmy had been a star athlete at Rogers High School in Newport, R.I., where he grew up, and he made the Navy football team as halfback in his plebe year, something unheard of before his time. Unfortunately he fractured two vertebrae. They wouldn't let him play in his second year. Football was his whole life, so he resigned and went to Brown University, played football and baseball for four years, and was halfback on the Brown team that played the first Rose Bowl game, New Year's Day, 1916.

Jimmy's work has been featured in a number of national magazines. When *Time* asked Jimmy what made his column so popular, he replied, "Human interest, sprinkled with humor, framed by common sense."

When the *Reader's Digest* ran a story on Jimmy, the magazine's Arabic edition brought an astounding reaction. He was invited by many "Jemails" to return to Lebanon for a visit. He flew back to Lebanon in 30 hours; it had taken 30 days to get here by steamer 50 years earlier. In Lebanon, Jimmy was greeted by the leaders and hosted by President Camille Chamoun. The Lebanese were especially captivated by Jimmy's charming wife, Natalie. Later, President Chamoun decorated Jimmy with the nation's highest honor for civilians, "Commander in the Order of the Cedars."

We asked Jimmy: "Of all your interviews, which remains most nostalgic in your memory?" There are several, but he thinks the one with President Kennedy tops them all. The security was the tightest he had ever seen, cops almost shoulder to shoulder. They all knew Jimmy and he got through to the reviewing stand on Fifth Ave. There the secret service men stood a few yards apart. How he got through them is a story in itself, but eventually he was sitting on the back of Mayor Wagner's chair in the reviewing stand. The President, flanked by all the brass, was standing, reviewing the parade. Jimmy nudged Wagner on the fanny. "How did you get here?" Wagner asked. "Never mind," replied Jimmy, "please introduce me." Later Bob Wagner confided to Jimmy that he was going to say, "Mr. President, this is Jimmy Jemail, the Inquiring Fotographer of the *Daily News.*"

He got as far as "Mr. President, this is Jimmy Jemail, the —" when Kennedy extended his hand and said: "Hello Jimmy, I've followed your column for years; I'm glad to catch up with you."

And Jimmy, taken aback, really taken aback, stammered, "After that greeting, how can I call you Mr. President? Jack, will you answer a question for my column?" "What is it?" asked the President. "My question is 'What is the height of your ambition?' " And everyone near him roared out laughing. As if the President hadn't already achieved it.

And when the laughter subsided, Jimmy said: "There isn't a good Inquiring Reporter in the crowd. Do you mean to suggest to me that just because Jack Kennedy is President of the

United States, he has no more ambitions; he is content to go along as he is? I refuse to believe it." Then, more formally, Jimmy said: "Mr. President, this is a legitimate question for a great newspaper. What is the height of your ambition?" And the President replied: "The height of my ambition is to always do well whatever I may be doing."

As he shook Jimmy's hand good-bye, Jack said: "Jimmy, my wife, Jackie, had a column like yours in the *Washington Times-Herald*. I used to read your column daily, pick out the best questions and answers, and suggest them to Jackie."

—JIMMY JEMAIL, April 1969

INDISPENSABLE CITY EDITOR,
NOT ALLOWED TO QUIT HIS JOB

The strangest city editor who ever sat in a newspaper office was the refined and poetic Caleb Dunn. He was constantly trying to lose his job on the *Star* and always failing. As a minor poet selling verse to some of the weeklies and once in a while to a magazine, with little monetary return, his ambition was to be one of the *Star* staff men, to wander in the outer air and pick up news for the paper to keep his pocketbook even with his necessities.

But this escape from his desk job was always denied him. He was too competent to be lost to the city desk for in his easy and graceful way he knew how to handle the men and the news. Again and again Caleb would inform the City Chamberlain (who was Chairman of the *Star* Board of Trustees) that he was quitting.

Ambitious Park Row newspaper men would be alertly after the job, for the *Star* paid the highest salaries in that period with the exception of the *New York Herald*. Word would come to Mr. Sandison, managing editor, that the Board of Trustees had appointed Mr. So-and-So to take over as city editor. But Sandison never made any effort to name a man in place of Caleb Dunn. He was too wise. Two such appointments came within six months of each other in 1880 before I was a full year on the *Star*.

John A. Greene, a well-built and handsome man, beardless and of deep olive complexion, from the *Tribune* was the first victim. His political background had won him the job for which he was well fitted—a fact he proved in after years of journalism. Mr. Greene was not aware that the *Star* staff would never let Caleb Dunn go for any long time. Most of its members would meet in Sweeney's hotel 200 feet from the office, agree that the newspaper would founder without the guiding mind of Caleb, then see the Chairman of the Board of Trustees and assure him that their fugitive city editor was too loyal to refuse to return.

The next move was to remind Caleb that the new city editor would bring with him four or five reporters of his own choice to displace Caleb's loyal followers. The poet in Caleb would take over. Sympathy would exude as this delightful man surrendered and avowed that, if asked to return, he would flll the old slot. I was one of five that Mr. Greene dropped from the *Star* with an extra week's pay. In another week, the combined genius of the staff, plus a little political pull caused the ousting of Greene and the return of Caleb.

The next victim in my time was William Muldoon of the *Brooklyn Eagle*. He was a bit blondish, about 30, tall, spare, and cold-looking. He wore a ruby pin in the centre of his shirt attached to a delicate gold chain which surrounded his neck. He entered the office in the early afternoon, attended by no fewer than six new members of a staff. He was sure he knew what he was going to do. I was among those told to take an extended rest. Well, there was an extra week's pay. The *Star* staff got to work at once. Mr. Muldoon lasted exactly two weeks and the cherubic Caleb Dunn, grieving but loyal, returned as of yore. Managing editor Sandison never intervened in these journalistic dramas. He knew how they would end, and he regarded Caleb Dunn as an irreplaceable genius in the handling of men and news.

But in the autumn of 1882, Caleb's heart was suffused with joy when he learned that Joseph Pulitzer was coming to New York the following spring to buy the then decrepit *New York World* from Jay Gould. Pulitzer arranged for the appointment of David A. Sutton of his St. Louis newspaper as city editor of the *Star*. He wanted Sutton to get the feel of New York for six months before he, Pulitzer, began his career in New York, and Dave Sutton was an instant success in the *Star* office.

On the second day he was calling all the men by their Christian names. He made it plain he was not making any changes and graciously told Caleb Dunn to make his own assignments and pick up news wherever his spirit guided him. When Dave Sutton departed to be the first of the Pulitzer city editors, Caleb was back in the slot once more and so remained for another year, when Tammany Hall sold the *Star*.

—JOHN A. HENNESSY, May 1951

"THE MONSIGNOR," FRIEND TO MANY, GENE FOWLER'S FINEST BOSS

Many of the able young men who came to Park Row at the time I arrived there in 1918 apparently were just as uncertain of themselves and as unsure of their abilities as I was. There were other greenhorns who owed much of their subsequent success—and some of them their very newspaper survival—to wise and helpful editors in their respective newspaper shops.

In my own case, one of the ablest but least "advertised" mentors was Martin Dunn of the *New York American*. Martin says he is semi-retired; but keeps in touch with his surviving fledglings by means of letters which seem to arrive when the spirits are a bit low.

"Don't let it get you down," he wrote to me two years ago, when it appeared as though my numeral was up once again at the hospital. "Unload your worries on the shoulders of the Lord. Worry is not easy to control. You need help from the General Manager in the sky. No harm in calling on Him."

How Martin Dunn knew of my state of mind, I cannot say. He always had a way of sensing things, as when some private trouble was bothering one of his reporters. And he would do something about it; quietly, efficiently, and, on occasion, with considerable risk to himself in shielding those whose morals were somewhat elastic.

I used to think that Martin kept me from being fired because he and I had been born in Denver, on the banks of Mullen's Mill Ditch. Later I found out that he not only loved his fellow men more than most editors did, but also loved the newspaper profession so much as to teach, guide, advise, and protect any young reporter who showed "promise."

We called him "The Monsignor" in the office. The nickname was given him either by Royal Daniel, Jr., or the late Martin Casey. I forgot which one of these bright young men gave him the handle, for somebody has mislaid the notes supplied me by that big-little veteran, Petey Campbell, everyone's friend. It seemed an appropriate title, affectionately bestowed, for its owner moved like a calm, reassuring army chaplain under fire on a battlefield—and our city room frequently was just that. Smiling always, and never losing his head or his sense of humor, he got the right things done at the right time.

Even the editors who disliked one another, and were constantly engaged in office intrigue, *all* liked and respected the Monsignor. His only ambition was to do his work well, and to help others do theirs efficiently, and to get out a good newspaper. He did not subscribe to Damon Runyon's advice to me when Damon brought me to New York:

"He who tooteth not his own horn, the same shall not be tooted."

The Monsignor never tooted his own horn. Nor did he have to toot it. There were many other members of the Hearst orchestra who got ahead because of their brassy solos; but most of them ran out of wind, and then out of sight. Three of them leaped from windows.

Martin Dunn got his early newspaper training in Denver, one of the fine schools for reporters and editors. He was a cub under that crabbed but remarkable Denver editor Josiah M. Ward. Martin worked alongside Charles Van Loan, Runyon, Nell Brinkley, Burns Mantle, George Creel, Paul Gregg,

Bide Dudley, Winifred Black ("Annie Laurie" in her San Francisco days), and many others. He left Denver to go to Chicago in 1908 to edit *The Railway Record*. That weekly trade paper had been financed by a group of railway executives.

Martin arrived in New York in 1909 to become a reporter for the *New York American*. Like some of the rest of us, he became homesick for the West. He was given a year's leave of absence, and returned to Denver, where he worked for the *Denver Times,* an afternoon paper owned by ex-Senator Thomas Paterson. He was successively a reporter, city editor, and editorial writer on the *Times*. Martin had friends on other Denver newspapers, including poet Arthur Chapman of the *Republican,* father of drama critic John Chapman, and author of "Out Where the West Begins," and William MacLeod Raine, and Courtney Ryley Cooper.

Martin returned to New York at about the time Damon Runyon was brought here by Charles Van Loan. From that time on he stayed in the Hearst Service, and held various posts: reporter, re-write man, city editor, and assistant managing editor.

When I last visited the offices of the *American* in South Street, I found Martin still interested in the careers of younger men. In fact he took great pride in telling me that Damon Runyon, Jr., was showing much ability as a journalist. Like several other sons of my illustrious colleagues, Damon, Jr. was fighting the shadow of a father's mighty name. It seems somewhat sad and unjust that this is so, but apparently any son or daughter of a celebrity has to overcome the "handicap" of having been born of an illustrious parent. Young Runyon is still working courageously and intelligently to prove that his very considerable talent is honestly come by, and authentic. I regret to say that a few of my old friends objected when the

----

lad wrote a revealing book which showed some of the human frailties of his otherwise great father.

Martin Dunn directed and planned the coverage of many well-remembered stories. His expert, steady editorial hand; his extraordinary sense of news values; his knowledge of politics, both local and national; and, above all, his integrity and his loyalty to his profession, are factors which set him apart as one of the finest editors during an era which produced some of the foremost editors and reporters and publishers of modern newspaper history.

—GENE FOWLER, November 1957

FURTHER MEMORIES—ROUNDING OUT THE CHERISHED PICTURE

From half a dozen obituary stories in *Silurian News,* the paragraphs here following seem to be necessary inclusions for our composite portrait.

Henry Beckett

Altogether, Henry Beckett was 57 years a reporter, beginning on the *Cincinnati Post,* then the *New York Herald* and the *New York Tribune,* then in 1924, going on to forty-four years at the *Post.* He saw active service in the Meuse-Argonne offensive in World War I, and at the age of 52 enlisted for W.W. II, where he became a sergeant.

Ike Gellis in his "Strictly Personal" column in the *Post* on Dec. 24, wrote about him:—

"The tennis world lost its biggest fan today. More important, the world lost the most decent, most gentle, most beautiful man I have ever known."

Here are a couple of incidents from Earl Wilson's column:—

"A city editor once complained to one of his reporters that Henry's expense account was about $2.75 and that this other reporter's, for covering the same assignments, was about $23.50.

" 'What's the trouble?' " the city editor demanded.

" 'Henry,' replied the other reporter, 'just never learned how to make out an expense account.' "

One day when he was alone in the news room, he answered a phone. An indignant reader protested the handling of a story in such vituperation that another reporter would have cursed back searingly.

"I am sorry," Henry answered gently. "I am just a reporter

and am not authorized to accept insults for the paper. You'll have to call one of the executives tomorrow if you wish to insult the paper."

Henry wrote an "overnight" covering his own departure. That is, he arranged with the Rev. Donald S. Harrington of the Community Church, his pastor and long-time friend, for the kind of memorial he wished, and left a concluding statement to be read, as follows, in part:—

"When I was five weeks old my mother died and with sadness for that I now express my thanks to her for giving me life. I am grateful to the grandparents and uncles and aunts who cared for me, to cousins and friends who instructed me and were kind.

"I am grateful for my years at Miami University, Oxford, Ohio, and for the aid and companionship of many men and women met in newspaper work. I am grateful for all of my military service, on the Mexican Border and in two World Wars, and for the comradeship there.

"I give thanks because of my feeling for four men who have lived during my lifetime: Theodore Roosevelt, Arturo Toscanini, Winston Churchill, and Dr. Albert Schweitzer.

"God to me is a mystery. I am uncertain of God's nature. But among God's creatures, I have found courage, faith, hope, kindness, compassion, goodness, truth, and most of all loyalty and love, and I have tried to live in the trust that they are the attributes of God and that I should cultivate them."

—**March 1970**

John Steinbeck

Five days before Christmas the Silurian Society lost its only Nobel Prize winner for Literature—John Steinbeck.

Steinbeck became a Silurian shortly after publication of his novel, *East of Eden*, in the winter of 1952–53, one of the 90 new members of that famous roundup conducted by Carl C. Dickey as membership chairman.

According to *The Times* obituary, he was fired from his job as reporter, and is not in recent Silurian rosters for the same reason as others who failed to keep paying their dues. There is a memo of his, however, resurrected from the archives, which pictures the young beginner:—

"When I came to New York in 1925 I had never been in a city in my life. My knowledge of the city was blurred. My uncle got me a job on a newspaper—the *New York American* down on William St. I didn't know the first thing about being a reporter. The $25 a week they paid me was a total loss. They gave me stories to cover in Queens and Brooklyn, and I would get lost and spend hours trying to find my way back. I couldn't learn to steal a picture from a desk when a family refused to be photographed, and I invariably got emotionally involved and tried to kill the whole story.

"But for my uncle, I think they would have fired me the first week. Instead they gave me Federal Courts in the Old Park Row Post Office. Why, I will never know.

"I wonder if I could ever be as kind to a young punk as those men in the reporters' room at the Post Office were to me. They pretended that I knew what I was doing, and they did their best to teach me in a roundabout way. I learned to play bridge and where to look for suits and scandals. They informed me which judges were pushovers for publicity and several times they covered me when I didn't show up. You can't repay that kind of thing . . . New York is the world with every vice and blemish and beauty, and there's privacy thrown in. What more could anyone ask? . . ."

(Who was the uncle? Anybody know?)

—April 1969

Paul Crowell

From the moment Paul joined the staff of *The New York Times* on March 8, 1928, he was a factor to be reckoned with on the New York scene.

A Silurian of many years standing, Paul in 1952 received a special award of the Society for his "integrity as a newspaperman."

Paul liked to say that his relations with the long line of New York's Mayors that he saw come and go were friendly. Nevertheless his penetrating writing and his gift for accurate analysis frequently angered—in particular—the "Little Flower"—sometimes known as "Butch."

One time the edgy LaGuardia wanted to make one final effort to bring Paul around to the Mayor's way of thinking on some issue over which the two had been in sharp disagreement. The Mayor invited Paul, at the end of a City Hall day, to ride up to Gracie Mansion with him and "talk it out" en route. Paul did so, but his disagreement was as definite as ever.

"Aw," said Paul, as Fiorello tried to make a well-worn point, "this is where I came in."

"No, Paul," snapped the enraged Mayor, "this is where you get out."

There, in the upper, remote reaches of the East Side Drive, the mayoral limousine was stopped, the door was opened and a rather surprised Paul Crowell was ushered out, to dodge traffic and make his way back to *The Times* City Room as best he could.

Many news executives take the attitude that "the customer is always right," when some one complains about their reporters. Not so, Arthur Hays Sulzberger, publisher of *The Times* during 25 of Paul's 36 *Times* years, in disputes that involved Crowell. Time and again LaGuardia sent letters de-manding that Paul be fired. Each such letter Mr. Sulzberger sent, through channels, to Paul with an intra-office memo checked: "What can I answer to this?" Paul would duly write a reply and send it to the publisher who would sign it and send it off to City Hall.

For all their differences, Paul respected Fiorello. But, in the sweep of his long tenure at Room 9 City Hall, there were some high city officials Paul did not respect. Such opinions, of course, never were reflected in his writings. But his personal comments could be acid. At one time, when a comment or action by a high civic figure particularly disgusted Paul, he turned to a Room 9 colleague and said:

"There are times when a man must rise above principle."

Another time Paul was expressing his personal contempt for an official we will call Commissioner X. Paul said he would very much like to write a news story saying:

"An empty limousine drew up in front of City Hall and Commissioner X got out."

—CHARLES G. BENNETT, October 1970

Frank MacMaster

Frank McMaster, 80 years old, died on June 20. He had retired in 1969 from the *Long Island Daily Press,* after hav-ing covered City Hall for half a century—longer, it was said, than any other reporter had ever done. Here is how one of his friends remembers him.

Against the drabness of New York City life and politics, the City Hall in general and Room 9 in particular were gayer, more lighthearted places throughout the many years Frank MacMaster worked there, because he was part of them.

There was the day at the Board of Estimate, at a jammed meeting in its own chamber. A certain item was called and several New Yorkers of substance rose and stood facing the board. Some reporters, including MacMaster, sat at the press table between the speakers and the board. One of the petitioners began to talk.

"Please give your name first," said Council President Paul Screvane, interrupting the speaker. The speaker, paused, incredulous that any New Yorker, let alone the Council President, should fail to recognize him.

"Why," he sputtered. "I'm Nizer. Louis Nizer." He paused.

Out of the momentary dead silence then came the stage whisper of Frank MacMaster—heard all over the room:

"Mr. Nizer, do you spell that with an 's' or a 'c'?" In the roar that followed, the name seemed to lose weight.

Over the years—before police guards began accosting people at City Hall's doorway—brides- and grooms-to-be often came to that historic structure looking for the Marriage License Bureau. In his kindly, fatherly fashion, Frank noticed them in the rotunda and would direct them to the bureau on the 2nd floor of the nearby Municipal Building. He rarely failed to recognize these bashful, giggling altar-bound couples.

But one memorable day the City Hall corridor was jammed with distinguished guests arriving for a ceremony. Frank was on hand. Through the front doorway then came a handsome young couple, the wife obviously soon to have a visit from the stork. Frank, all solicitude, stepped up and spoke to them: "Would you like to know how to get to the Marriage License Bureau?"

The couple looked at him blankly, then broke into laughter. The husband, a well-known scientist and educator, was arriving to participate on the program, one of the speakers at the ceremony.

Came a day when the National Democratic Club was about to hang on its walls, with appropriate ceremony, a portrait of one of its recently retired former presidents.

An invitation came to Frank MacMaster. It so happened that the portrait's subject had served for some time at City Hall in an official capacity and during that interval had made himself particularly obnoxious to the press. Frank's recollection of him was scarcely pleasant. His reply to the Club's invitation deserves its own place among classic documents.

"I very much regret," Frank wrote, in effect, "that a previous engagement will keep me from attending the hanging of the portrait. But if, at any time in the future, your organization decides to hang the original of the portrait, the undersigned will be pleased to break any and all previous engagements in order to be on hand."

Frank insisted, to the end of his life, that this story was apocryphal. But the twinkle in his eye that accompanied it failed to convince.

—CHARLES G. BENNETT, October 1972

Barry Faris

Barry Faris died in Kansas of a heart attack on November 6, 78 years old. He was a former president of the Silurians, also editor of the *Silurian News*. As everyone knows he ran the International News Service, dominated it, personified it over more than forty years.

Faris owned the first motorcycle in St. Joseph, Mo.—this was in 1908—and Homer Croy, the writer and a colleague of Faris's on the old *St. Joe Gazette,* remembers that on the rough cobblestones of that city it was possible to ride on a motorbike for seven city blocks without once coming in contact with the seat. "Faris on that motorcycle was the Spirit of St. Joseph," said Croy.

Faris excelled in that deceptively simple quality known as a nose for news. Once he came across a routine one-paragraph story about a suicide in a Carolina tobacco empire. "This was murder, not suicide," he told an INS desk man. Turned out he was right.

Another time an angry accountant turned over to Faris the expense accounts filled out by Pierre J. Huss, who was assigned to cover Hitler's armies in the spring of 1941. The various expense slips all had been dated ahead into June and were for non-existent expenses in Minsk, Pinsk and Kiev. Faris took one look. "Holy smoke," he said. "Hitler's going to invade Russia."

Once he fired and rehired a man three times in the space of four weeks. Following one of his interviews with the boss, the man emerged from Faris's office with a glazed look. Asked what Faris had said, his answer was, "All I know is, the count's 3-and-2 and everybody runs on the next pitch."

—March 1967

George H. Lyon

George H. Lyon, who died at 80 on February 16, left a heritage of incredible personal anecdotes to the newspaper world.

The former reporter for the *Binghamton Morning Sun,* city editor of the *New York Evening Telegram,* city editor of the *World Telegram,* editor of the *Buffalo Times,* first managing editor of *PM,* deputy director of the OWI, and consultant to Pan American Airways, was a muckraker, a hell-raiser and, above all an individualist. As befits a Silurian, he always did his own thing.

One of his great contributions to journalism was his success in the war in getting full coverage of D-Day and the drive across France and into Germany. As personal representative in London of Elmer Davis, head of the OWI, George attended a pre-D-Day meeting of top brass and discovered that the command had planned to take five correspondents on the invasion. The Signal Corps said it could only allow enough communication channels for that many. A sergeant said more channels could be used, and Lyon urged he be heard.

After the meeting, George got the sergeant aside and said, "Son, don't you know you're not supposed to talk to generals that way?" The sergeant gasped, and George got busy. Before the next meeting, the sergeant was commissioned a major by order of General Eisenhower.

And with the new major's planning and George's bellowing assistance, provision was made for 200 correspondents on D-Day. And while there were delays at deadline peaks, the communications channels kept flowing.

As Davis's representative at SHAEF, George realized the futility of going through channels to influence division commanders who censored correspondents, refused to give them adequate briefings, lend them jeeps, or give them billets.

Instead, George would wait until they came to Paris. Sometimes he would suggest to Commander Butcher, a newspaperman himself, that a certain general ought to be called in for a conference, and George would contrive to get the general up to his room in the Scribe Hotel. Sometimes George would hire a girl from Les Moulins for window dressing.

George would have a few drinks and pretend to be roaring drunk. Then he would say to the general, sometimes shoving him against a wall, "Do you think the war is going on forever? What do you think is going to happen to you when you go back to the States, with every newspaperman in the country ready to call you an enemy, ready to tell the world the first time you got arrested at a smoker?"

George was at a party on the evening of March 1, 1932, when he received a phone call: the Lindbergh baby had been kidnapped. George lined up the guests and said, "Each one of you can keep enough money for a taxi home. I want the rest."

He got more than $2,000, hurried to the phone, routed every reporter out of bed, gave each expense money, and assigned each to an angle to the story. The party guests, of course, got the money back the next morning.

In Brooklyn in early *PM* days, Lyon took a staffer with him to call on Joseph Bonanno (Joe Bananas), the gangster. Since George was spending up to 18 hours a day at *PM,* he had a room at the hotel near the office and near Bananas' bar. At the saloon, Lyon denounced Bananas in a torrent of invective and abuse because Bananas had sent a whore to George's hotel room. He threatened to run Bananas out of town.

Bananas meekly protested he hadn't sent the woman. George slammed his business card down on the bar. "You lying——!" George shouted. "This is my card I gave you the last time I was here. And that's how she got by the room clerk. She gave him my card."

Bananas protested that he didn't do it and wouldn't do it again.

—ELMER ROESSNER, March 1971

.

VII.

ON FROM NOSTALGIA

Where Do We Go from Here?
Into Change, of Course.
But Silurian Jubilee
Asserts a Vital Confidence

HAPPY MEMORIES!

GOOD FELLOWSHIP!

Published by The Society of The Silurians, Inc.

An organization of veteran New York City newspapermen who gather twice annually for an evening of good fellowship—founded in 1924 by Charles Edward Russell, William O. Inglis, Perry Walton and David G. Baillie.

Volume XXV   New York City, Monday, October 4, 1971   No. 1

Silurians Go Co-Ed; Sky Hasn't Fallen as Yet

WELCOME SISTER!

Brady Drawing

Forty-seven Year Tradition Flips, No-Women Rule Yields to Modernity

Silurian gates—and arms—now stand wide open to newswomen on equal terms with newsmen. A select bevy of femininity impends.

After forty-seven years of exclusiv- masculinity the citadel has fallen, the tradition collapses. This day for history was Wednesday, September 15, monthly luncheon of the Silurian Governors, unanimous vote, and Number One is Miss Helen M. Staunton, formerly of Editor and Publisher, now managing editor of Publishers-Hall Syndicate. And then, Ruth Preston of the Post, both now members.

Breaks the Ice

Change has not overtaken us, in quite the slick fashion here indicated. For nearly two decades cracks and erosions have been appearing in the wall. The more sensitive gray counters noted underground snorts and blasts from Silurian forebears, but at last the time came.

Last January our Membership Chairman Harold Blumenfeld received an application with check in due form — a certain Miss Staunton—and what should he do about it? Victor House, our counsel, reported nothing in the constitution to obstruct. The momentous issue went to membership vote. Yes, said the members, 230 to 143. So the Governors made it official.

One voter commented "keep the bums out," no special reasons. Several threatened to resign, although until now still not beyond hope of redemption. Another advised the girls to form their own "granny 'ph,'" another said the move had nothing to do with women's lib. But everything with men's.

Helen M. Staunton

Our first, or even pioneer, woman Silurian makes such an engaging approach that one must wonder how she was kept waiting eight months at the door. "Just why, Miss Staunton," the question was put, "did you ever want to break into this masculine re- .reat?"

Yet to be Converted

The same gentleman also wanted to know where the Board of Governors stood. The official answer is that the board voted in favor of the girls by a majority before putting it to a general membership vote.

Some in favor of admission dragged out the old saw, "women are here to stay," one pointed out that this country wouldn't be what it is today without women. An erstwhile New York Journal-American probably nailed down the verdict more firmly than 230 to 143 by saying, "Yes, any sex other than the one to charge will help!"

The thaw has quite gradually sapped Silurian defenses. Dorothy Kilgallen made perhaps the first inroad when she could not be denied her honorable mention for covering the Coronation of Queen Elizabeth in 1953. Followed then in 1958 the series about Russian women which won an award for Marilyn Bender of the Journal American, now of The Times.

"On Editor & Publisher," she answered, "I covered the New York newspapers, mechanical stories, some union and legal stories, syndicates, personals, etc.—and it seemed to me all the good newspapermen joined the Silurians as soon as humanly possible. Why did I want to join? That's why. I wanted to be where the company was good."

As if this were not enough, here's more about her.

Born in Binghamton, she has ample memories of South Bend, Ind. where her father was a professor of English at Notre Dame. In fact he started the now-accomplished union of Notre Dame with St. Mary's, where she was a freshman. After a lapse from college she entered the University of Chicago, and there as she recalls, "I was probably the first student to take advantage of their examinations-instead-of-courses program to complete three years of credit in one to get my bachelor of arts degree." One quarter of graduate work then qualified her to teach—and so "I walked into the South Bend Tribune news room, grass-green, and asked for a job."

Brogan Tells Them It All Comes True

Begin back in the year 1962 with an alert and prophetic youngster by the name of John A. Brogan, Jr. He lived in the former Gas House District—First Ave to the Riv- er, 14th to 23rd Sts — then transformed into the quiet Stuyvesant Town - Peter Cooper Village apartments of the Metropolitan Life Insurance Co. Into this sylvan dell had crept the urban commonplace of mugging, rape, bike-stealing and burglary. The local weekly, Town & Village, published by one Charles G. Hagedorn, carried a young girl's Letter to the Editor, "almost afraid to walk to and from school."

Brogan got riled up and himself wrote in, breathing such fire and zip that the editor played up the letter under a two-column head, "Tenant Suggests a Volunteer Patrol To Rid Community of Hoodlum Fear." The letter pointed to lots of able-bodied youngish men in the community. If interested volunteers would each give just four hours every month to patrol in pairs two hours of an evening, they could strip violence of its popularity. He suggested, also, a community collection to buy badges, caps and nightsticks for the volunteers.

So the idea caught on. Not exactly like wildfire, you might say, but this year, nearly nine years later, spring of 1971, and with the agitation of the T&V weekly, the first volunteer Auxiliary Police equipped with badges, caps and nightsticks, stepped out on their rounds. The community, it seemed, had finally wearied of hoodlums. The city cops welcomed them and provided training. The T&V news report gave credit as due. "Prediction Comes True, Just for Your Inf," Commissioner Murphy was there to see them off. And they have cleared out lurking menaces, actually nabbed several and chased others into police grasp.

Yes, that Brogan of 1962 is the same, this brass-tacks, looking-ahead Silurian John, sometimes with Hibernian flourish called our Modern Hebrew Prophet Isaiah.

Brogan

And in Nine Years Fishermen Still Catch 'Em, Ecologist Finds Frustration

By Jesse Brodey

The life of an ecology reporter is a frustrating one.

From that day in 1609 when Henry Hudson saile i his "Half Moon" upriver to the site of Albany and his galley boy toasted his first bucket of slops over the rail, the Hudson has b en going steadily down-stream in more ways than one. For every sewage or industrial treatment plant now completed, another putrid outfall is discovered. Yet, strangely enough, despite man's worst pollution, marine life still survives in it and men who know the river will tell you that Havenstraw Bay offers the best fishing west of Montauk Point. There are some fishermen also who eat their catches, and some who won't.

Governor Rockefeller points to plans on drawing boards for new treatment plants up and down the Hudson while the U.S. Attorney's office, after 14 years of fishermen's complaints to the Army Corps of Engineers, finally gets a 100-count indictment against Anaconda Copper for polluting the Hudson at Hastings. The Penn Central, fined once for polluting, still drips oil into the Hudson at Harmon and into the City reservoir system at Brewster. General Motors, fighting a delaying action in Federal Court, continues to pour 500,000 gallons of industrial waste into the river at North Tarrytown.

And down in the southern part of Manhattan where all human sewage, as it has for decades, flows raw into the Hudson and East Rivers for lack of any treatment plants, Rockefeller family money is helping build the world's two

Silurian Brodey, New York News, received the 1969 Striped Bass Award of the Hudson River Fishermen's Association (no reference to the bass he brought home) "For His Distinguished Reporting on Conservation." He recently received the 1971 Scarsdale Elks Lodge Special Award plaque for distinguished reporting on youth and community news.

polluting, still drips oil into the Hudson at Harmon and into the City reservoir system at Brewster. General Motors, fighting a delaying action in Federal Court, continues to pour 500,000 gallons of industrial waste into the river at North Tarrytown.

tallest treatment, the World Trade Center. So, the World Trade Center will add its raw human sewage from its expected population of 21,000 to the outflow into the rivers.

Officials now say a treatment plant should be ready by 1975 if all goes well to handle all (Continued on Page 5)

The Dinner

Monday, October 18, is the date, fall dinner of the Silurians, extra special, to be held this year at the distinguished club of the Players, 16 Gramercy Park — same as 20th St., just east of Fourth Ave.

The fall dinner traditionally is the year's fun session, beer and relaxation at the Grand Street Boys. Grand Street being for the moment closed for adjustments, fun still invites. And the Players extends its cordial welcome. Gather at 6 o'clock, dinner about 7:30.

Cheering the 25-year Award Winner will be part of the fun. Peter Kihss of the Times will be presented.

But especially — don't overlook — the girls! On this historic occasion, first time women tread these areas precincts. Two new feminine Silurians will be present. Well turn out and meet them. See and admire! October 18, The Players, 16 Gramercy Park.

Next in Line For Fem Seniority

She is listed among the current New Members as Ruth L. Peskin, and a lot of identification that is. Add a Mrs. to the name, so what? Well, out with the secret—she's Ruth Preston of the N.Y. Post. Her daily column pulls in the woman readers, telling them how to be better dressed, better groomed and coiffed, in short more seductious, and she's been adding that sort of appeal to the Post for twenty-five years. (Very young indeed when she starred; before that 1944-45 she was with Harpers' Bazaar.)

Ruth Preston's application was sponsored by Oliver Pilat, old colleague on the Post, not wanting her to miss out when the walls of Jericho came tumbling down. To her goes what someday will be a proud distinction, No. 2 among the Silurian gals.

Their best response was to allow her to hang around, without desk or salary. At the end of a week they put her on the payroll. So she got on the track toward becoming a Silurian. In between she taught a couple of years, and worked on a neighborhood paper in Chicago. Editor & Publisher provided the start in New York.

Dudley Martin to V.P.

Dudley B. Martin, one of the board of governors and a Silurian of long and useful devotion to the society, was elected second vice president at the September board meeting to fill the vacancy created by the death of Lee Margolin. Silurian Harold Blumenfeld, our active membership chairman, then was elected to the board.

1947 OUTLOOK, ACCEPTING NOVELTY
OF RADIO, EDITOR KEEPS COOL

The following article is from the speech delivered at the Silurian dinner in November 1947 by the executive editor of the *New York Daily News.*

When I started newspaper work—that was in 1913, on the *Boston Traveler*—the rules for success in the editorial department were simple. Some of the more important were: learn how to talk to cops, and get to know as many as you can; same with politicians and lawyers and crooks (I think we never referred to them as gangsters in those days); cultivate a memory for names, faces, and telephone numbers; learn to spell names correctly.

All these elementary rules hold good today, but there is a vast difference between then and now in the rewards the young reporter might expect if he displayed exceptional ingenuity, perseverance, and writing ability.

Then, he might aspire to three or four top writing jobs; he might become a star reporter and have news stories appear regularly under his by-line; he might achieve dignified anonymity on the editorial page; perhaps he could join his paper's Washington bureau; best of all, he might eventually become a foreign correspondent.

If the possible rewards for skill and effort in the newspaper world were as limited today as they were 25 years ago, I doubt if we should find many youngsters anxious to devote themselves to our profession.

However, the field has broadened to such an extent that the beginner may now try for a job on a newspaper because he sees it as a springboard to prestige and even wealth in any of the so-called "media of mass communication." That's a tag our intellectual folk have thought up to include the press, both daily and periodical, the movies, and the radio.

Twenty-five years ago, every young reporter I knew was thrilled when the results of his labors appeared in print under his by-line. In those days it was customary to keep most of the staff members anonymous as far as a paper's readers were concerned. The by-line was an award of merit, passed out seldom—perhaps becauses management felt that the honor might inflate the reporter's ego to the point where he would demand a raise.

Today, the by-line has lost all significance except as a means of identification—that is, when it appears above a news story. But the by-line which blossoms in the same spot on the same page day after day—that is something altogether different.

The real glamor boys of today's newspaper world are those who have been able to convince their employers and their readers of their ability to diagnose any political ailment of mankind, then prescribe the proper treatment—generally surgery.

Should the treatment be carried out and the patient die, no public announcement or apology need be made.

So, it seems to me, almost every young writer today yearns to become an editorial columnist. Some no doubt, have an honest urge for world saving. Others, of more practical mind, have figured out that such a job may become highly remunerative.

In any case, the hope of one day becoming the proprietor of a signed pillar of opinion attracts many young folk into newspaper work. And some of them turn out all right.

Now for the nostalgic touch—25 years ago there were 13

English language newspapers circulated generally throughout New York City. This total does not include publications originating in Brooklyn or the Bronx. Two of the 13 papers carried signed columns of editorial opinion—the *American* had Brisbane, *The World* had Broun. On rare and momentous occasions a publisher or editor-in-chief might set forth his views (generally on page 1) and acknowledge them by his signature.

Today, the line-up of editorial columnists in New York newspapers is close to overwhelming. The number of papers of general circulation has dropped from 13 to 8, Brooklyn and the Bronx still excluded.

The 8 papers present 23 columns of opinion, each with its writer's by-line. Not all 23 columns appear every day, perhaps because the strain of diagnosing and prescribing cures for global ailments five days out of every seven is more than the mind of man can stand.

It seems unnecessary to add that in the tabulation of columnists, then and now, I have excluded all writers on special subjects, from art to philately. Today's list might be lengthened by the use of fractions, since some of the specialists consistently split themselves between their proper fields and pure editorializing. For instance, it is not uncommon that a columnist supposed to record the activities of Broadway folk leaves that fascinating subject flat while he gives his opinion of the atom bomb as a guarantee of world peace. But in my count I have ruled out all writers who are even theoretically restricted as to subject, and have included only those who are free to discuss whatever they choose.

He may deny the dubious distinction, but I believe I know the man who popularized the by-lined editorial column in New York. At least, it was during the time he directed the *World* that the paper's page opposite editorial was turned over to a crew of opinion-expressers higher-powered and more amusing than any other newspaper has since assembled.

That op-ed page during the Herbert Bayard Swope regime was the envy of the nation's editors. They tried to imitate it —with the result that columnists hatched out at a fantastic rate.

If he admits the responsibility which I think is his, I wonder if Mr. Swope hasn't an occasional twinge of conscience as he ploughs through column after column of opinion in some of our gazettes.

Any pain he feels might be eased by the knowledge that he started a fine recruiting job for the nation's editorial rooms— there are now so many youngsters eager to learn the business, in the hope of eventually enjoying the prestige and salary that reward a popular columnist.

It was just about 25 years ago that radio broadcasting gave definite promise of becoming an important medium of public information and entertainment. Many newspaper publishers sensed the possibility that spoken words, widely disseminated, might challenge printed words in the contest for popular acceptance. Accordingly, these publishers got into radio in droves. The rush to the radio bandwagon was more furious outside New York City than in it. The lords of the metropolitan press missed the wagon, as evidenced by the fact that not one major radio outlet in the city is under newspaper control today. In most of the rest of the country, the reverse is true, with newspapers owning and operating a good proportion of the leading stations.

As radio became stronger, newspaper proprietors began to fear the public might quit reading in favor of listening, which requires less effort. That fear was dispelled in 1939, with the outbreak of World War II. The radio did its damndest to get the news out quickly. It outsped the press, of course, since it had no problems of mechanical composition, printing and delivery—but it helped boost newspaper sales to figures undreamed of before. The public just had to read print in order to clarify the rather hazy idea of the news it had got from the airwaves.

Some New York publishers then determined they ought to have a larger part in radio news presentation. Several set up separate staffs whose sole purpose was the processing of news for radio transmission. The quality of news programs immediately improved—and a lot of new jobs were made.

I well remember my paper's start in news broadcasting. We went on the air for five minutes each hour over station WNEW. The scripts of about 800 words were tossed off by three or four regular staff members, mostly from the telegraph desk. They stood the grind for two or three weeks; then they were near collapse. So we set up a separate department, which now has 22 members, with 13 classified as writers.

Since the broadcast desk was established, we have had a steady line of applicants for jobs on it. Many of our early script writers have gone on to better paying work elsewhere in the radio field. So the pattern has become fairly clear—the newspaper office is an excellent place for a beginner to get into the writing end of radio. He may even learn to be a commentator—the equivalent of a newspaper columnist.

In the last year or so a new field has opened up. It holds greater promise of rich reward to those who get into it than either column writing or radio. I am talking about television. 25 years ago I had never heard the word. This is an eye appeal medium, allied more closely to the movies than to voice broadcasting. As a method of news and entertainment dissemination it is potentially the greatest, for it gives the public an opportunity to see and hear what is happening in the world, often while it is happening.

I am glad newspaper publishers generally have jumped into television with much more alacrity than the New Yorkers displayed climbing aboard the radio bandwagon. Six of the 15 stations now telecasting are newspaper-owned; so are six of the 14 due to get on the air in the next half year.

Present indications are that news, in one form or another, will be the backbone of television programs, with entertainment and educational features in second and third place. Consider the time now devoted to telecasts of sporting events—that's news, isn't it? Although such programs have plenty of entertainment value.

I believe that newspaper-trained personnel can handle the news end of television better than operators whose experience has been wholly in movies or radio.

At a luncheon of the Radio Executives club the other day, one speaker estimated that in two or three years 250,000 men and women would be employed in all branches of television. Where all these people are going to get their training I don't know, but if I were 25 years younger and wanted to get into a non-mechanical branch of this new business, I think I'd head for a job in the editorial department of a newspaper, preferably one owning or affiliated with a television station. This goes for both sexes. There isn't yet any such thing as a television star—but I have no doubt we'll see plenty in a couple of years.

Now that you have listened to all the words I have poured forth, you can't be in much doubt how I answer the question: "Do you think the newspaper business is more attractive now than it was 25 years ago to a young man starting on a career?"

My father was a newspaperman, and I hung around editorial offices almost from the time I could walk. I always thought newspapering was a fascinating occupation, although my father assured me it would never bring in much money.

Today it is far more fascinating, far more varied, and offers far greater possibility of financial reward than in the good old days of 1922.

—RICHARD W. CLARKE, May 1948

NEWSPAPER SURVIVAL A BIGGER
PROBLEM THAN LABOR CRISIS

The saddest part of the death of the *Herald Tribune* was how few people really cared. Once the television cameras were turned away from the last rites, most New Yorkers were ready to forget there ever had been a *Trib*. A cenutry and a third of journalistic tradition slid down the drain without the slighest sign that anything important had gone out of the city's life. A couple of people wrote letters to Mayor Lindsay; a half-dozen wrote to *The Times*. But the only real mourning was done at Bleeck's and in the hearts of newspapermen, a strange and increasingly irrelevant breed.

I suppose it is accurate to say that the unions killed the *Tribune*. Certainly, it would have been alive today if the unions had not decided that a strike was the way to save jobs in a merger born of pernicious financial anemia. But, in a real sense, the *Trib* began dying long ago and few of its own editors believed it could have survived very long even if all the unions had stayed on the job.

It was always the unwanted child in this strange marriage of Hearst, Scripps-Howard, and Whitney. Yet it was the only unit involved with a genuine claim to distinction. It ranked among the first ten in the country's dailies, and it had a liveliness and originality few could match. Now it is gone and the survivor, flung together from elements of *Journal-American, World-Telegram and Sun* and *Trib,* is a composite as devoid of independent character as a TV dinner.

The contrasts between the community indifference that attended the passing of the *Trib* and the sense of personal loss, even grief, that gripped millions when the old *World* died is a dismaying indication of how far newspapers have slipped in public esteem in the last three decades in this communications capital. Part of the answer, of course, lies in the senseless cycle of strikes that have blacked out large sections of the metropolitan press for long periods in the last four years. The surest way to become convinced that you can do without newspapers is to have to do it, over and over again, for weeks or months on end.

But in this case, too, it is much too easy to point to labor strife as the culprit. The problems of New York's newspapers extend far beyond primordial labor-management relations; they are problems of function and meaning in a society that is changing faster than our capacity to comprehend or interpret it. The mirror we hold to the world often gives back a foggy image; our readers don't always recognize themselves in it. And other media of much greater immediacy—if not of perspective or penetration—have come along to challenge our hold on public attention.

What can be done about both heads of this Hydra: First, making sure that newspapers will not disappear yet another time when present citywide union agreements run out next March 30, and Second, making them better when they do appear?

On the labor front, the ingredients for a more wholesome relationship seem plain enough, but they have been plain since the 114-day strike of 1962-63—without any adequate will on either side to fit the pieces into place. The first necessity is for the publishers to convert their association from a body subject to eternal paralysis whenever any single owner says "No" into a unified bargaining council, with clear ideas on overall strategy and trust in the negotiators it sends to the conference table to carry out that strategy.

Up to now the owners have alternated in yo-yo fashion

between eagerness to fight and eagerness to settle, and their negotiators have been kept on such short tether that any momentum they were able to build up for resolution of key issues would ooze away while they sought a go-ahead from their disputatious principals. The creation of the *World Journal Tribune* as a third force to share power with *The Times* and the *News* inside the association has improved chances for achieving a unified over-all position in the 1967 talks. The big question is whether the strong resolve all the association members now have to find a "better way" will not once again melt under the strain of actual negotiations.

For the unions the problem is essentially the same. The ten unions must work out some mechanism for joint negotiation on basic issues or the odds in favor of a strike will remain ten to one every time citywide contracts run out. The hopeful element is that the two strongest men on the union side— Bertram A. Powers of the "Big Six" Typographical Union and Thomas J. Murphy of the New York Newspaper Guild— have become ardent partisans of the joint bargaining concept.

The holdback comes from the Pressmen's Union, which delayed settlement with the *World Journal Tribune* for a full month after all the other unions were ready to go back to work. One factor that helped the pressmen hold out was the lack of any financial squeeze on the union pocketbook or even on its idle members while the merged paper was down. All the supposed strikers were working five days a week at *The Times* or the *News*. That kind of privileged sanctuary would not exist if all the papers were closed, and the pressmen's treasury is too barren to finance benefits for a single week if the local tried to go it alone in another strike. Such factors may prove controlling when the real push is made for welding all the unions into a joint bargaining mechanism.

The model for such an arrangement already exists in Great

Britain, where all the papers of national circulation and the eight press unions negotiate successfully through a joint council. They also meet jointly on a year-round basis to promote increased efficiency and develop equitable programs for sharing the benefits of automation. In New York the composing-room doors remain locked to new technology. The test in the forthcoming contract talks will be whether they can be opened and whether overall machinery for lasting labor peace can be established. One way to start toward both goals would be to begin negotiations in the next few weeks, with a view to getting final agreements with all ten unions well before the March 30 deadline.

The alternative to that idyllic outcome could be a very gloomy one indeed—a choice by the unions to exercise the option, opened under a recent National Labor Relations Board decision, of insisting on dealing separately with each paper. The ability to pay of the most prosperous publisher would become the lowest common denominator of settlement, and each union would feel an obligation to outdo the next one in militancy. The result almost certainly would be a whip-saw pattern so chaotic and so costly that more tombstones would eventually arise in New Yor's journalistic graveyard.

On the quality front, the need for change is less in the realm of structure than of spirit. For me the most disquieting aspect of the three-paper merger was the very fact that three publishers of such differing orientation and tradition as Hearst, Scripps-Howard, and Whitney had so few qualms about their ability to fit comfortably into a single bed. So far as I can gather, the negotiating difficulties preceding the consolidation were primarily of a business nature—what plan of operation would contribute most to a healthy balance sheet for the new corporation.

Apparently no one worried nearly as much about the reconcilation of editorial viewpoints or philosophies on how to do a more significant job of conveying the news. The consensus idea is certainly a popular one these days, and it is probably old-fashioned of me to question the Mix-master road to progress. But maybe one of the things that is causing a downhill slide in metropolitan journalism is too much malted milk in the daily diet. Newspapers—all of them—must have some clear idea of where they are going if their readers are to take them seriously. Or stay readers.

—A. H. RASKIN, October 1966

SECURE IN PLUSH PR SET-UP,
GUILD MAN HEEDS OLD CALL

(From another point of view, that of a *World-Tele-gram & Sun* man caught in the midst of it, has come in a letter which looks like a companion piece to Abe Raskin's, above. Bernie Brown first told of his lifelong affair with newspapers and of his then landing safely in a plush public relations job. From there he goes on.)

Less than a week after the *World Journal Tribune* began publication, I received a call from Ted Levine, the chief copy editor, offering me a daytime copy desk job. Overnight I had to make up my mind. Visions of the lovely, air-conditioned, fountain-bedecked Seagram Building, imposing decor and desk in my office and beautiful, but really beautiful, typists and secretaries almost beclouded my judgment. But the following morning I gave Ted Levine my decision. I would be ready to report for work within a week.

There would be nothing much else to say except for this, which I consider the supreme irony of my 57 years on this planet: Under the Guild agreement I must be paid my severance pay (12 weeks), dismissal notice pay (4 weeks), and, if I wish, accrued pension and vacation monies. I won't tell you how much it comes to, but it will make my creditors very happy. And the check for it happened to arrive on my birthday.

If there is any moral here it is this, and I hope all newspapermen everywhere of any age, Silurian and junior journalism student alike, take it to heart:

The American Newspaper Guild, founded by Heywood Broun and a small group of other farsighted newsmen, including, if I must say so, myself, as one of the first chairmen of the *Brooklyn Times-Union* unit, has brought a large measure of justice and a reasonable portion of that unattainable commodity, security, to the working stiffs in this profession. And if some young columnists or young reporters, rewrite men and others who have had the five-day, 35-hour week and all the other decent working conditions handed to them on silver platter, largely through the blood, sweat and tears of men like Broun, Morris Watson, Carl Randau, Milton Murray, Tom Murphy and others far too numerous to list here, don't like the responsibilities imposed upon them by membership in their big labor union, it's high time they found out what it was all about.

Like almost everybody else in the industry, I am sick unto death of strikes and mergers. A better way must be found or the four remaining dailies in this city face untold difficulties.

I no longer look with distaste upon voluntary arbitration as a substitute for the strike. I regard myself personally as one of the luckiest fellows in this indescribably exciting, inspiring, frustrating, but in the long run satisfying profession. And I am glad to be a part of it, probably until the day I cash in my chips.

But any time anybody wants to argue with me, in public or private, about the merits of the Newspaper Guild and the generally high motives of its leaders, I am willing to meet him anywhere, anytime or anyplace, on or off the television camera—or even in a dark corner of Gallagher's Steak House, if I can afford it.

—BERNARD D. BROWN, October 1966

1967 EDITOR GAZES FROM GOOD OLD DAYS INTO BRIGHTER TOMORROWS

Since a Silurian is by definition a man of a certain age he has a natural inclination to nostalgia. Since he's a New York newspaperman, he has a lot to be nostalgic about. And being a sentimentalist, he isn't always nostalgic about the right things.

My own nostalgia begins with the mid-1930s. Armed with a fresh sheepskin, a Phi Beta Kappa key, and a sheaf of clippings from Tar Heel newspapers, I found no enthusiasm for my services among the city's bustling journals. So in due time I wound up with the New York City News Bureau, that co-op which covered the city's news for all the member papers and which served as a pasture for worn-out old reporters and eager young colts.

It's easy to wax nostalgic about City News. It taught me how to find the best coffee in the city at 2 a.m., broadened my acquaintance to include the drifters, whores, pimps, and muggers for whom night court was a sort of neighborhood club.

And it made me acquainted with Pop Henderson's filing system which consisted, when asked about some past event, of squinting at the ceiling, recollecting that it happened about March of '34 and then digging out a clip folder which might or might not have what you were looking for.

I can be equally nostalgic about the old Broad Street quarters of the *Wall Street Journal,* which later hired me, and about the old barn of a city room at the *Evening Sun,* where I had many friends and was once spoken to by Keats Speed. I can also be sentimental about that special atmosphere of composing rooms I have known, the smell of which was compounded of a good bit more than ink.

I have affectionate memories too for all the old-timers who were kind to a young stripling; most of them were good reporters even though quite a few couldn't write a simple English sentence. At City News all I was asked to do was get the victim's name and the reason he became a corpse; some unknown Damon Runyon back in the office would supply the prose.

But if I find happy memories in all this, I can also see in retrospect that dry rot was then already attacking the newspapers of our greatest city. The source of the rot was too much nostalgia for the old way of doing things.

Consider just one example. If Horace Greeley had walked into the back shop of the *Herald-Tribune,* circa 1935, he would have felt perfectly at home. The linotype, that somewhat awkward robot type-setter, would be about the only change he would note. Come to think of it, Horace wouldn't have felt too strange if he had walked into the same shop circa 1965.

Or to put the matter briefly, the newspaper industry is about the only one in America that made no important technological progress from about 1880, the date of Mergenthaler's handy-dandy gadget, until the day before yesterday.

It's fashionable, I know, to put all the blame for this on the labor unions and no one who has suffered through the agony in our business of the past twenty years can absolve them from blindness, short-sighted selfishness, and stupidity. It may well be true that a little more vision by union leaders in the past decade could have saved one or more of New York's dead newspapers.

But surely a part of the problem is also the lack of vision on the part of newspaper management in the years before that.

And if we are honest with ourselves we ought to admit that on the editor's side of the table there has been also a certain reluctance to welcome, and to learn to use, the new technology.

Even today, if I may judge by the bull sessions at editors' meetings, there's a great fear of "automation"—a catch-word for technological progress—and what it will do to the editors' functions. The fear is unjustified. The new technology will help us to gather, edit, and present the news better than before.

Take one simple example. In most news shops today the news has to be fed to the composing room all day long, even for a morning newspaper, because the present equipment won't handle an avalanche of stock market reports, sports results, and the like. Only the "big story" can be handled late.

New equipment can revolutionize this situation. High speed transmission wires combined with automatic typesetting and phototype can produce volumes of type that would make old Horace's eyes bulge.

The advantage of this on the business side is self-evident. It can also be a tremendous advantage for the reporter or editor. On a running story the reporter can have a little more time to check his facts, the editor can have a little more time to organize the story, before everything must be rushed into print.

With the new equipment we can have something better than Pop Henderson's filing system. Electronic memory retrieval systems on a computer can not only store mountains of information, but can organize it in almost any way anyone wants it organized and deliver it in most any desired package.

Think what this could mean in the handling of many sudden stories—the death of a president, a holocaust at sea, another Cuban-type confrontation. The bare facts could far more quickly be put into perspective than is possible today in most newspaper shops.

The real question for us Silurians, and the Silurians to come after us, is whether we learn to use these new tools. The new tools are really no smarter than a linotype; that is, you only get out what you put in. What is important, then, is that reporters and editors not abdicate the handling of the new tools to the technicians.

If we do learn how to use these new tools then I, for one, think there's a glorious day ahead. If we don't—well, nostalgia can be fun but you can't eat it.

—VERMONT ROYSTER, November 1967

BACKWARD AND AHEAD,
DECADE BY DECADE

Of the Society's rather scattered records the one reaching farthest back is a twenty-year souvenir booklet and roster of 1944, adorned with congratulatory messages from President Roosevelt and Governor Dewey, but helpfully including also the Silurian memberships for both 1927 and 1934. No full list has turned up for the initial enrollment of 1924. In lieu of charter members, the 1927 names will have to serve, a group of assured authenticity, fully entitled by their service at least back into the mid-1890s to call themselves New York newspaper veterans.

These men knew Charles A. Dana as a living presence. They were there while Pulitzer and Hearst slugged out their rivalry and when Adolph S. Ochs bought *The Times.* Unobstructed by radio microphones or TV cameras, these forebears had covered the international cup races for autos and flying machines by which the younger James Gordon Bennett was encouraging the future. The Boer War was current news for them as from across the ocean they watched a hero's fame descend upon a young British correspondent, Winston Churchill. The Spanish-American War drew in, among others, our future president, Bob Livingston, who was sent to Cuba by the *Herald* and shared reflected glory from the Rough Riders.

The news stories of early Silurian memory had, or seemed to take on, unique spangles. Charles M. Lincoln, our revered honorary president, eminent on *Herald, World,* and *Times,* voiced the lament, "Why are there no first-class murders any more? What would not a city editor give for something even approaching the Harry Thaw-Evelyn Nesbit-Stanford White story? Or Herbert Swope's 'Becker Case'? Or that Roland Molineux-Harry Cornish drama?"

Many of the original Silurians had got their first stories into print without benefit of either typewriter or linotype. Albert Payson Terhune's copy could be followed through the *Evening World* shop by the purple ink he used in his pen. Samuel G. Blythe, that matchless political reporter so far ahead in so many ways, brought his typewriter with him— yes, a blind Remington—when he started work on the *Rochester Democrat and Chronicle* in 1886. Our late president, Hugh Baillie, born in 1890, wrote, "I can remember when there were very few typewriters on Park Row. As a child I was taken to the City Hall reporters' room, and all the journalists were writing their copy with pencil. When my father began using a typewriter the copy desk objected, as they couldn't calculate the length of his stuff (he was working on space) and he was making too much money at $8 a column."

The Silurian Society was formed in 1924 at the famous old Hotel Lafayette, Ninth Street and University Place, following a dinner: "It was called," says the twentieth-anniversary booklet, "by Charles Edward Russell, Perry Walton, and William O. Inglis, and was attended by these three or four other founders, William A. Hoy, Isaac D. White, Hartley Davis, and Caleb H. Redfern. The name Silurian was proposed by Russell, who had previously discussed with Walton and others the idea of forming this distinctive general alumni association of New York newspaper men."

Our only "I-was-there" account is a paragraph in *Silurian News,* May, 1950, from John A. Hennessy: "I attended the organization meeting of the Silurians twenty-six years ago, called by Charley Russell, Bill Inglis, Dave Baillie, and Perry Walton. About forty-seven of us were at baptismal rites." The seeming discrepancy between these two accounts is a triviality, herewith brushed aside. Hennessy had one of the longest and clearest memories in the society, and a record of distinction as city editor of the *Star,* managing editor of the *Press,* later editor of the *Providence News.* At the founding in 1924 he could look back half a century to his first job as copy boy on *The Times,* and he lived to be 91.

Although omitted from the 1944 anniversary jotting, David G. Baillie was the Society's first secretary, continuing until his death in 1937. Scottish-born and a friend of Robert Louis Stevenson, he came to New York in the 1880s, wrote politics for the *Tribune, World,* and *Press,* and became literary secretary to Andrew Carnegie.

Of the named founders, Caleb H. Redfern disappeared from the records between 1927 and 1934, while Perry Walton faded into the distance. Early clippings refer to him as "formerly of *The Sun,*" and the printed rosters, 1927 and 1934, place him on the Society's executive committee; his address, was given as 88 Broad Street, Boston.

William O. Inglis, the last survivor, died in 1949, 87 years old. From the *Herald* he proceeded to the *World,* then on to *Harper's Weekly.* With his editor there, Colonel George Harvey (who also became a Silurian), he was credited with being of major influence in bringing Woodrow Wilson into active politics—and so to become Governor of New Jersey, then President. In later years he was a close associate of the senior John D. Rockefeller

William H. Hoy, our second president, was night city editor of the *World.* Then, admitted to the bar, he took up the practice of law. Previously he had worked on the *Philadelphia Press,* the *New York Sun,* and *The Times. The Times* obituary in 1938, when he was 77, mentions him as a Silurian founder, saying he was "three times elected president of the organization and until his death was one of its leading spirits."

Notable also among the founders was Isaac D. White, a *New York World* man continuously from 1886 until 1931 when the paper was sold. He died in 1943, 79 years old. "One of New York's great reporters," *The Times* called him, and told of "the murders he solved when the police couldn't . . . how he almost started a revolution in Yucatan . . . his exploits fighting pirates in Chesapeake Bay . . . how he founded the *World's* Bureau of Accuracy and Fair Play . . . how he was one of the country's leading authorities on the law of libel."

Hartley C. Davis died in 1938, an ex-reporter and advertising writer, semi-retired as publisher of the weekly *Great Neck News.* In advertising he was famous as the originator, for a memory-improvement course, of the oft-repeated phrase —the mark of a phenomenal memory—"Mr. Addison Sims of Seattle." At 21 he joined *The Sun,* worked on the *Paris Herald* and the *World,* and for a time was editor of *Munsey's Magazine.*

Charles Edward Russell, the leader in organizing the Silurians, was first president and then honorary president until his death in 1941. The *Sun* of November 28, 1931 notes his attendance at the Silurian reunion the night before and includes this bit of joshing:

"There was a lot of talk in the course of the dinner about the good old days when Park Row was the newspaper hub of New York and real whisky was procurable at Andy Horn's at the Brooklyn Bridge entrance or Oscar Lipton's at the old *Times* Building or Perry's Drug Store at fifteen cents a shot or two for a quarter. . . . Charles Edward (Iron Face) Russell, the city editor of the *New York Morning Journal* (now the *American*), used to call the head office boy to his desk about 4 p.m. and say, 'Mike, go over to Lipton's and see if any of my reporters want to work today.' " At the March dinner that year the *Sun* had also observed Russell, "who as city editor was at one time or another the boss of many Silurians, to their journalistic benefit."

Thirty years before the society was formed, Russell became city editor of the *World;* he went on to the *American* and then to Chicago, as publisher of Hearst's *Evening American.* He then had a hugely effective career as writer for the muckraking magazines; in 1928 he won a Pulitzer Prize with his biography, *The American Orchestra and Theodore Thomas.* The Socialist Party nominated him successively for mayor, governor, senator, and in 1916 for president, which latter he declined. The following year the party expelled him because he advocated America's entrance into the war against Germany.

* * *

The Silurian founders in 1924, joining together in an association of old-timers, acted with acute historical perception. The New York papers, to be sure, were still sovereign in the national scene, brilliant in enterprise and talent. Radio rivalry was yet but an upstart; Hollywood was not yet seducing away the bright young writers; New York City itself was still proud and confident, the mecca and paragon. But an Indian summer climate had crept in; winter was in the air. Men's thoughts turned back to the old days.

Most disturbing was the magazine publisher, Frank A. Munsey—what he represented and what he had revealed about the newspapers. A cold-blooded financier, he viewed the field as economically overgrown and himself as the agent for weeding out excesses. After earlier newspaper failures he bought the successful *New York Press* in 1912. In his hands the *Press* slumped and in 1916, first buying the *Sun* and the *Evening Sun,* he killed it. In 1920 he realized a fond ambition by buying the *Herald,* with its evening mate, the *Telegram.* In two weeks he merged the morning *Sun* into the *Herald.* In 1923 he bought and killed the *Globe,* an event on which John T. Flynn has given his personal report in these pages. Then came 1924: in January he crossed off the *Evening Mail,* in March he proposed to buy the *Tribune* for merger with his *Herald.* Rejected, he sold instead, and thus again it was one in place of two, the *Herald Tribune.* Four papers in four years, and a fifth only slightly earlier.

These historic giants were blotted out and gone, their staffs turned into the streets. To the survivors these papers had been a deep and sacred element in their city's life. When Russell and his nostalgic handful, ample in prestige, sounded their call, the response was a cheer.

Membership in the Silurians was not for juniors. By definition it meant seniority. Covering the fall dinner of 1929, five years from the starting line, the *Sun* noted the attendance of its own Al Steimer, former sports editor of the *Herald.* "Mr. Steimer," said the *Sun,* "holds the seniority record of the organization with fifty-one years of newspaper work." This placed him on the job in 1878, five years before the Brooklyn Bridge, eight years before the Statue of Liberty.

Another name on the 1927 roster is "Conkling, Frank W., *New York Evening World,* Brooklyn Edition." Ten years after this he was with the *World-Telegram,* and the paper celebrated his anniversary, on March 15, 1937, with a full-page story headed "55 Years of News," telling all about this superb reporter and beloved character. He had gone to work for the *World* on March 16, 1882, a 13-year-old boy, and when Joseph Pulitzer took over the *World* a year later he chose Frank to be his personal copy boy.

The 1927 membership was filled with rampant distinction and fame. Here is the top brass: Van Anda and Birchall of

----

The Times; Chester S. Lord and Frank O'Brien of the *Sun;* Arthur Brisbane and Bradford Merrill of the *American;* Don C. Seitz of the *World* and Jack Tennant of *The Evening World.* Also included were the early Pulitzer Prize winners of the *World,* John J. Leary, Jr., and Louis Seibold; Jesse Lynch Williams, first Pulitzer winner for playwriting; and Ralph D. Blumenfeld, editor of the *London Daily Express,* once of the United Press, the *New York Telegram,* and the *Herald.*

The 1934 roster includes reporters who became notable in different professions—still cherishing Silurian fellowship: George B. McClellan, former Mayor; Charles B. Dillingham, Broadway producer; Stephen T. Mather, director of the National Park Service; Thomas W. Lamont of J. P. Morgan & Co.; Louis McHenry Howe, president-maker of 1932; James Branch Cabell and Irving Bacheller, novelists. Later came Lincoln Steffens, and in 1953, John Steinbeck, our only (thus far) Nobel Prize winner.

But even the least conspicuous Silurian has his own distinction, that of being a New York newspaper man, and as such he remembers the injunction that reporters should keep their hats on when talking to the boss. Membership here is different from the Society of the Cincinnati, clutching a handed-down exclusiveness; ours has been always an open-door fraternity of congenial interests, open to time's revising.

Especially aware, also, of the personal diversity so essential to vital newspapers, the Society early enacted a ban on irrelevant issues. "Whatever may be their beliefs as individuals," says a statement dated 1930 or earlier, "the Silurians have not as an association any political or social causes to advocate, except that they would do whatever is in their power to do to maintain the freedom of the press and the dignity of the newspaper profession."

There is a rather wonderful photograph labeled in the corner, "Spring Dinner of the Silurians—Hotel Brevoort, May 2, 1928," spread across a page full-width in *Silurian News* twenty years afterward, the Society's earliest extant group portrait. About a hundred obviously qualified veterans are seated at their tables in bland respectability, and they arrest the eye, these inhabitants of an antique day.

That same summer just three months later Broadway raised the curtain on one of its greatest all-time hits, *The Front Page*. No imagination could cast these Silurians of the photograph for the antics of that raucous comedy. Yet those present that evening in all likelihood included characters as bizarre as a playwright could ever conceive—for example, Morrill Goddard, uninhibited as a burglar, who set the continent athrob with his exclusive story of the stag dinner featuring "The Girl in the Pie"; or again, the garrulous Roy L. Mc-Cardell, who invented the whole idea of Sunday comic pages in color. Essentially, this 1928 Silurian turnout brought together the eyes and the wit, the tireless footwork, and the unmatched talent of an age. This crowd, as inclusive as was ever assembled, still were keeping the New York newspapers at undimmed preeminence.

* * *

And what about ourselves? And our present Society? Entranced by memories, eager for reunions but with fewer and fewer of our own old friends still attending, the Silurians surely would need additional elements for survival. Since that old photograph time has shaken up the Silurians as it has their city and their world. The changes make the story, and the record shows that the Silurians have adapted and alerted themselves.

The Society changed most naturally and essentially by becoming more numerous—at first 80 or 100 at a reunion, then up to 500, with enrollment of 800. The requirements for membership were made less stringent.

In 1938 the 30-year qualification for admission was cut to 25 years, then associate members were taken in at 15 years; then members were taken from papers all over the metropolitan area. In 1958 the Society voted to admit newsmen from radio and television.

At last came women members, bringing change of far-reaching promise. From the beginning newswomen had been excluded and ignored. The first issue of *Silurian News* carried a query (anonymous), "Why not women?" The editor answered, "You're a lovable dope. Besides, who could ever induce a woman to admit that she'd been an editor or reporter for 25 years?"

Twenty-four years after that we still held out. Then in 1971 the gates—the vote was 230 to 143—swung open; the reunion of October 18 seated our first women Silurians.

Helen M. Staunton, qualified from the *Editor & Publisher* staff, presently managing editor of the Publishers-Hall Syndicate, broke the ice. Her approach was simple. She filled out an application blank, got sponsors, enclosed a check, and mailed it in. The Governors sat on it, delayed, balked, dithered, finally referred it to vote of the general membership, and the answer was Yes. Second to join was Ruth Preston of the *New York Post*. Others have joined since then, although in no stampede.

Another basic change was the conversion in 1947 of this informal dinner companionship into the Society of the Silurians, Inc., complete with charter and constitution. The ensuing structure turned the casual style into something resembling order, created a board to mull over decisions and carry them out, and established financial and legal responsibility.

Without loss of conviviality or reminiscence, also, the Society was now pointed toward "giving direction and assuring continuity to its efforts to promote the traditions of the American newspaper profession."

Eugene E. Early, president at that time, gave the effective push to this move. Early was a gregarious, florid, sparkplug of a man, one of the most amusing of table-mates in a poker game, a Silurian who notably served the Society three terms in office. Beginning on the *Brooklyn Times* at $8 a week, he later crossed the bridge to the *Globe,* for which he reported major trials and sensations of the day. Finally with his Silurian brother, Joseph J. Early, he started a local weekly and developed it into the *Queens Evening News.*

For the professional techniques demanded by a constitution and charter, Early called on his friend, Victor House, a *Herald* reporter from 1912 to 1917 during his student days at NYU and at Columbia University Law School, then a practicing lawyer, and to this day, the ever-ready counsel to the Society.

"Gene enlisted me," House writes, "but Bill Orr and Charlie Hand supplied me with much of the background and worked closely with me on the very careful formulation of the constitution. Both were even then legendary figures among newspaper men."

The phraseology, House recalls, was "hammered out the hard way." Orr had "one of the most sensitive feels for words and their nuances that I have ever encountered." House and Orr struggled with the writing, "as often as not calling on Charlie Hand if neither of us felt we had captured the exactly right turn, and getting from him generally in an inspired flash just the words that fitted."

In that same year 1947, also, Early started *Silurian News,* from which come the stories here collected. If this book had a dedication, it would assuredly name Gene.

For help Early enlisted his friend, William J. Brede, and the following year when ill health forced him to give way, he pushed the editorship onto Brede. Then for fourteen years, twice yearly through 1961, with help uncertain, Brede put out the paper. Next editor was Barry Faris, then in 1964 with the fall issue, George Britt, then with spring, 1973, Newton H. Fulbright.

In the tenth anniversary issue, November 1957, Bill Brede describes the struggle of getting started. Turning through the pages back to Vol. I, No. I, the reader wonders if any later issue has ever equaled its merits.

As Brede tells it, Early personally made it happen. "Funds or no funds," he insisted, "we will have that paper ready for the fall dinner."

Brede continues: "Gene had done most of the typesetting at his newspaper plant in Jamaica. He had arranged with a local printer for forms, correction facilities, revised proofs, etc. We decided to make-up on Saturday afternoon. . . .

"The printer was most willing, but his facilities were the most primitive imaginable. The printer's gas had been shut off, so we proceeded under candlelight. . . . We handled type, lifted and corrected lines, and did about everything that is forbidden under union rules today. That we managed to complete that eight-page paper without a pi mishap seems a miracle. The job was finished around midnight. . . .

"There are no records available to show how much of the cost of that first edition was absorbed by Gene Early. I do know, however, that the *Queens Evening News* set up the major portion of more than fifteen thousand words of text and never submitted a bill."

Looking back over the Silurians' cheerful and animated half century, great years in memory, one peak dominates the scene as highest and foremost—and that, of course, is the Fund.

As the Depression years plodded their course, with the loss of more and more jobs, the Silurian elders realized their helplessness at meeting crises for old friends in a jam. Recurrent facts called for action. In 1953-1954 President Neil MacNeil acted, after first consulting a devoted group—Bertram B. Caddle, Gene Early, Walter T. Brown, and Charles A. Donnelly. With the indispensable lawyer, Victor House, they organized the Silurian Contingency Fund. House obtained tax exemption. And by an inspired sense of personal fitness, MacNeil appointed George E. Sokolsky to be chairman.

For years thereafter every dinner program included an evangelical exhortation—"Come across for the Fund"—and every issue of *Silurian News,* the same. Profit margins from the dinners went to the Fund; spring, 1966 did especially well, $746.81. Sokolsky screamed alarms, "The Fund has been hard hit! It has had to pay out more than comes in! Send me a check!" The members contributed. They wrote it into their wills.

After two decades the Fund enjoys a certain confident health. Sokolsky's hard sell brought in the money. At his death the Society gratefully made the Fund his memorial, the George E. Sokolsky Silurian Contingency Fund. Lee B. Wood as his successor and after him, Henry Senber, have carried on as chairmen, the work undiminished.

The Fund is strictly off-the-record, with only contributions noted. Two of the trustees must sign any check withdrawing money from the savings bank, and professionals audit the accounts. Occasionally some money comes back although no one is billed for repayment. Silurian membership is no insurance policy; news people who are not members receive help on the same terms. Payments to a single established need have reached $1000. Tens of thousands of dollars have been paid out; beneficiaries are not counted. That part is confidential; the Fund has magnificently lifted despair, no one knows whose. But the Silurians do know that the Fund is their deepest credit and satisfaction.

* * *

Silurian News in its issue of November, 1950, three years from the start graphically announced hard times by its acute emaciation—an issue in mimeograph, cut to half-page size. Other half-size and single-sheet issues followed intermittently. The Society was in trouble, its treasury a victim of neglect; the more affluent members were digging up for deficits.

President Charles M. Bayer paid sharp attention. For professional help he turned to our Wall Street reporters and financial editors, to Charles A. Donnelly, Joseph M. Guilfoyle, C. Norman Stabler, and J. Louis Donnelly. They gave prescriptions, warned of a slow recovery, themselves worked so valiantly that all of them in due time became presidents, Charley and Lou Donnelly the only pair of brothers to be so honored. One move was a working finance committee, its O.K. required on any expenditure of $100 or more. Coming on, too, was an alert line of treasurers—financial writers Thomas J. Keller, Joseph D'Aleo, Jesse G. Bell, and others. As a natural accompaniment, Carl C. Dickey as chairman led an extended membership campaign. In 1960, President Lou Donnelly reported membership of just under 700, dues were raised sensibly from the old $2 rate, and all activities were within the budget.

Editor Bill Brede, following Charlie Bayer as president, made a special contribution by bringing in Alden D. Stanton to act, until his death a dozen years later, as executive secretary. The two occupied neighboring offices in the Real Estate Board building. Stanton had long been controller over the vast real-estate holdings of the Trinity Corporation, having no newspaper past except that his father had been city editor of the *Brooklyn Eagle,* and he had two aunts on the *Eagle* staff. But Stanton volunteered to share Brede's double burden and so became an honorary governor and one of the Society's most essential servants.

In the year 1943 President Neil MacNeil appointed a Watchdog Committee which took the Society into the arena of battle for freedom of the press. He appointed a galaxy of notables to the committee, the chairman being Reuben Maury of the *Daily News,* a Pulitzer Prize winner, followed by the beloved Bo McAnney of the *World-Telegram.* Over the next ten years they dramatically established the Silurian point that official brass must never get away with suppression of legitimate news.

At the insistence of Emmet Crozier, Civil War buff and historian, the Watchdogs took up an ancient wrong and set themselves to right it; the case of two young war correspondents, from *The Times* and *Tribune,* who had reported in 1861 the incompetence of a certain Union general. In his memoirs years later the general attacked their news stories as both false and a menace to the national interest. Vigorously presenting Crozier's evidence to the Library of Congress, the committee placed their challenge on file for the attention of future historians.

Memorable reunions staged by the Silurians followed through the years. In April 1940 the speaker was Al Smith, the first non-member ever so invited. President Orr in presenting him with a plaque saluted the Governor as one of the few

"who never weasled out of a tight spot by saying that the reporter had misquoted him."

In May 1944 the Society honored the pioneer syndicate and
magazine editor, S. S. McClure, by conferring on him its first
honorary membership. Another standout evening was in
May, 1953, honoring the Hagerty father-and-son combination, "Old Jim," *The Times*'s great political reporter, and
"Young Jim," then press secretary to President Eisenhower.
On numerous other occasions, dinner programs have been
sparked unforgettably by the graceful wit who ever repeats,
"I'd rather be a Silurian than anything else"—Harry Hershfield.

One of the dinners in 1941 gave the audience a fresh new
item of history from the *World*'s old political reporter and
friend of Theodore Roosevelt, John J. Leary, Jr. He was quoting his predecessor and colleague, John W. Slaight, on the
Spanish-American War. The words now are Slaight's:

"While the army was assembling in Tampa, we all sent
reams of stuff to our papers, telling of the arrival of troops,
the generals, and all that sort of thing. When the papers arrived back we found the blue pencil of the censor had deleted
about everything except the date lines. In this emergency a
conference was called. It had degenerated into a lodge of sor-
row when Jimmy Hare, the war photographer, sitting on a
table swinging his legs, had a happy thought.

" 'You are up against it and you might as well realize it. I
know censors. If you want copy, why don't you take up this
Roosevelt outfit? He's a New Yorker, he's got a picturesque
crowd that will make good copy and the censor will let you go
as far as you like.'

"It was a life-saver. That night the wires were loaded with
Rough Rider copy. Thus by a strange kink of fate, regular

army officers who have always protested against the prominence given Roosevelt in the war, were themselves strictly
responsible for that prominence."

The most notable Silurian dinner came on November 17,
1945. Bill Laurence, our speaker, freshly recalled his aerial
view three months before, the sole eyewitness for the world's
press, of the fatal dropping of the bomb on Hiroshima. On
almost mystical impulse the year before, the Society had voted
to award citations for superlative news performance. The first
award went that night to Laurence.

Amid today's multiplied and well-publicized awards from
every direction, the Silurians' pioneer position has remained
clear, a firm commitment to excellence. By this time the
Society has distributed a hundredweight or more of honorific
bronze.

Another first, in 1953, was the citation to a woman—for
coverage of the coronation of Queen Elizabeth II, to the
Journal-American's Dorothy Kilgallen. At that time, of course,
no woman could be admitted to the select presence and the
token was accepted for Dorothy by her father, Jim Kilgallen.
The first woman winner to receive her honor in person and as
a guest at dinner was Kitty Hanson of the *News* in 1962.

But in 1973 the dinner speaker was Katherine Graham,
publisher of the *Washington Post,* the most timely of appear-
ances, since it immediately followed the Pulitzer Prize awards
for Watergate exposure to two of her reporters.

Another dinner highlight was back in 1959 when Silurian
playwright Russell ("Buck") Crouse was a guest of honor.
Present also was Howard Lindsay, co-author with him of *Life
With Father* and other Broadway sensations. Greeting the
guest by tape were Ralph Bellamy and Ethel Merman, stars of
Lindsay-Crouse productions, and Roy Roberts, publisher of

the *Kansas City Star,* who recalled Crouse's early newspaper days on that publication.

But for the brightest elements of the Society's history, not excepting the writings presented in this volume, the single proper reference must be to the men themselves who have been Silurians. Our honored senior, Albert Stevens Crockett, once suggested, "As I look back and think of the great contributions made to journalistic progress by men within our time, I sometimes wonder what our Society is doing to perpetuate their names and deeds." As our summation we can do no better than to cite a few more names and deeds, remembered with vivid interest, high points that meant much in their generation.

Here's first to the Silurians!—a group credit—for behavior not entirely common at a merry-making banquet. It was a long, long evening: a once-brilliant senior mumbling through the reading of interminable memoirs, and more than a hundred Silurians—wearied, sturdy, and sympathetic—kept their seats as politely as if in church.

And with "In Memoriam" never missing an issue of *Silurian News,* there was the special name of Joe Lilly, member of a Pulitzer Prize team, devoted in Silurian activities, designated in two months to become our president, suddenly stricken. As one says, "Always the wrong one!"

Certainly not to be forgotten was James W. Barrett, city editor of the *World* in 1931 who led the forlorn effort of the *World* men to keep the paper alive. Later overtaken by blindness, he learned Braille, and *Silurian News,* November, 1953, quotes a published article of his concerning major public problems. His solution: "The call is for Faith; the kind that believes that bigger things can be done, that problems can be solved; Faith that simply will not accept 'No' for an answer." Jim Barrett disclaimed credit for his writing: "All I did was to type the article from some Braille notes which I had been jotting down with plate and stylus as thoughts came to me while looking over the news by radio. My seeing-eye wife read copy and proofs."

In the fall of 1969 the Silurians' Quarter Century Achievement Award was instituted, a sort of marathon of merit. Surely to be recorded is our first winner, Walter Cronkite, whose quarter century of news coverage extended from Normandy, D-Day, 1944, for the United Press, to reporting the first men on the moon, 1969, for CBS-TV.

We must also give tribute to our resourceful president, Budd Stahl, who got our Silurian mugs across the ocean to the appointed dinner in 1968. The mugs were so painstakingly shaped by the potters' hands, the whole venture so diplomatically arranged, only to be stalled on the docks by the British longshoremen's strike, until Budd wangled them over cost-free on one of his employer's coal boats, on time.

Another unforgettable was Poultney Bigelow, living until almost 99, boyhood schoolmate of Kaiser Wilhelm II, expelled from Czarist Russia in 1892 for his "capitalistic political views." He enjoyed quoting his first boss, Dana of *The Sun,* who never forgave President Rutherford B. Hayes the dubiety of his election, referring to him always and only as "that rancid fraud."

There are so many others, overdue for mention, such as:

The reporter who covered the inauguration of T.R. as Governor of New York in 1899 and went on to forecast precisely in 1936 that F.D.R. would carry every state except Maine and Vermont—George D. Morris of the *Sun* and of the *World-Telegram;*

The city editor credited as first to give assignments with the admonition, "And don't come back without it!"—John L.

Eddy, who succeeded Charles Edward Russell on the *American;*

The interviewer to whom Pulitzer expressed his appraisal, "Every reporter is a hope. Every editor is a disappointment." —Henry Noble Hall of the *World;*

The reporter through whom J. P. Morgan calmed the panic of 1907 by his announcement on October 24, "Tell your office the banks have loaned $35,000,000 to the call-money market at 6 percent"—Oliver J. Gingold of the *Wall Street Journal;*

The artist, humorist, and sage who advised his contemporaries at a Silurian dinner, "This longevity is only a matter of procrastination"—Rube Goldberg of King Features;

And one other, the one whom Lord Northcliffe called "The greatest reporter of our age"—Herbert Bayard Swope.

Today's members cherish their Society for its occasions of good fellowship, with undiminished warmth. They revere its prestige of talent and renown, while they are also aware of its deep significance—beyond the perception of the glamorous founders. Its history flows through a lush anecdotage, with sweat to compress it. Honoring this heritage, they carry on as vital links—past to future—each Silurian a part in the moving pageant.

—George Britt

CREDITS, as definite as possible: The files of *Silurian News* are a major source, together with the rosters, year by year back into history. But in addition, are clips from the New York newspapers, the unfinished manuscript of our late historian, Robert J. Kennedy, who died in 1956, the salvage of devoted archivists, such as former Presidents Senber, Charles G. Bennett, and J. Louis Donnelly, notes from our counsel, Victor House, and from our former secretary, Maurice G. Postley, and so on, bit by bit, together with the ambience of common interest which makes this a production by the totality.

PAST PRESIDENTS

Honorary Presidents
Charles M. Lincoln (elected 1941)
Charles Edward Russell

Presidents   Date of Service

Charles Edward Russell	1924–1929	Walter T. Brown	1954–1955
William A. Hoy	1927–1929	Charles A. Donnelly	1955–1956
Robert E. Livingston	1929–1933	George E. Sokolsky	1956–1957
John Langdon Heaton*		Joseph M. Guilfoyle	1957–1958
Frank Parker		Barry Faris	1958–1959
Stockbridge*		C. Norman Stabler	1959–1960
Harold M. Anderson	1933–1937	J. Louis Donnelly	1960–1961
Maurice Campbell	1937–1938	Hugh Baillie	1961–1962
Joseph J. Canavan	1938–1939	Carl H. Pihl	1962–1963
Col. Reginald L. Foster	1939–1940	Murray Davis	1963–1964
William Anderson Orr	1940–1941	Marshall Newton	1964–1965
Charles E. Still	1941–1942	Eugene S. Haggerty	1965–1966
Charles S. Hand	1942–1945	Henry Senber	1966–1967
Robert E. MacAlarney	1945	Donald D. Hoover	1967–1968
Edward R. Anker	1945–1946	Charles G. Bennett	1968–1969
Eugene E. Early	1946–1949	Rodney L. Stahl	1969–1970
Dwight Perrin	1949–1950	William R. Hart	1970–1971
Charles M. Bayer	1950–1951	Kalman Seigel	1971–1972
William J. Brede	1951–1952	Oliver Pilat	1972–1973
Bertram B. Caddle	1952–1953	Dudley Martin	1973–1974
Neil MacNeil	1953–1954		

* Dates of Service Not Available

THE CONTRIBUTORS

BAEHR, Harry W.—editorial writer for the *Herald Tribune,* later for the *New York Herald* of Paris; author, *The New York Tribune Since the Civil War.*

BECKETT, Henry—graduate of Miami University, Oxford, Ohio; soldier in World Wars I and II; 44 years a reporter on the *New York Post.* Died 1969, 80 years old.

BEECROFT, Chester—reporter, *Press, World,* and *Sun;* movie producer and manager of Cosmopolitan Studios in New York; For more than 20 years as a quartermaster on round-the-world cruise ships, avidly earning his name, "Sinbad." Died 1959, at 77.

BENNETT, Charles G.—covered City Hall for *The New York Times;* New York reporter since 1929; returned to native Vermont, director of Bennington Historical Museum; past president of both the Inner Circle and the Silurians.

BINNS, John R. (Jack)—first celebrity of sea rescue by radio; worked for *New York American* and *New York Tribune;* chairman of Hazeltine Corp. Died 1959, at 75.

BIRD, Robert S.—correspondent for *Times, Herald Tribune, Saturday Evening Post;* died February 1970.

BREDE, William J.—president of the Silurians and for fifteen years editor of *Silurian News; New York Evening Post,* 1898; *New York Globe;* later with New York Real Estate Board, real estate representative at New York Legislature. Died 1968.

BRITT, George—from Chicago to New York, 1924;

with NEA Service, *Telegram* and *World-Telegram, New York Post, Survey Magazine;* taught writing classes at Columbia (General Studies) and John Jay College of Criminal Justice.

BROWN, Bernard D.—*World-Telegram and Sun, World-Journal-Tribune;* associate editor, *Financial World.*

CLARKE, Richard W.—from Chicago to New York, 1921; assistant Sunday editor, *The World;* editor, *New York Daily News* 1961.

COHEN, Edward Carey—*Brooklyn Citizen* in early 1900s; entered practice of law. Died 1969, at 83.

CORNISH, George A.—*Birmingham Age-Herald,* 1921–23; *New York Herald Tribune,* 1923–1960, concluding as executive editor; then editor-in-chief of encyclopedias.

CROWELL, Paul—*The New York Times,* 1928 until retirement in 1965, mostly covering politics, later a consultant to city charter revision commission; received Silurian award in 1952 for study of city transit problems. Died 1970, 78 years old.

CROZIER, Emmet—*The World,* the *Globe* and the *Herald Tribune,* reporter, rewrite, city desk; also editorial writer and special correspondent for *The Times;* with Navy analysis during World War II.

CURRAN, Henry H.—*New York Tribune,* 1898–1903; alderman, president of borough of Manhattan, deputy Mayor, and judge of special sessions.

DALEY, Arthur—"Outstanding coverage and commentary of the world of sports," says his citation for the Pulitzer Prize, local reporting in 1956; with *The Times* since 1926; before that, while a team player, he covered campus sports for the *Fordham Ram*.

DAVIS, Murray—from *Kansas City Star* to the *World-Telegram* in 1933; Silurian Award to him in 1948; the newspaper reporter chosen to represent the craft in *Saturday Evening Post* series on "Men at Work," March, 1949.

DEL VECCHIO, Tom—retired from the Associated Press in August, 1971, with one of the AP's thirty-year pins.

DODGE, Wendell Phillips—born 1883, reporter and war correspondent for *The World* and other papers; explorer, voyaged around the world in a square-rigger; publicity man for David Belasco; wrote his contribution to this volume at 89, still active and ambitious.

DONNELLY, John B.—began on *Amsterdam* (N.Y.) *Morning Sentinel*, then to *Bronx Home News, Wall Street Journal, New York Telegram;* then twenty-six years at public relations with I.B.M. Died 1965.

EDWARDS, Deltus Malin—long an acknowledged star of the *New York Herald*'s galaxy, but also with the *Washington Times*, Associated Press, International News Service; retired to San Antonio, Texas, he was applauded at many Silurian dinners as the one who had traveled farthest to get there. Died 1962, at 88.

ENGELKING, Lessing L. (Engel)—from Texas, the *Austin American,* to the *Bronx Home News* in 1925;

to the *Herald Tribune* 1927, to become an institution as city editor, until the final closing in 1966; then, Port of New York Authority.

EWAN, Earl O.—from Honolulu to San Francisco; from Columbia School of Journalism to *The New York Times;* later with public relations, U.S. Steel.

FARIS, Barry—first, *St. Joseph* (Mo.) *Gazette;* for more than forty years the active boss, with mounting titles, of International News Service; editor, *Silurian News.* Died 1966, 78 years old.

FLYNN, John T.—born 1882; from *New Haven Register* to *New York Globe,* to become that paper's last managing editor before it was folded; prolific writer of magazine articles and books.

FOWLER, Gene—*Denver Post;* managing editor of *New York American* and of *Morning Telegraph;* author of numerous books. Died 1960, at 70.

FREEMAN, Andrew A.—foreign correspondent for the *New York Post;* faculty member of the Columbia School of Journalism, Andy is best known as editor for two years of the King of Siam's newspaper, the *Bangkok Daily Mail;* "Remember," the king told him, "in Bangkok you call me Boss."

FRENCH, Herbert M.—"Mr. French has done it again," says a *Times* citation, referring to a star performance of his as late man on the foreign desk; from the *Springfield Republican* and Associated Press he came to *The Times* in 1927; A Mayflower descendant and sergeant in W.W.I.

GRAYSON, Robert E.—for many years and until the closing, librarian of the *Herald Tribune*.

GREEN, Martin—began, *Burlington* (Iowa) *Gazette; St. Louis Republic;* to *New York Morning Journal,* 1896; to *The World* until its folding in 1931; then *The Sun;* an all-time notable and legend, honored at dinner at Delmonico's in 1913, Irvin S. Cobb presiding. Died 1939, at 69.

GRUTZNER, Charles—began 1926, with the *Brooklyn Times;* then with *Brooklyn Eagle* and *Long Island Daily Star;* to *The New York Times* in 1941, his reporting including the war in Korea in 1950.

HALL, Henry Noble—born in England, 1872; European journalism, 1890–1900; *Philadelphia North American; New Orleans Item; New York World,* 1908–1917, including war correspondence; Washington correspondent for *London Times.* Died 1949.

HANSEN, Harry—*Chicago Daily News,* war correspondent and literary editor, 1914–1926; literary editor *World* and *World-Telegram;* editor World Almanac.

HEARST, William Randolph—the original. Died 1951.

HENNESSY, John H.—managing editor, the *New York Press.* (See extended note following his article, "Old New York Press Club.")

HERSHEY, Burnet—*New York Post; New York Sun;* correspondent for *The New York Times, Philadelphia Public Ledger;* president, Overseas Press Club. Died 1971, at 75.

HERSHFIELD, Harry—from San Francisco and Chicago, New York's man since long ago; 80 years old when he wrote these stories in 1966, Harry belongs to the whole race of mankind, the Silurians' pride and joy.

HORNE, George—coming to Columbia University from Oklahoma, he worked at ship news for *Morning Telegraph* and the *American;* on graduating, went to *The Times,* soon received ship news assignment for keeps; met his wife while covering her arrival as a young actress from England; retired 1969.

JEMAIL, Jimmy—the *New York News;* since he tells his own story, you may read it by turning back through these pages; retired 1973, at 79.

JOHNSON, Malcolm M.—from the *Macon* (Ga.) *Telegraph* in 1928 to the *Sun,* he stayed on until the paper's last day, picking up a 1949 Pulitzer Prize en route; now vice-president, Hill & Knowlton. (His son, Haynes Johnson, *Washington Star,* received a Pulitzer in 1966.)

KATZ, Ralph—to *The Times* at 18 in 1929 as night office boy; went on to police, night rewrite, and general assignments, until retirement after the 1963 newspaper strike; then to the State Commission on Human Rights.

KIERAN, John—*The New York Times* sports, 1915–1943; *New York Sun* columnist, 1943–44; notable writer on nature.

KILGALLEN, James L.—from the *Indianapolis Times* in 1922 he went to join International News Service in Chicago; continued in the Hearst services, most recently, the Hearst Headline Service, to receive in the spring of 1973 the Silurians' Quarter Century Achievement trophy.

LANDER, William H.—United Press specialist in Spanish-speaking revolutions (about a dozen in a couple of hemispheres); then a hitch with Dupont P.R.; now Journal of Commerce.

LAURENCE, William H.—Retired from *The Times* after many years; see page 3.

LEWI, Maurice J.—elected in 1950 an honorary member of the Silurians; himself a longtime president of the New York College of Podiatry, he was a brother of Isidor Lewi, a *Tribune* reporter in the 1890s and an early Silurian; his nephew, Joseph L. Cohn, was also a Silurian. Died in 1957, a few months short of 100 years old.

LINDLEY, Ernest L.—*World;* then *Herald Tribune* in Washington; for years *Newsweek's* Washington bureau chief; charter member of Sigma Delta Chi's Washington Correspondent's Hall of Fame.

LOCHNER, Louis P.—Associated Press correspondent in Germany throughout the rise of Hitler to power; Pulitzer Prize winner in 1939; author and editor of books on Nazi history.

LYON, George H.—city editor of the *World-Telegram;* editor, *Buffalo Times;* managing editor, *PM;* press officer, deputy director of OWI with Allied Supreme Headquarters in Europe, W.W. II; later public relations, Pan American Airways.

MACMASTER, Frank—covered New York City Hall for half a century, longer, it is said, than any other reporter ever did; retired from *Long Island Daily Press.* Died 1972, 80 years old.

MACNEIL, Neil—for twenty-one years, assistant night managing editor of *The New York Times;* before that, night city editor; headed *Times* teams covering national political conventions and organization of United Nations at San Francisco. Died 1969, 78 years old.

MACVANE, John—United Press and American Broadcasting Corp.

MASON, Frank E.—a foreign correspondent who became general manager and president of International News Service; vice-president, National Broadcasting Co., 1931–45.

MCCOY, Samuel Duff—the son of Presbyterian missionaries to China, he went from Princeton in 1903 to newspaper work in Washington; served the *Philadelphia Ledger, Brooklyn Eagle, New York Sun,* and the *World,* where he won a Pulitzer Prize in 1924. Died 1964.

MERIWETHER, Walter Scott (Skipper)—when he wrote his story of frustrations over the North Pole affair, he was 88 years old and retired to Charleston, Miss.

MORGAN, Thomas B.—Associated Press war correspondent in W.W. II; became United Press bureau chief in Rome, covering that news center between the two World Wars; assisted in writing Mussolini's book, *My Twenty-four Hours;* later a radio commentator and special events director. Died 1972, 87 years old.

MOSCOW, Warren—political reporter and Albany correspondent, *The New York Times;* assistant to Mayor

Robert F. Wagner; editor *New York Law Journal;* author of political biographies and memoirs.

NEWTON, John W.—Brooklyn editor of *New York Journal-American;* in April, 1955, received a gold watch in token of fifty years service with the Hearst organization.

NEWTON, Marshall E.—assistant and acting city editor, *The New York Times;* army for W.W.I. and W.W. II, emerging a colonel.

NOMBURG, Mack—Began *New York Globe,* 1916; a veteran of City Hall press room; long in public relations, Commerce and Industry Association.

PECK, Marshall H., Jr.—*Herald Tribune* from 1951 until its closing in 1966; special adviser to Ambassador Sargent Shriver for Paris peace talks in 1968; with New York State Division of Human Rights.

PILAT, Oliver—forty years a newspaperman, eleven with *Brooklyn Eagle,* twenty-nine with *New York Post;* president of Silurians and of New York Newspaper Guild; author of various books, latest being *Drew Pearson.*

POSTLEY, Maurice G.—former member of Silurian Governors and secretary of the Society; *Bronx Home News; New York Evening Journal;* writes column for weekly *Walton* (N.Y.) *Reporter;* president of Delaware County Conservation Association.

PRETSHOLD, Karl—from Middle-west newspapers to New York; *PM;* public relations for City Health Department; retired.

PULITZER, Joseph—the original. Died 1911.

RANDALL, Ed—*New York Daily News,* 1919; a syndicated cartoonist.

RASKIN, A. H. (Abe)—second recipient of Silurian Quarter Century Achievement Trophy; born in Alberta, Canada, he was graduated from City College and there was campus correspondent for *The Times;* since 1934, he has served *The Times,* mostly as national labor reporter; now a member of *The Times* editorial board; during W.W. II, he was special assistant to the Secretary of War, a lieutenant-colonel.

ROESSNER, Elmer—from San Francisco to NEA Service; *World-Telegram; PM;* Bell-McClure Syndicate; city editor, columnist, of all-around capacity.

ROYSTER, Vermont C.—*Wall Street Journal,* 1936–1958, through all ranks to editor; Pulitzer Prize in 1953.

SCANDRETT, Richard B.—a New York lawyer and friend of many newspapermen; active in politics, he saw news from inside the locked doors, especially in association with Senators Dwight Morrow and Robert A. Taft; in 1944 he enrolled as a Democrat. Died 1969.

SENBER, Henry—having apprenticed on the *Oil City* (Pa.) *Derrick* he joined the *Morning Telegraph* in New York in 1926, eventually conducting the "Beau Broadway" column; stagestruck, he achieved a part in Walter Hampden's production of *Cyrano de Bergerac;* now, for many years, with the New York Telephone Co.

SHAINMARK, Lou—with the *New York Journal-American;* before that, managing editor of the *Chicago*

American; later in city government, including the Economic Development Administration.

SLATTERY, Dan—on *The Sun* as a 14-year-old office boy during the blizzard of 1888; became a stage manager in the theater and active in production.

STABLER, C. Norman—financial editor of the *Herald Tribune* in 1929, being then 28 years old, the youngest of that rank on any metropolitan newspaper, anywhere; continued until the paper closed in 1966; columnist for *The Bond Buyer* and *The Money Manager.*

STEINBECK, John—yes, the novelist and Nobel Prize Winner.

SULLIVAN, Frank—the *Herald* and *The World;* contributor to the *New Yorker* and other magazines; author of numerous books.

TASTROM, Edw. P.—his long Wall St. career began as a Columbia University sports stringer for the *Brooklyn Eagle,* 1915–19; then to the *Tribune*'s financial page; then into financial business; then returning 1942–1959 to the *Journal of Commerce,* concluding as associate editor.

TYNG, Ed—from the *Telegram* to *The Sun* to the *Journal of Commerce;* as a change from financial subjects, he varies to fishing; out of a half-century background he still writes with authority on banking and finance.

WAGONER, Clyde D.—three years with the *New York Journal;* then to radio, the newcomer in news. Died 1964.

WELCH, Ned—identified in footnote to his contribution on Page 271.

WHITE, Charles T.—began in 1894 on the *Herald,* continued until 1926, covering politics; resigning from the *Herald Tribune,* he became publisher of the *Hancock* (N.Y.) *Herald.* Died 1951, at 89.

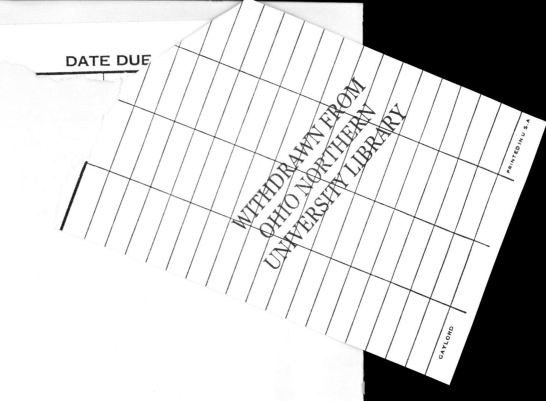